POETRY AND HERESY
Selected Essays

POETRY AND HERESY
Selected Essays

Joe Safdie

MadHat Press
Cheshire, Massachusetts

MadHat Press
MadHat Incorporated
PO Box 422, Cheshire, MA 01225

Copyright © 2024 Joe Safdie
All rights reserved

The Library of Congress has assigned
this edition a Control Number of
2023952396

ISBN 978-1-952335-73-0 (paperback)

Cover art and design by Marc Vincenz
Book design by MadHat Press

www.madhat-press.com

First Printing
Printed in the United States of America

Table of Contents

Introduction: On the Secular	ix
DORN	
Once Upon a Time with West Ed	3
Ed Dorn and the Politics of Love	11
Politics and Time: *Gunslinger*	23
Satire, Edward Dorn and the Via Negativa	35
Poetry and Heresy	45
OLSON	
Letter to Olson	61
Charles Olson and Finding One's Place	67
Projective Verse, Space-Time and Attention	85
Charles Olson and Brooks Adams	99
Charles Olson and the Bolinas Nexus: Avant-Pastoral?	109
ALCALAY	
Unmasquing a Whole Hole Chapbook	125
From the Warring Factions	133
Resurrection of the Ancillary & Ghost Talk	139
SATIRE & ROMANCE	
A Defense of Satire (on *A Modern Dunciad* in Three Parts)	149
Kent Johnson and the Future of Poetic Satire	171
Isn't It Romantic?	177
SELECTED SHORTER REVIEWS	
In the House Un-American by Ben Hollander	191
Like A Dark Rabbi by Norman Finkelstein	197
Dreamland Court by Dale Herd	207
Damage by Mark Scroggins	211
jes' sayn' by Heller Levinson	215

IMAGE & NATION

Musing about the Muses — 221
Image & Nation — 237

Acknowledgments — 257
About the Author — 259

Introduction: On The Secular

One tremendously windy day when I was a graduate student in Boulder, Colorado, I was trying to walk up a hill to a bus stop and kept being blown back down. When I finally got there, the only other prospective passenger was a wiry gray-haired old woman, who looked at me critically up and down and then said "You need to carry a rock in your pocket; otherwise you'll get blown away." And ever since then, I've done just what she said; my current rock is on my desk while I type these words, worn smooth by constant handling.

Maybe carrying a rock in my pocket is a way of being grounded; maybe that woman saw that I was like many assorted white citizens, head in the clouds, full of theories and speculations. Maybe, as an essay here about the Muses suggests, carrying rocks can be a means towards what's called "embodied cognition." But what I know is that two weeks or so after I thought this introduction was finished, I came across the following passage in Charles Olson's *Causal Mythology*: "among American Indians, the Sioux, for example ... say that the stone is the truest condition of creation, that it is silence and it is solidity and all that. Well, I like that. I mean, I think the Earth is nothing but a pebble, a marvelously big stone." That made me think about my rock in a new way, as did this nugget from Northrop Frye's *Fearful Symmetry*: "from the imaginative point of view the physical world is a rock, within which all life is 'vegetable' in the sense of being anchored to it." All this reinforced what I had already written, that what these essays and writers share is a concentration on the secular universe.

So one might ask: Don't *most* writers concentrate on the secular? Or maybe: What else is there? But considering the title of this book, the main question might be what being secular has to do with heresy. One answer is that for Olson—and for other subjects of these essays—the secular was never separate from the divine. Indeed, terms for that union percolate throughout Olson's late work: whether he was writing about Corbin's "terrestrial angels," the "subterranean and celestial" in "Maximus from Dogtown IV," or even Gertrude Stein's "geography and the dictionary," he was always at pains to show (and say) that sociology and politics alone weren't worth cultivating, and what was all around us, as he said in his "Talk at Cortland," was mythology: "these big essential things ... aren't going to run away, and you can't just sort of arrive there by fine new ways of travel." But at the same time, he wrote in his short essay "Bill Snow," "it's the secular I don't think is going to go out of our bones yet." That comports with what Jack Clarke—the substitute teacher for Olson's mythology class at the University of Buffalo—wrote in his dissertation on William Blake (1963) about "the changed existential status of the world with which modern commentators now believe Blake's poetry to be actually dealing," namely "a movement from the divine to the human. The prevailing emphasis in Blake studies today is 'the *human* form divine,' not 'the human form *divine*.'"

Still, most poets vacillate: relatively few identify as heretics. I thought it was funny that when I floated this book's title to some poet friends, one wrote back and suggested it be called "Heresy and Heresy." Those were the days: it's been a while since poetry could be called heretical, especially American poetry, and it seems a real stretch in the age of Instagram poets and the metaverse and whatever constitutes the latest incarnation of language poetry. But seen another way, heresy only exists when there's an orthodoxy to define it, and if today's "mainstream"—sanctioned by contests, federations, associations, academic conferences and tenured university jobs—qualifies as orthodox, these essays explore an alternate belief, that the secular is all we know of the sacred. That might be heretical even in these straitened times.

I found some historical backup for this position in an old issue of the *New York Review of Books*, an article called "Apotheosis Now" by Fara Dabhoiwala:

> Above all, the very idea of a binary division between humanity and divinity was itself a peculiarly Christian dogma. In most other belief systems, the two were not strictly separated but overlapped. Reincarnations, communications with the spirit world, living gods, avatars, demigods, ancestor deities, and the powers of kings and lords—all were part of an interwoven spectrum of natural and supernatural authority.

Dabhoiwala then mentions some ancient Greeks and Romans who participated in this common spectrum: "Oh dear, I think I'm becoming a god," Vespasian is said to have joked on his deathbed in 79 CE, which seems fairly heretical. But this secular/spiritual mix isn't only Western: Victor Sogen Hori, a scholar of Zen, wrote that if *kensho* (insight) "is to be described as a breakthrough, then it is a breakthrough not out of, but into conventional consciousness": freedom, he wrote, lies in gravity, not beyond it. Or as V. A. Kolve, a Chaucer scholar I quote in one of the Olson essays, wrote, "The Miller's Tale" is "a look at life uncomplicated by transcendent idea or ideal,"

> a world temporarily—by an act of imaginative exclusion— unshadowed by Last Things ... Characters in such stories live,

for the most part, as though no moral imperatives existed beyond those intrinsic to the moment. They inhabit a world of cause and effect, pragmatic error and pragmatic punishment, that admits no goals beyond self-gratification, revenge or social laughter.... It finds the physical world enough—its plenitude, its charm, its energy, its rules.... an idea of order sufficient to man's needs.

As Blake, again, had it in "A Descriptive Catalogue," "The characters of Chaucer's Pilgrims are the characters which compose all ages and nations; as one age falls, another rises, different to mortal sight, but to immortals only the same." These ideas about the secular are also entertained in the title essay and the review of Norman Finkelstein's *To A Dark Rabbi*.

To see the secular in these terms requires care and attentiveness, but etymology is instructive as well: "from Latin *saeculum* 'generation, age,' used in Christian Latin to mean 'the world' as opposed to the Church; c. 1300, living in the world, not belonging to a religious order." That is, the world is larger than the Church (any Church): the secular is *larger* than the religious. But there's more if we go even further back: "from Proto-Italic *sai-tlo-, PIE instrumental element *-tlo- + *sai- 'to bind, tie' (see sinew), extended metaphorically to successive human generations as links in the chain of life." That is, "The Great Chain of Being," the Pythagorean cosmology that defined intelligent life for thousands of years, is actually secular: who knew? I'm not a scholar of religious history, but one last look inside the etymological treasure chest reveals that the word "cosmos" usually suggested "the universe as an embodiment of order and harmony." And that includes *this* world: "an idea of order sufficient to man's needs." Still, Rebecca Solnit, acute reader of the zeitgeist, might say it best:

> there's an Etruscan word, *saeculum*, that describes the span of time lived by the oldest person present, sometimes calculated to be about a hundred years. In a looser sense, the word means the expanse of time during which something is in living memory. Every event has its saeculum and then its sunset, when the last person who fought in the Spanish Civil War or the last person who saw the last passenger pigeon is gone.

Rock in the pocket. I repeat myself every now and then in these essays, so I hope readers will pardon the occasional lapse: I've always believed Allen Ginsberg's "first thought best thought," but it doesn't mean second thoughts are inauthentic. For example, readers who get through the entire three-part sequence about satire and Richard Nason's "A Modern Dunciad" will see many of the same ideas repeated in "Satire, Ed Dorn, and the Via Negativa," employed for a slightly different purpose. As the chapter headings show, the great majority of these essays are about poets and poetry, but the final one needs a few words of explanation: it's the introduction to a book I was writing during my one and only sabbatical (six months) about "visual literacy," and it contains ideas about developing writing skills by improving visual skills. As I spent most of my teaching career teaching college composition classes, I thought to include one essay that reflected those conversations: as you'll see, poetry shows up there as well.

Finally, I owe the publishers of these essays my gratitude; the journals are all listed in the Acknowledgments, but I especially want to thank Michael Boughn and the late Kent Johnson, editors of *Dispatches from the Poetry Wars*, for bringing some of these pieces to light. Thanks as well to George Quasha, who—after I had presented one of these essays at the Louisville Literature Conference in 2020—recommended a book by Michael A. Sells, *Mystical Languages of Unsaying*, which became essential to both my poems and my prose. Actually, I hope these essays give some of the pleasure one comes to poetry for; they were written for different occasions, but I was always conscious of the rock in my pocket while they took form.

Dorn

ONCE UPON A TIME WITH WEST ED

> The opening scene ... is famously without words—
> an opera where the arias are stared, not sung.
> —Sydney Pollock on *Once Upon a Time in the West*

In the introduction to *Internal Resistances*, a book of essays on the poetry of Ed Dorn published in 1985, Donald Wesling writes about Ed's first class at UC–San Diego in La Jolla in the spring of 1976, when, "after a prolonged silence," he dramatically unrolled a map ("There is your domain") of the railroads stretching across the Western United States. I had a similar experience of Ed's teaching style at the University of Colorado some 18 months later. He had been hired to teach in the creative writing program that had started up the previous year; the teaching assistants, of whom I was one, were directed to attend once-a-week lectures by the permanent faculty to the undergraduates, who were then broken up into smaller sections taught by us.

These lectures were given in a cavernous lecture hall with green walls, mostly used for chemistry classes; I remember a row of Bunsen burners arrayed across a long slab of formica. One afternoon early in the semester, Dorn strode in, wearing cowboy boots and a vest, and started taking out a series of books from a leather bag. After three or four had emerged, he squinted balefully out at the assembled students, took out a match, struck it against the edge of the formica slab, lit his cigarette, and took a deep drag, not saying a word for about five minutes: the ritual was impeccable. Finally, he said "The subject of these lectures is obviously what I've been reading"...and started talking about Cioran's philosophy, Samuel Johnson's *Life of Richard Savage* and W. E.

Woodward's *Meet General Grant*, weaving them together in a brilliant para-logical narrative the likes of which I haven't come close to hearing since. I'd been lucky enough to have experienced some great teachers in my university experience, but this was something else again; I was 24 years old, and I was hooked. Ed's work and presence were my most important instruction in poetry, and they still inform almost everything I write.

Lots of critical essays have been written about his work—the aforementioned *Internal Resistances* has some good ones in it, and Tom Clark's biography *A World of Difference* provocatively interweaves the facts of Ed's life with reflections on his writing and the peculiar indeterminacy of his authorial persona—but here I'd like to informally remember a little bit of what it was like being, first, a student of Ed's, and then a friend and occasional correspondent until the pancreatic cancer (what he would call "the alien" in *Chemo Sábe*, the record of those last years) finally took over in December of 1999.

"I saved myself by … establishing a ritual of my own person" he wrote in "Driving Across the Plains," and I don't think it's possible to explain how special it was being around him without talking about his presence, always a little larger than life. A few years after I'd left Boulder for San Francisco, I organized a benefit reading for *Zephyr*, the magazine I was editing at the time, to coincide with a visit from Ed and his wife Jenny, and called all the writers I knew. Richard Grossinger, writer and publisher of North Atlantic Press, said he had just seen a Clint Eastwood movie that reminded him of Ed, and if you can picture *Pale Rider* or that first scene of *Once Upon a Time in the West*, that wariness and rock-hard cragginess … that was definitely part of the image. He both was and wasn't Slinger, the demi-god of his most famous work—certainly those of us who were privileged to have kept company with him often assumed those adventures were continuing—but I think people who didn't know him well thought that a certain splenetic sarcasm was all there was. That's too bad, as he was one of the most generous people I've ever known.

But he did have a fiery temper. Perhaps our most unusual contact was in 1992, when he and Jenny drove from Southern France (where

"Languedoc Variorum," originally called "Languedoc Around the Clock," had its origins in the early '90s) to Olomouc, a small town in the Czech Republic where my wife and I were teaching as Peace Corps volunteers, and where I had arranged for him to give a talk and a reading. I'd mailed what I thought were fairly accurate maps, but apparently had left out a crucial segment ... anyway, they got lost, and when they finally arrived, an hour or so late, it didn't seem as if the vodka I'd made sure to chill in our freezer would be enough to calm him.

It reminded me of a time back in Boulder when he and Jenny needed a place to stay for a few nights before the fall semester of 1978 began. They had been in San Francisco over the summer, winding up their affairs in North Beach, and were traveling with their kids and most of their possessions.[1] I was sharing a house near the university at the time with a young single mother, and gladly gave up my room and slept on the deck outside. I didn't know, however, that my roommate had managed to offend Ed with a stray remark during the evening, and I woke up at about 6:00 in the morning to the whole family tramping out to a motel.... "Tell your roommate she won't have to bother with us anymore," he growled. I was mortified, but visited him in their motel room a day later, and all was forgiven ... the remark, whatever it had been, forgotten.

He calmed down after the long drive to Olomouc as well—"I never thought I'd get this far East," he said—and learning they would stay in a guest house that Mozart had once stayed in didn't hurt. We had a great dinner at a Chinese restaurant, paid for by a visiting law professor from Georgetown we were sure was a member of the CIA. (He kept on getting Ed's name confused with Bernadine Dohrn's). The next morning, Ed gave a well-attended talk about Black Mountain at Palacky University, and that afternoon, a reading, complete with Czech translator. I remember that the poems he was going to read had to be arranged in advance with the rector of the university, who wanted

---

1. They left me their parakeet to take care of while they were gone. One day my roommates let it out of the cage and it flew into a nearby tree; I almost had heart failure. I had lost Ed Dorn's bird! My life as I knew it was over! We put the cage on top of the car hood and whistled, and after a few minutes, the bird, amazingly, flew back in. Two days after I proudly returned it to them, a cat got in its cage and tore it apart.

him to read pieces that had already been translated into Czech from *Hands Up* and *Geography*, personal lyrics like "Are They Dancing" and others written to his first wife Helene, with which Ed felt quite uncomfortable and read awkwardly. The next day, we drove to Prague to pick up his check from the U.S. embassy, a photo of George Bush the Elder gazing down at us. It was the summer of 1992, and the first tales of Bill Clinton's infidelities were in the news, this time with Jennifer Flowers. "He fucked her," he said at our table in the Grand Hotel on Wenceslas Square, "but he didn't come" (a version, for those too young to remember, of "I smoked, but I didn't inhale").

He was constitutionally unable to support anyone in power; although he once allowed as how he had voted for Jimmy Carter, his scorn at what he felt was the amateurish nature of that administration in the late 1970s was relentless. As Wesling said about him, "Dorn is not a poet of causes. In fact, he is suspicious of anyone who *favors* anything." I laughed when Clark revealed one of Ed's earliest intellectual influences, a Methodist preacher who said "It's not okay, and it's not going to be okay." When I saw him in Seattle in 1994, he and Jenny were engaged in a project called "Negativity," collecting notes about public signage that expressed hostile sentiments. One favorite was "The King is rolling in his grave" (a reference to the ill-fated marriage of Michael Jackson and Lisa Marie Presley).

It seemed at times that he purposely picked on popular received ideas, if only to pierce any of them that had been accepted lazily, without a thorough examination: the word "gadfly" comes to mind. Once, when we were walking quickly across the CU campus (he always moved quickly), a squirrel was attracting some attention from the coeds. "Everybody has these Walt Disney feelings about them," he snarled…"they're just bushy-tailed rats." I also remember, in the midst of a popular boycott of the Coors brewery, Ed going up to the bartender at the Boulderado Hotel and loudly demanding a Coors. As Anselm Hollo said, in Clark's biography, "Almost any take endorsed by the U.S. media, and perhaps especially by the 'liberal' wing of same, was instantly suspect, and Ed's m.o. was to assume the diametrically opposed position." An e-mail correspondent a few years ago sniffed disapprovingly about his references to the "jackbooted purveyors of multiculturalism," and his famous air bag poem—one of the first of the short, twisted epigrams that were to make up most of his work in the late 70s and 80s—was in part a diatribe against Ralph Nader.

But as a student, I took his rants as an opportunity to sharpen my attention to what he thought were the pernicious forces forever threatening us, "conning the present to hustle the futcha / By a simple elimination of the datadata" ("The Cycle") "They ALWAYS want to screw you, Oscar," he once admonished one of my roommates, who had innocently complained about his utility bill. Things assumed heightened importance whenever he was around, no matter what the subject of conversation was, which made me (and hundreds of others) want to explore and learn a little about what he knew.

For me, specifically, that was American history: in my standardized English department education before grad school, I'd thought of the eighteenth century only in terms of Pope and Swift, and (of course?) favored the romantics to come. No, no, no, he insisted: this was the century of the American revolution; this is where we came from! He got me reading epochal books of American history, W. E. Woodward's *Washington: The Image and the Man* and *Meet General Grant*, and Claude Bowers' *Jefferson and Hamilton* (much more inspiring than the aesthetic theories and confessional poems of the late '70s) and gave me a lifelong preference for poetry that incorporated and explored historical fact rather than the intricacies of its own syntax. I didn't get to all of Olson's recommendations in the famous "Bibliography on America," but I found quite a few—Walter Prescott Webb's *The Great Plains*, Kathleen Coman's *Economic Beginnings of the Far West*, Carl Sauer—all of which rescued me from any possibility of repeating the mainstream lyric effusions then in vogue. (As I went to the "Bibliography" to remember the spelling of Ms. Coman's name, I found Olson's remark that "our own 'life' is too serious a concern for us to be parlayed forward by literary antecedence. In other words, 'culture,' no matter how great"... which seems relevant.)

But this was a creative writing program, after all, and eventually a few of us, who felt we had progressed "beyond" the regular workshops, got a chance to take an advanced class with him. The required reading was a letter from Tom Raworth containing an acidic review about a European poetry festival (it might have been Spoleto) at which many American friends had read, Ed Sanders' *Investigative Poetry* (which had started as a Naropa class project investigating the infamous Trungpa Rinpoche-W. S. Merwin dispute at a Buddhist retreat and set off "The Great Naropa Poetry Wars"; see Tom Clark's book of that title), and another letter from Jeremy Prynne about Sanders' essay, to which he was hardly sympathetic—that one started "But Edward— …"

Think about that for a minute: a famous poet letting graduate writing students read his own personal correspondence, in order to talk about the issues involved. Writing programs may be problematic (I agree with a lot of the criticism I've read), but if examples of such generosity are on the curriculum, one would be small-minded indeed to criticize them.

The classes were held around his dinner table, scene of many raucous gatherings ("where one place / is the center of this terrific actualism" as Book III of *Slinger* had it), but the conversation was serious: he wanted us to fully consider Prynne's objections before we too rapidly signed on to a trendy new "movement," even one (or especially one) with which he was sympathetic; he wanted us to consider everything that poetry could possibly do and be, and then find our own way.

One thing that established writers can do for novices in such situations is simply to recognize them. I still remember Ed saying "That's really masterful compression" after he'd read a short poem I'd written "about" Alexander Hamilton's plan to revamp the currency in the 1790s: simple encouragement that allowed me, simply, to go on with what I'd been doing. He felt, I think, that serious practitioners need only tell the truth, and that any device that would lead to the expression of that truth should be exploited…including historical documentation of course, but also jokes, bad puns, sarcasm, irony and "samplings" of other poems! If you weren't somehow telling the truth in your poems, though, there was nothing that he, or anyone, could do for you. (One early criticism came when I showed him a sequence of poems I'd inscribed "For E. M. Cioran" …"You can't say that," he said, disgusted; "you don't know him.")

On March 25, 2000, I helped organize a memorial reading for Ed in Seattle: many writers came from various far-flung regions to participate. English poet Tom Raworth flew in that morning from Albany, NY; John Daley, who'd met Ed in Buffalo in the 1970s and became a lifelong friend, took a few days off from his criminal defense work in Los Angeles; Charles Potts, author and editor of *The Temple* and a student of Ed's in Pocatello in the early 1960s, drove in from Walla Walla, etc. I've been listening to the audio cassette of that reading—readings of and in response to Ed's writing—while I finish these recollections, and I'm struck, as I have been so often, with that curious combination of fierce morality and side-splitting humor that he practiced so well. As he said, in the late reading tour of Eastern Washington that Potts arranged, "My problem is how to make pain funny."

That was something he managed to pull off pretty well in his last book of poems, Chemo Sábe, and in this wonderful quote from a late letter to Clark:

> But now I'm leveling off again and feel much better. I've stopped taking that fucking Zoloft for starters, and feel a *lot* better already. That has to be something invented by some New Age Torquemada, mindless nasty stuff. It is said, and I believe it, that the whole English dept. at CU is "on" it, and that theorists in general everywhere can't function without it. No wonder they detest the past in which it didn't exist. (September 30, 1998)

The seriousness was always there, from "The Rick of Green Wood" on, but it took a while to register the humor, encased, as it so often was, in bitterness. Another thing about Ed that Raworth mentioned at the memorial was that he knew about work; he knew what it meant to be poor and live on food stamps (see Clark's bio, and his own semi-autobiographical *By The Sound*, for vivid descriptions of that poverty), and he never failed to indict the people responsible for the maintenance of that situation. Yet the humor made the social commentary even more pointed: "1 billion Chinese are telling me / the gang of 4 are wrong? / Doesn't this seem out of proportion?" he asked in *Yellow Lola*, a book of "offshoots" from *Hello, La Jolla*. (I'm not sure if I've ever seen any comment that *Yellow Lola* is an approximation of a Japanese person trying to pronounce the name of the earlier book; Ed was hysterically politically incorrect before the term was even invented).

And finally, that's what matters most: he was just such a gas to be around. As John Daley said at the memorial reading, "One was never bored around Edward." Which made it such an honor, in the winter of 1979, when my roommate and I drove down to Santa Fe to, among other things, meet Max Finstein, the éminence grise behind the Taos World Championships of Poetry, to be accompanied by a note that said: "Max—these are my friends, Stokes and Joe. Show them a good time. West Ed."

Ed Dorn and the Politics of Love

From his early verse, written in the late 1950s and '60s before the mock epic *Slinger*, to his "middle period" of satirical epigrams, to his late reports on the cancer that was consuming his body, Edward Dorn wrote demonstrably "political poetry." That he did so is easy to show; more arguable is the proposition, advanced here, that his political poems achieve their efficacy and success because they're grounded in love. If I have a formal thesis, it's to demonstrate what Duncan McNaughton, in a 1997 letter, wrote … that Dorn "had been one of the faithful of love."

These are large terms, so it might be well at the beginning to present a few definitions: Dorn's practice of political poetry was something broader than what might, in 2004, come to mind. Indeed, many current practitioners resist the term outright, thinking that it leads to preaching, agitprop, or telling readers what to do; they equate it with literalness, or a paucity of expression.[1] But Dorn's poetry, while unabashedly "referential," incorporating historical fact and commenting on it, eschews any immediate political goals. The function of a poet,

---

1. Ron Silliman, on his blog, is typical: "themes, for me at least, don't work. That is to say, I literally can't read them. Them, in this instance, being *poems with a point*. When I try, the poem invariably loses my interest before I complete the text. My experience as a reader is that it feels like coercive sentiment & I find myself physically repelled by the poem. The affect is nausea. It doesn't matter whether I agree with the sentiment or not." Such thoughts contradict Walter Benjamin's, who wrote, in *One-Way Street*, "The tract is an Arabic form. Its exterior is undifferentiated and unobtrusive, like the facades of Arabian buildings, the articulation of which begins only in the courtyard. So, too, the articulated structure of the tract is invisible from outside, revealing itself only from within." (*Reflections*, 83)

he told Stephen Fredman in a 1977 interview, was "to stay as removed as possible from all permanent associations with power"; he was responsible only for delivering the best product he was capable of to his readers (*Interviews*, 66). "Dorn is not a poet of causes," agrees Donald Wesling, in his essay on Dorn in *Internal Resistances*. "In fact, he is suspicious of anyone who *favors* anything" (35).

In a letter to Amiri Baraka (then Leroi Jones) in 1961, Dorn pronounced himself "embarrassed" at "the poor prospect of fellow poets singing the praises of any thing so venal as a State.... *Sides* are a bigassed drag. The biggest small-talk of all, like which one are you on? Motherfucker." (quoted in von Hallberg 58).

In other words, he believed that he could "write around the ideological encampments that are usually the governing forces ... in political poetry" (58). James Scully, in his collection of essays *Line Break: Poetry as Social Practice*, makes a useful distinction between this broader practice, which he calls "dissident poetry," and "protest poetry," which

> is conceptually shallow. I think of the typical protest anthology: poems in opposition to the Vietnam War [or, in 2003, to the invasion of Iraq] or to the coup in Chile, ecologically concerned or anti-nuke poetry ... Such poetry is issue-bound, spectatorial—rarely the function of an engaged artistic life.... Dissident poetry, however, does not respect boundaries between private and public, self and other. In breaking boundaries it breaks silences: speaking for, or at best *with*, the silenced; opening poetry up, putting it into the middle of life rather than shutting it off into a corner. It is a poetry that talks back, that would act as part of the world, not simply as a mirror of it (5).

If "speaking for, or at best *with*, the silenced" is an important characteristic of this more valuable poetry, Dorn's translation, with Gordon Brotherston, of *One Word: Guerrilla Poems*, would seem to qualify on the basis of its title alone; "putting [poetry] back into the middle of life" and "talk[ing] back" were, of course, central concerns throughout his career. He would also have shared Scully's disdain of conceptually shallow protest poems. In the Fredman interview, making the argument that poetry "of a certain ambition and size will attempt to treat its culture in an instructive way," he speaks of the perils of basing poetry on an event,

> Like the Vietnam War was an event. I don't mean to disparage anyone's experiences of that. I'm saying that in terms of poetry, it's not stable enough.... The people who talked directly at it really dropped their tongues. (I 92, 94)

Two years later, he described the difference between such attempts and what he was doing as "a difference in morality":

> There are some people who have power and a certain kind of means at their disposal who are trying to get the society to think in a certain way, to do a certain set of things, and so forth. I think any responsible writer is never that. No writer is ever trying to get anybody to do something; what they're trying to create is a cognizance in the society of itself, to furnish the means—through clarity of language—for a self-appraisal and self-evaluation. (I 109)

Or, as he has it in *Yellow Lola,*

> The common duty of the poet
> in this era of massive dysfunction
> & generalized onslaught upon alertness
> is to maintain the plant
> to the end that the mumbling horde
> bestirs its prunéd tongue. (63)

The admission of the other, however—the recognition and articulation of forces outside one's person—is also characteristic of love. In this, Dorn's work is very much in the tradition of the love poems that have shaped western practice, which includes, as Louis Zukofsky reminds us in *Bottom: On Shakespeare*, the "configurations of Dante and Cavalcanti" (15). Dante, in the course of *La Vita Nuova*, changed the lyric from a narrow complaint of personal despair to a broader and more nuanced exploration of the effects his love for Beatrice was having, and could potentially have, on Florence (and eventually in the *Paradiso*, to the sun and other stars): "I felt impelled to take up a new and nobler theme than before," he writes in Section XVII of *La Vita Nuova*. "I had said almost everything about my state and I thought it right to be silent and say no more, for I felt I had explained enough about myself" (53).

This passage would surely have resonated with Dorn, who, as Wesling said, is unique "in the extent of his scorn for personality and inwardness" (*IR* 17). When "I" dies in Book II of *Slinger*, it's not just a clever linguistic turn, but the end as well of an entire mode of poetry based on individual complaint or report—"I didn't want to have any truck with that first-person-singular excuse," he said in a 1972 interview, "which I find one of the most effective brakes on current verse practice" (I 30). Before "I" becomes the receptacle of Kool Everything's five gallons of acid, though, he asks Slinger about love, offering a chance for Dorn to update Cavalcanti's "Donna mi Prega" (which, in Pound's translation in Canto XXXVI, reads "A lady asks me / I speak in season / She seeks reason for an affect, wild often / That is so proud he hath Love for a name" [177]) with this dialogue:

> What do you know
> of Love?
> Know? Nada, if I knew it
> it couldn't be Love.
> Even a mortal knows that.
> Then, what is it?
> IS is not the link
> it takes nine hundred years
> to explain one blown
> spark of Love
> and you don't have
> that much time Amigo.

Not long after this first book of *Slinger* was written, Dorn would publish *Twenty-four Love Songs*, #22 of which contained a similar sentiment: "The agony is beauty / that you can't have that / and sense too. There is / no sense to beauty." That poem ends with a surprising couplet for a book of love songs: "really, the world is shit / and I mean all of it" (*CP* 248). Dorn would adopt radically different forms, voices and techniques throughout his career, but this interpenetration of love and politics would remain a constant theme.

In the poem that usually appears first in collections of his work, "The Rick of Green Wood," Dorn explains to the woodsman that he prefers "cherry or alder or something strong / and thin, or thick if dry, but I don't / want the green wood, my wife would die" (3). He goes on to explain that "Her back is slender" (as in fact it was, Helene Dorn having suffered excruciating back pain for several months—Dorn seldom felt the need to "make things up," and there's a strong connection between realism and the strident positions he often takes in his poems).[2] As this conversation is going on, "my daughter was walking / singing / ... in the november / air, in the world, that was getting colder" (4). This poem inaugurates the co-existence, in much of his work, of a "cold" outside world combined with expressions of affection toward the people he loves who would be most threatened by it. In another early poem, "The Air of June Sings," Dorn's daughter is examining some of the inscriptions on the tombstones of a country cemetery; he himself is "moved to tears" as he hears "the depth in 'Darling, we love thee,' and as in 'Safe in Heaven'" (11). But he avoids

> the largest stone, larger than the common large, Goodpole Matthews,
> Pioneer, and that pioneer sticks in me like a wormed black cherry
> in my throat, No Date, nothing but that zeal, that trekking
> and Business, that presumption in a sacred place, where children
> are buried, and where peace, as it is in the fields and the country
> should reign. A wagon wheel is buried there.

This is a visceral recognition of the forces Dorn would be engaged against throughout his career, the ones that trivialize the "love of common object, / and of woman and all the natural things I groom, in

---

2. In another essay in *Line Break*, Scully expounds on this point: "Realism and partisanship are inseparable. It's not simply that partisanship without realism may be toothless, but that the dependency is the other way round: there can be no realism without partisanship. (We can't describe anything accurately without entering into a relationship with it and accounting for that relationship in our description. This doesn't mean we must be 'subjective' rather than 'objective,' though these are question-begging terms, but that we must struggle to be objective about our subjectivity") (67). Also see Robert Holub, in *Reception Theory: A Critical Introduction*: "Prejudice, because it belongs to historical reality itself, is not a hindrance to understanding, but rather a condition of the possibility of understanding" (41)

my mind" (13) and obliterate the "possibility" inherent in the common ground of the cemetery, with the less pretentious stones and inscriptions like "Budded on earth and blossomed / in heaven" (12). These forces sometimes assume the shape of characters, such as Howard Hughes/Robart in *Slinger*, but are always marked by a ruthless, a-historical ("No Date") lust for power and "Absolute Authority," like the Catholic Church during the Crusades ("Languedoc Variorum"). Sometimes their economic nature is emphasized: "the oblivious process / of a brutal economic calculus," for example, in "Problem of the Poem for My Daughter, Left Unsolved" (*CP* 93) leads to "the elimination of freely disposed / intellection" (96). For Dorn, whose poetry is "theoretical in nature and poetic by virtue of its inherent tone" (v), the "Entrapment" brought about by such forces is total:

> To a poet all authority
> except his own
> is an expression of Evil
> and it is all external authority that he expiates
> this is the culmination of his traits (*Slinger*, Book III)

The focus of Dorn's political poems would change: while the early poems concentrated on perceptions of his local environment (seen occasionally through the lens of Carl Sauer's cultural geography), *North Atlantic Turbine* investigates an overall theory of global and monopoly capitalism pushed along through the turbines of world trade. He would, though, come to look on that book as "over-reached" and "the most uncomfortable of my work to me" (I 24): "I wanted to stop looking through these binoculars at the horizon," he said, and instead "look at who was standing next to me. Like who was in the immediate room because I had never done that" (25). But, in fact, he had—in his first three books. Dorn was always to deny that he wrote domestically, but his examiner at Black Mountain College, Robert Creeley, disagreed: "Ed writes from a domestic base all the way—and it really underwrites his politics" (Clark 36).

One way to resolve this seeming contradiction is to realize that Dorn is at his best when he combines the personal and the political, as in Part I of the "Oxford" poem in *Turbine*. Sitting on a train and ruminating about the rich and beautiful women who come to Oxford from would-be imperialist countries in search of "The Good Life," he realizes that "The woman opposite me / by no other act than Murder / is permitted existence. Nothing less / will shape and spread / those legs" (CP 197). One of the last poems in that book again attempts, as Zukofsky had it, to "Perfect the composition of a two-point view" (A8 49):

> And I would not believe it
> If Europe or England
> Could in any sense evoke her without me,
> The guitar of her presence the bearer of her scent
> Upon my wrist
> The banding of her slightsmiling lassitude … (CP 230)

This poem is probably addressed to Jennifer Dunbar, soon to become his wife, who also inspired "the Song about a woman" at the end of Book I of *Slinger*. The previously mentioned *Twenty-four Love Songs*, which celebrates their marriage, again combines political awareness and indignation with the contrasting values of sex and the body. While asserting, in a lovely early passage, that "we are / everyway locked / inside the warm halls of flesh" (CP 238), he acknowledges later that his partner "will permit / any property of herself / any slanted permission / but make you know / any property is a careful / waste of time" (248). This union is ecstatic; it partakes of the cosmos:

> I am nothing
> anymore at all
> than in myself, you be
> a still center
> which has about it pivoting
> ramifications of my strain
> a marvelously pure crystal
> the center still and in me
>   located (243)

This is reminiscent of an early dream Dante writes about in Section XII of *La Vita Nuova*, when Love admonishes Dante to put aside pretenses: "I am the center of a circle to which all parts of the circumference are in a similar relation, but you are not so."[3] Soon afterwards, in a weakened state after another vision of Beatrice, Dante realizes that his love for her has "set his feet in that part of life beyond which it is not possible to go with any hope of returning" (XIV 48). Charles Williams, whose *The Figure of Beatrice*, according to Norman O. Brown,[4] "breaks through the literalism and poverty of our thought about love," expounds:

> This is the present climax of self-preservation and self-loss. Love itself says "Flee," and the stones say "Die." The beauty and the joy are too much for him; they are absolute over him; there is in them a high and dreadful conclusion; it is either flight or death. But if he stays? if he dies this little death? if he, so far, understands this new centre which is Love? It is, I think, true to say that from this point the quality of Love is found illuminating in a new way. (25–26)

This "new way" is perhaps equivalent to Dorn's in these love poems and in *Slinger*, in which the death of "I" was soon to follow. But even from this new center, Dorn doesn't forget that the New World to which he's returning with his new bride is where "Diego de Landa / the glyphic books destroyed" (CP 236) and where "the agent's dark eyes / burn from the dark short past / represent, handles the claims / of those we over ran / and they scream with their / fixed smiles / for satisfaction" (CP 245).

Dorn's work of the late seventies and eighties would mostly consist of the fierce and funny political epigrams of *Hello La Jolla, Yellow Lola*

---

3. Dorn's attainment of the center, though, more closely approximates St. Bonaventura, who wrote, at about the same time: "God is a circle whose center is everywhere and whose circumference nowhere." (Being compared to a Catholic theologian, however, wouldn't have pleased him.)

4. Brown's late essay "Revisioning Historical Identities" in *Apocalypse and/or Metamorphosis* is a central stimulus for this one. Directly after this sentence, he adds "Love, believe it or not, is what moves the sun and all the stars; as well as any political or social movements that may be moving.... There is a connection between Beatrice and the Revolution; communist politics must be grounded in Amor" (167168). Scully, in *Line Break*, asks (rhetorically) "Can you imagine looking Dante in the face and saying poetry and politics don't mix?" (5)

and *Abhorrences*, books in which love can be intuited only through its absence: "Environmental carcinogens / and large bowel cancer / go together like marble steps / and fancy dancers" (*YL* 18). He does, however, insist "I'm no hater" (54), even while noting (about Henry Kissinger) that "Moved was a bit too classy / to be used to note an emotion / and I doubt that it occurred to him" (71). These fierce moral discriminations dissecting the simulacra of love persist throughout his work, even to the last months of his life. "There is a certain amount of mail unconsciously addressing me in the past tense" he said in a letter to Tom Clark in June of 1997; in another letter on July 1, he vowed to ignore these "we're-scared-so-shitless-we-assume-you're-dead people … when I die I'll be dead but until then I'm living. Hope is beside the point." (qtd. in Clark 406). At the same time, he acknowledges in *Chemo Sábe* that

> My tumor is not interested in what
> or who I love,
> My tumor is not interested in love,
> no neoplasm is—the blind cells thereof are not interested in love
>   or affection,
> she sends out little colonies, chipped genes mark their crossing
>   the river
>
> ("The Decadron, Tagamit, Benadryl and Taxol Cocktail Party of
> 1 March 1999")

It's hard not to remember an echo of Pioneer Goodpole Matthews here, that arrogant usurper of what was common. The Alien of Dorn's tumor, like other enemies and rogue capitalists in his previous poems, assaults the condition of peace and common humanity that was always at the center of his work. Cancer is also "Catholic—it loves to / evangelize, and it will intermarry with anything / to claim the progeny" ("White Rabbit") and "was environmentally / Induced and politically generated" ("Enhancement"). The last poem in the book, and possibly the last poem he ever wrote, "The Garden of the White Rose" also echoes "The Air of June Sings" in its invocation of Dante's White Rose ("Budded on earth and blossomed / in heaven"), which, unlike himself, "will return next year" and "whose house is light against the / threatening darkness."

I mentioned a letter from Duncan McNaughton at the beginning of this piece, from which I'd now like to add a bit more context:

> you might say the nyad of his being has taken over—a radiant sweetness, even joy, which his tears ... etc. His being is literally flooding with this grace. It is "because of" his love. He has been one of the faithful of love. He was never finally capable of being otherwise.

Casual readers of Dorn would probably not think of him in exactly that way; many, after all, know his work only through *Slinger*, or the acerbic epigrams of the late '70s and '80s. Breaking through "the literalism and poverty of our thought about love," though, would mean realizing that love can co-exist with scorn and disdain for anything that would thwart it, and that it's closely aligned with what Dorn said was the function of the poet: "to stay as removed as possible from all permanent associations with power." Such a breakthrough might extend as well to our notions of politics and political concerns in poetry. Rather than limit these to the latest outrages of an illegitimate administration, we might more profitably realize that such a practice would be an "Art designed"

> to keep us apart, but more than that, to keep
> our senses apart, to make dormant at least
> and at best to make wrecked
> to have made inoperative the mechanism
>   whereby we track
> with the capturing powers of our own love
> the expanding universe, as it goes
> in our brief time beyond us (CP 100)

Only then, perhaps, might we experience "the return / onto the land again / the spore of politics / the ringing arrangement of love" (CP 144).

Works Cited

Alighieri, Dante. *La Vita Nuova*. Tr. Barbara Reynolds. Harmondsworth, England: Penguin Books, 1969.

Benjamin, Walter. "One-Way Street." *Reflections*. Tr. Edmund Jephcott. New York: Harcourt Brace Jovanovich, 1978.

Brown, Norman O. *Apocalypse and/or Metamorphosis*. Berkeley: U of California P, 1991.

Clark, Tom. *Edward Dorn: A World of Difference*. Berkeley: North Atlantic Books, 2002.

Dorn, Edward. *Chemo Sábe*. Boise, ID: Limberlost Press, 2001.

———. *Collected Poems*. Bolinas, CA: Four Seasons Foundation, 1975.

———. *High West Rendezvous*. South Devonshire, England: etruscan books, 1997.

———. *Interviews*. Ed. Donald Allen. Bolinas, CA: Four Seasons Foundation, 1980.

———. *Slinger*. Berkeley: Wingbow Press, 1975.

———. *Yellow Lola*. Santa Barbara: Cadmus Editions, 1981.

McNaughton, Duncan. Letter to the author. 3 November, 1997.

Pound, Ezra. *The Cantos*. New York: New Directions, 1975.

Scully, James. *Line Break: poetry as social practice*. Seattle: Bay Press, 1988.

von Hallberg, Robert. "'This Marvellous Accidentalism.'" *Internal Resistances: The Poetry of Edward Dorn*. Ed. Donald Wesling. Berkeley: U of California P, 1985.

Wesling, Donald. "'To fire we give everything': Dorn's Shorter Poems." *Internal Resistances: The Poetry of Edward Dorn*. Ed. Donald Wesling. Berkeley: U of California P, 1985.

Williams, Charles. *The Figure of Beatrice: A Study in Dante*. New York: Octagon Books, 1978.

Zukofsky, Louis. *A 112*. Garden City, NY: Paris Review Editions, 1967.

Politics & Time:
The Continued Relevance
of Edward Dorn's *Gunslinger*

Marjorie Perloff, in her short foreword to the fiftieth anniversary edition of Edward Dorn's *Gunslinger* (Duke University Press, 2018), finds herself surprised that she had mentioned Donald Trump in her previous introduction to the second edition, in 1989, when she had had no real consciousness of him at the time. Maybe, she thinks, he was already "part of our collective unconscious and hence of my own."[1] In much the same way, I think this poem has charted our collective unconscious, which might help to answer the elephant-in-the-room question: why is there a need for a fiftieth anniversary edition?

Gunslinger had its genesis in late 1966, when Dorn was in England teaching at the University of Essex and wrote a poem called "An Idle Visitation": it was the first appearance of the Gunslinger, "of impeccable personal smoothness / and slender leather encased hands" (3), who was probably based on Robert Vaughn's character in *The Magnificent Seven*. Dorn laid aside that poem for almost a year before returning to it and writing Book I of *Gunslinger* in the autumn of 1967. The longer poem developed over the next seven or eight years, eventually encompassing four books, a philosophical interlude called "The Cycle" and a one-volume newspaper, *Bean News* (not included here), and was published by Wingbow Press in Berkeley in 1975 and then, as mentioned, again in 1989. Maybe there'll be another edition in 2049, if books are still being printed then.

That is, maybe this isn't a poem that "maintains relevance," but is one of those works of art that fades in and out of consciousness as historical conditions determine. It's too easy to say that it was originally written during the Nixon administration, reprinted for the first time in the Reagan era, and now reappears during Trump's: that's just coincidence. While it's true that Dorn was playing the organ of the public mind in much of his work, especially the short and savage epigrams that made up his work of the late '70s and '80s—*Hello La Jolla, Yellow Lola,* and *Abhorrences*—in this poem he seems to agree with Charles Olson (in the "Bibliography on America for Ed Dorn," reprinted in this volume) that "History as *events* ... is now mostly hogwash" (247). *Gunslinger*'s treatment of history, and its subsequent politics, is much more complicated than that. I say "the poem's politics" rather than using words like genre or form because all of Dorn's work makes an argument, sometimes through specific political references, but even then only as a means to argue about poetry itself. In this poem, the central argument revolves around time, its relativity, and the threats to its proper functioning. At first, Dorn seems to be declaring his independence from the concerns of Olson, his teacher at Black Mountain College: Olson had started *Call Me Ishmael,* his study of Melville, with the thundering declaration "I take SPACE to be the central fact to man born in America, from Folsom cave to now." The Slinger sees it differently:

> Time is more fundamental than space.
> It is, indeed, the most pervasive
> of all the categories
> in other words
> there's plenty of it. (5)

While it's true that space in this poem isn't any longer the "simple location"[2] of the Western United States treated in Dorn's earlier work, it's also true that Olson never recommended that it should be: in the "Bibliography," he constantly denigrates "the local" and promotes space-time, the "human universe" the travelers of this poem are moving through. That's made clear in the next lines after the ones quoted above:

> And it stretches things themselves until they blend into one,
> so if you've seen one thing
> you've seen them all. (5)

Although it begins in Mesilla, New Mexico, and the travelers progress across the Colorado Plateau through other recognizable towns (Truth or Consequences, Farmington, and Cortez), "There are no degrees of reality / in this handsome and singular mass" (146). Indeed, this journey, which started on the trail to Las Vegas and Howard Hughes, ends—anticlimactically for some—near the Four Corners region, an abstraction created by the boundaries of four states. "The central question of Dorn's poem" wrote Thomas Foster in a 1997 essay, "is whether there is any 'place' outside the system of late capitalism where either poetic language or political resistance could be grounded."[3] I think there are such places, but that they can only be evoked through a language of space-time, as in this poem.

* * *

I suppose there may be some readers of American poetry unfamiliar with *Gunslinger*, so for them, here's the plot of this narrative-lyric-epic-mock epic poem: the narrator meets the Gunslinger in Mesilla, New Mexico and realizes he's in need of some instruction, which is provided by not only the Slinger but also Miss Lil (a frontier madam), the Talking Horse (of course), the Singer/Poet (because all epics need a bard), and Kool Everything, a '60s acid freak. In Book II, the narrator—heretofore known as "I"—dies, but is preserved by the administration of five gallons of uncut acid and then resurrected, in Book III, as the secretary to the Greek philosopher Parmenides. In between those books comes the famously difficult "The Cycle," which is actually the cycle of Rupert's wallet (Hughes morphs into Rupert and, later, Robart) and borrows some details from Hughes's actual trip from Boston to Las Vegas in 1966. Following are more speculations about the nature of time and reality and a lot of rapid-fire puns, as the company is joined by other characters—Dr. Flamboyant, Tonto Pronto, Taco Desoxin, Portland Bill, and the Speaking Barrel—and near the end, Robart escapes to Chile (or Siberia) riding a cow and the company disperses with affectionate farewells.

Not your average Western, even one like Jodorosky's *El Topo*. But what about that "relevance?" The first pictures of black holes were published just this year, but Rupert's "Winged Car" seems eerily similar:

> There are no *things* there as such
> Material is a not with the K detached
> All is transhistorical, functions
> Have no date … nothing occurs
> Dates have no function anyway …
> There is no light as we get it
> Nor any dark as such and the atmos
> Is the medium of variable tubes of spectra
> Like nothing yet gleaned from the Sunne (98–99)

A little later in "The Cycle," we meet Al the Atlante, one of Rupert's henchmen, who

> holds a tablet as a waiter holds a tray
> And upon the tablet rests an urn
> Which in turn bears the inscription
> EMIT NO TIME …
> Inside this urn are the ashes
> The final remains of a colossal clock
> Which stood in the hallway
> At the beginning of Organized History (104)

These lines introduce us to Rupert's main technique, his manipulation of time, in order to

> [suspend] the messengers in the formula
> of another instant
> That they may never see, feel and conceive
> And inhabit themselves for in *No Way*
> May they occupie their instant …
> They get sent for Burgers Everytime. (93)

"Oh Children! *The hour has struck by the clock* / Don't mean shit to him" (106). There are other moments in Dorn's poetry where things have no date, and they're usually ominous, like the tombstone of "Goodpole Matthews, Pioneer" in the early poem "The Air of June

Sings": "that pioneer sticks in me like a wormed black cherry / in my throat, No Date, nothing but that zeal, that trekking / and Business, that presumption in a sacred place."[4] That presumption is shared by Hughes, the original target of the Slinger and his company, who, as he morphs into Rupert and, later, Robart, becomes more of a caricature, with plans to invade our sacred, private places and freeze us there:

> The shrill scream
> Of metal to metal across the switch-yard
> The scream of the Accomplished Present
> A conglomerate of Ends, The scream of Parallels
> All tied down with spikes These are the spines
> Of the cold citizens made to run wheels upon ...
> Thus rhythm has a duty to de-tour the Vast
> Contra Naturam? Baby you ain't heard nothing yet (97, 100)

These threats to time's proper functioning—so that our attention is diverted by phantoms and "The shades are drawn against / The organ of the Imagination" (101)—constitute a major theme of the poem. It also seems like what's going on today, with our collective attention locked onto our screens, many of which are monitoring our every impulse and action. Shoshanna Zuboff, in her magisterial new book *The Age of Surveillance Capitalism*, gives a new name to this instrumental power, calling it "a new global architecture of behavioral modification ... based on total certainty" and accurately points out that the digital oligarchs are the robber barons of the twenty-first century, their business model premised on deliberate "psychic numbing" and our unconscious awareness of what they've been doing. "There's vivid precedent for this kind of encounter with an unprecedented new species of power"[5] she writes. I agree: part of that precedent was this poem. Today Hughes/Rupert might be a rogue manager from Google or Facebook who's figured out new ways to profit from what's been uncovered about our habits through our phones and laptops. "And Rupert cackles and grabs for Breath / And hollers This! / Is what we keep the slums awake with." (103)

This endless flow of digital entertainment can't be fought with normal weapons: that would be mere materialism, "a stutter / of some deep somatic conflict" (74). Since the digital universe has assumed cosmic status, something new has to arrive on the set to combat it, and that's what the Slinger and his company provide, primarily through their mutual conversation and repartee: resolutely anti-Cartesian, they move through a lively world where there's no distinction between subject and object. Or as Charles Potts has it, in his essay "On Ed Dorn's *Gunslinger,*" In order for a poem to be an epic, something heroic has to take place. In the case of *Gunslinger*, that heroism is language itself."[6] This is a poem that finds normal, referential language fatally compromised and in need of an upgrade, one that would retain awareness of its ambiguities, its capacity for puns (even groaningly bad ones) and its ability to incorporate random quotes from Shakespeare and Keats. Anything goes, one feels while reading, except language that names or explains or takes itself too seriously: reality is always going to be more slippery than that.

In that connection, it's important to remember that the goal of the recitation of "The Cycle" is for the poet to "make / their azured systems warm *Make your norm* / their own deliver them / from their *Vicious Isolation*" (89). While so isolated, it's impossible to apprehend anything real:

> That is, if you see a chair to sit in
> You sit in the image of that chair
> You fry an egg in the image of the skillet
> Which looks at you like you're Killin it
> Goodbye anything which dares purport to Be (102)

But that's exactly what the Slinger and his company do "purport." Their goals and desires are most often seen in the introductions to the various books, as in this lovely section from the beginning of Book II:

> This tapestry moves
> as the morning lights up.
> And they who are in it move and love its moving
> from sleep to Idea
> born on the breathing
> of a distant harmonium, To See
> is their desire (45)

So the real battle is between sensate beings, who "wander estranged / through the lanes of the Tenders / of Objects" (45), and those ruled by calculation—those living in space-time or out of it—and that battle is waged, and won, throughout the poem. But it has to be fought again and again, or more precisely, we have to continually reorder our minds and senses and reorient ourselves so as not to sink into stasis, because Rupert has "only named the game / you know, He AIN'T DELT YET" (101).

Einstein wrote, "the distinction between past, present, and future is only a stubbornly persistent illusion," which is why there's no "resolution" at the end of the poem. In space-time, there is no last battle at the OK Corral; indeed, every supposed confrontation, like the gun battle in the first book in which the Horse is threatened by a stranger or the attack by the owner of a horse who had been set free in the second, is revealed as a false stage set:

> speed is not necessarily fast.
> Bullets are not necessarily specific.
> When the act is
> so self contained
> and so dazzling in itself
> the target then
> can disappear (30–31)

On the contrary, in Rupert's car, there's no process or forward time anymore: "there is indeed inside only / The No No No" (99). That Dorn labeled Rupert's time distortions as "inside only" recalls his scorn—when I knew him in the late 1970s and in many interviews—about people's self-involvement: "e-mail" he wrote in "Languedoc Variorum," "is me mail."[7] It's instructive to remember that the prevailing mode of verse during the time this poem was written was called "confessional" poetry, which might describe some of his early work, but not this poem or anything after it:

> I think now the ego is pretty obviously dead. One of the most obvious facts of present life is people talking about themselves or referring to themselves or being preoccupied with themselves. That's about the most boring thing around. It's a habit that really

has seen its day. It's not that it doesn't persist, but it turns out that everybody's everybody else. All our stories are so interchangeable. [8]

Thomas Gardner, in his *American Poetry of the 1970s: A Preface*, quotes John Ashbery saying that his poems were marked by "an individual consciousness confronting or being confronted by a world of external phenomena."[9] I think that's probably still the mode of mainstream poetry, which can fill a lot of bandwidth before ever approaching the wit of James Wright on his hammock. Dorn, on the other hand,

> does not work within the largely egocentric, expressivist, or personist modes of his predecessors on the avant-garde scene ... does not believe that one can so simply identify oneself with the landscape without encountering prior manipulations of the scene. The 'self' is not some autonomous generator of emotions, opinions, feelings, or yearnings; like the landscape, it is subject to material and social forces beyond.[10]

In one of his more direct proclamations, the Slinger prays for the horse (and us) to "feel"

> and in your feeling move your bones
> for the want we now have of your access
> in this time so little beyond you ...
> needs your moving nerve
> as it dries tacked
> on the warp of its own flat sedimentary internalism (121)

This is why "I" becomes the secretary to Parmenides and why, as one of Dr. Flamboyant's paradoxes has it, "Everything is prehensible / for from that which is not / we fall off" (137). In a poem filled with philosophical jokes, my favorite is spoken by the Horse, "What makes Process and Reality heavy / is the &!" (134). In this way, "Our company thus moves collectively / along the River Rio Grande" (46).

This collective movement is yet another reason why "I" had to be transformed: at the beginning of the poem, he's like any other preconscious human, inattentive "and expect[ing] reason to Follow /

as some future chain gang does / a well worn road" (16). The Slinger challenges him:

> you want to know
> what something *means* after you've
> seen it, after you've *been* there
> or were you *out* during
> That time? (29)

That question might also be addressed to anyone analyzing what a poem means instead of just appreciating it.

* * *

And all of this is intensely political. For example, one recurring image in Dorn's work is the metaphor of a scar, from the early "Dark Ceiling"— "Broad black scar the valley is"[11]—to "The Sundering UP Tracks" from *The North Atlantic Turbine*: "Every little bogus town / on the Union Pacific bears the scar / of an expert linear division."[12] It also finds its way into the Prolegomenon of Book IIII

> where the green mesas give way
> to the Vulcan floor, not far
> from Farmington and other interferences
> with the perfect light
> and the glittering trail
> of the silent Via Lactea
> there is a civil scar
> so cosmetic, one can't see it (146)

Dorn always knew, and wrote about, the divisions of American life, its poverty, its injustice: "I BELIEVE in the insensitivity of America,"[13] he said in a 1980 interview. In *Slinger*, he's just dealing with those issues in another way, analogous to Chaucer, in the *Canterbury Tales*, standing outside the system of medieval political life he had always served. Near the end of the "Bibliography," Olson posits the "law" that "the real *power* contemporary to one is *kept hidden*," and recommends that we try to find out "how the money or 'ownership' really keeps its hidden hands on the machinery" (248). Similarly, Howard Hughes—in this poem and while he lived—is a non-presence, not to be found: "*this Howard is kinda / peculiar about bein Seen / like anywhere anytime"* (10). He's a shapeshifter, living "in the dangerous disguise of Nobody," (92) thus joining the tenuous nature of other things and characters in this poem, like the dissertation of Dr. Flamboyant, *"The Tensile Strength of Last Winters Icicles"*: "it doesn't exist. Like the star whose ray / announces the disappearance / of its master by the presence of itself" (82). But if, as Alan Golding argues, "Hughes and his cronies control also the terms for understanding history ... *then new terms, or new possibilities of understanding, must be created."*[14] When billions of dollars change hands in seconds through a few keystrokes, we have to "reverse the stream" of the turbine, not through material solutions but a shift in consciousness.

There's a certain impatience with the overly rigid square world—an inheritance, perhaps, from the '60s—against which "our mission is to encourage the purity of the Head" (63). But it's not an exclusive club: "All may wake who live" (46). The goal isn't scorn, as in many of Dorn's later poems, but the inauguration of a different way of seeing: "and we concur To See / The Universe" (46). In this sense, the poem can be seen as idealistic, promoting a better look at things: a new world, one in which humans can consort with the semidivine.

Finally, though, it's a poem, not a manifesto, and like the man said, it has to stay news. And *Gunslinger* does that by its humor and through its language: "We're *Here!* laughed Everything / Sounds like an adverb / disguised as a place, commented the Slinger" (65).[15]

Notes
1. Marjorie Perloff, foreword to *Gunslinger*, 50th anniversary ed., by Edward Dorn (Durham, NC: Duke University Press, 2018), viii.
2. For more on this term coined by Alfred North Whitehead, see Ferdinand Santos and Santiago Sia.
3. Thomas Foster, "'Kick[ing] the Perpendiculars Outa Right Anglos': Edward Dorn's Multiculturalism," *Contemporary Literature* 38, no. 1 (Spring 1997): 79.
4. Edward Dorn, *Collected Poems*, ed. Jennifer Dunbar Dorn (Manchester, UK: Carcanet, 2012), 109.

5. Soshanna Zuboff, *The Age of Surveillance Capitalism* (New York: PublicAffairs, 2019), 352.
6. Charles Potts, "On Ed Dorn's Gunslinger," Electronic Poetry Center (University of Pennsylvania, Ed Dorn Author Page), Ed Dorn Materials (formerly at *Cento Magazine*).
7. Dorn, *Collected*, 825.
8. Edward Dorn, *Interviews*, ed. Donald Allen (Bolinas, CA: Four Seasons Foundation, 1980), 49.
9. John Ashbery, quoted in Thomas Gardner, "American Poetry of the 1970s: A Preface," *Contemporary Literature* 23:4 (Autumn 1982): 407.
10. Donald Wesling, introduction to *Internal Resistances: The Poetry of Edward Dorn* (Berkeley, CA: University of California Press, 1985), 6.
11. Dorn, *Collected*, 186. 11. Dorn, *Collected*, 283.
12. Edward Dorn, "Ed Dorn's Views," interview by Tom Clark, in *Views* (Bolinas, CA: Four Seasons Foundation, 1980), 15.
13. Alan Golding, "History, Mutation and the Mutation of History in Edward Dorn's *Gunslinger*," in *World, Self, Poem: Essays on Contemporary Poetry from the "Jubilation of Poets"*, ed. Leonard M. Trawick (Kent, OH: Kent State University Press, 1990), 46. My italics.
14. Besides Olson's "Bibliography," this edition also reprints Michael Davidson's fine 1981 essay "To Eliminate the Draw: Edward Dorn's Slinger" and a short foreword by Marjorie Perloff, along with her 1989 introduction to the second edition. I'm also indebted to Tom Clark's biography of Dorn, *A World of Difference*, Alan Golding, "History, Mutation and the Mutation of History in Edward Dorn's Gunslinger," "'Kick[ing] the Perpendiculars Outa Right Anglos': Edward Dorn's Multiculturalism" by Thomas Foster, "On Ed Dorn's Gunslinger" by Charles Potts, and the fine collection of essays about Dorn edited by Donald Wesling called *Internal Resistances*.

Edward Dorn, Satire, and the Via Negativa

A talk given at the Louisville Conference on Literature & Culture
February 22, 2020

> Satire is not reasonable; it tends, in many versions, toward explosive and disorganized force; and because the powerless see power as theater, it is often theatrical: it mocks, parodies, devours literary genres that in other contexts make the world seem reasonable and orderly. So it can be formally antagonistic to form.
>
> —Robert Haas, *A Little History of Form*, 328

"Satire," said George S. Kaufman, famously, "is what closes on Saturday night." It certainly seems to have closed in American poetry: by and large, and despite its long history—Archilochus, the second poet of the western world after Homer, was rumored to have killed people by means of his iambs—examples of satire in our poetry since 1950 have been few and far between. There are reasons for that: for one thing, satire traffics in shaming, and it's hard to defend holding anyone up to ridicule; for another, one person's vice is another's kink, and we've become, these days, notoriously shy about inhabiting any sort of moral high ground. And then, I think, there's one more reason: satire might just seem too simplistic for academia.

A defense of satire, then, including some of the works of Edward Dorn discussed here, *Abhorrences* and *Yellow Lola*, needs to do more than state its ideal aims: to expose vices, follies and shortcomings in society in order to expose and eliminate them. One virtue of satire not talked about often enough is humor—another element in short supply—but there's also support from an unlikely source: theology. Negative theology is a form of thinking and religious practice which attempts to approach the Divine by negation, to speak only in terms of what it isn't rather than to presume to describe what it is. Kierkegaard, in a development of that idea, wrote that negative thinkers "have something positive, namely that they are aware of the negative; the positive thinkers have nothing whatever. They are deluded." This anti-idealistic sentiment has been promoted today by Barbara Ehrenreich, not a literary writer but a good one, who argues that the all-positive approach, with its rejection of the possibility of failure, helped bring on the great recession: anti-idealism is also promoted in much of the paradoxically positive late work of Edward Dorn.

*　*　*

Whether or not satire is unpopular in academia, there may also be periods of time in which it's unnecessary: people who think that think we might be living through one of those times now. Still, I detect some of the old moralistic taint around this sentiment, and think we need a new, more positive feeling about negativity.

When we think of the great ages of satire, besides the ancient Romans, we might think of the Restoration and the eighteenth century. But the "Restoration" was a total fraud, a complete masquerade: as is clear from Samuel Pepys' reportage of Charles II's return from exile, most Brits had just decided to forget that they had executed his father eleven years before. If there had been a *Washington Post* in that age instead of *The Tatler*, it would have been full of an astonishing amount of court lies, even more, perhaps, than were generated by the Trump Administration.

I'll return to the eighteenth century, but for now, a more congenial place to start might be with the negative everyone likes, Keats' negative capability, which seeks to mute the persistent and irritating rational ego so as to more fully appreciate the mysteries surrounding us. But that's not really controversial, especially for poets: a more telling defense might be found on Barry Watten's website. "*Negativity* has become a social threat, a thought crime that may be punishable—a moment of social reinforcement that has everything to do with normalizing our current extreme circumstances" … which, depending on how you feel about Barry, might even be prescient. Or we might invoke the spirit of Adorno's *Negative Dialectics*, which parodies Hegel's famous dialectic in the *Phenomenology of Spirit*; that was too programmed, thought Adorno, because "the whole is the false."

Samuel Freeman, in a review of a recent book about the Frankfort School, devoted a few paragraphs to *Negative Dialectics*, thought by some to be Adorno's "masterpiece":

> A major theme of this work is the mistaken focus on the subject of self-consciousness that has epitomized modern philosophy since Descartes and that is especially pronounced in the idealism of Kant and Hegel. Their "fallacy of subjectivity" ignores what Adorno calls "the primacy of the object" (remembering here Charles Olson's "objectism" in Projective Verse) or the crucial part played by material and social reality and historical circumstances in shaping consciousness and self-awareness. According to Adorno, idealism misconceives the subjectivity of the self and its relationship to the world: it regards the self as ultimately constituting reality "the absolute I as the world's source." The "sovereign mind" refuses to tolerate the idea of the objectivity of nature as prior to and independent of the self's subjectivity. This is idealism's "rage against nature," which aims to conquer and subdue all that is "not-I" or different from itself, and regard it as inferior.

Which finally isn't that different than Keats, just more wordy; it also reminds me of Melville's Captain Ahab, obsessed with conquering and subduing the white whale. Freeman adds, completely unnecessarily, "Adorno and Horkheimer were consummate pessimists."

But I'm not sure pessimism and negativity are all that worrisome. "It is never a positive image of redemption that one finds reproduced in his writings," writes Richard Wolin in *Walter Benjamin: An Aesthetics of Redemption*; "rather, by viewing the world from the standpoint of a hypothetical intelligible realm, it is his intention to set its degraded condition in relief all the more vividly" (91). This is true in Benjamin's surrealism essay, as in most of his post-messianic thought, from *One Way Street* on: he was suspicious of any easy surreal "cheerful images of reconciled life" (Wolin 134). What interested him was revolutionary nihilism, profane illumination, the negative, anarchistic dimension of the revolutionary process:

> And that means pessimism all along the line. Absolutely. Mistrust in the fate of literature, mistrust in the fate of freedom, mistrust in the fate of humanity, but three times mistrust in all reconciliation: between classes, between nations, between individuals. And unlimited trust only in I. G. Farben and the peaceful perfection of the *Luftwaffe*. ("Surrealism," *Reflections* 191)

Which will give any Western reader pause, but it does bring us closer to satire: "For only such 'profane' works of art (fragmentary, e.g., Kafka, Baudelaire) undercut the illusory Enlightenment vision of cumulative historical progress and its concomitant myth of the infinite perfectibility of man; and thus, *by setting in relief the incorrigible depravity of the human condition*, they refute the false semblance of reconciliation in fallen, historical life" (Wolin 59, my italics). I think all satirists, from Archilochus and Juvenal down to Ed Dorn, share similar goals, whether or not they envision a future Messianic age.

Speaking of the Messianic, here's Adorno in *Minima Moralia*: "Perspectives must be fashioned that displace and estrange the world, reveal it to be, with its rifts and crevices, as it will appear one day in the messianic light. To gain such perspectives without ... violence, entirely from felt contact with its objects this alone is the task of thought." Those "perspectives" are paradoxical, he said, because "negativity, once squarely faced, delineates the mirror-image of its opposite." Adorno and Benjamin were later to find fault with each other's positions, but on this they were united. In fact, Benjamin's ideas about allegory are still relevant:

> Just as a force can, through acting, increase another that is acting in the opposite direction, so the order of the profane assists, through being profane, the coming of the Messianic Kingdom. The profane, therefore, although not in itself a category of this Kingdom, is a decisive category of its quietest approach. ("Fragment")

Wolin develops the idea in different words: "For if the Messianic age is deemed the absolute antithesis of the historical age, the deepest insight into the most sacred truths of the former realm are allegedly indicated, albeit *negatively,* by the most thoroughly profane and forsaken aspects of the latter." (60–61)

So this might be a good time to mention the exercises in *negative theology* in which the Kabbalists engaged. Wikipedia says:

> Apophatic theology, also known as negative theology, is a form of theological thinking and religious practice which attempts to approach God, the Divine, by negation, to speak only in terms of what may not be said about the perfect goodness that is God. It forms a pair together with kataphatic theology, which approaches God or the Divine by affirmations or positive statements about what God is.

Dionysisus the Areopagite, in his work the *Mystical Tradition*, wrote about the "attempt through negative thinking to tear themselves loose from all that frustrates their pursuit of wisdom." There's some scholarly dispute about whether there actually was such a figure in the century after Jesus, and most people consider the source of this work as *Pseudo*-Dionysisus the Areopagite in the 6th century AD, but like the similar historical controversy about Hermes Trismegistus, the quality of the ideas is what matters: "God is better characterized and approached by negations than by affirmations. All names and theological representations must be negated." According to pseudo-Dionysius, when all names are negated, "divine silence, darkness, and unknowing" will follow.

Don't believe it? Let me give you a prime example of its opposite, the kataphatic or affirmative way. This is from a poem by the so-called "master of satire," Alexander Pope:

> All Nature is but art, unknown to thee;
> All chance, direction, which thou canst not see;
> All discord, harmony not understood;
> All partial evil, universal good.
> And spite of pride, in erring reason's spite,
> One truth is clear: Whatever is, is RIGHT. ("Essay on Man")

I don't think six more disgusting lines exist in English poetry. His buddy Voltaire, who had mercilessly satirized this Deist idea of intelligent design in *Candide*, calling it Panglosses' "best of all possible worlds," probably choked on his croque monsieur; it may also have been why Swift wrote "almost obsessively about dirt and shit, insisting that the opposite [of Pope's blind faith] was true" (Stubbs, *Jonathan Swift: The Reluctant Rebel*, p. 171). In this, he agreed with Benjamin, who wrote, in "Theses on the Philosophy of History," that "there is no document of civilization that is not at the same time a document of barbarism," and Horkheimer and Adorno, who were heavily influenced by that idea, wrote in the preface to their *Dialectics of Enlightenment* that they had set out to do "nothing less than to explain why humanity, instead of entering a truly human state, is sinking into a new kind of barbarism."

All of this is a long introduction to the subject of satire and satirical poems. Let's see what Wikipedia has to say about that:

> Satire is a genre of literature, and sometimes graphic and performing arts, in which vices, follies, abuses, and shortcomings are held up to ridicule, ideally with the intent of shaming individuals, corporations, government, or society itself into improvement. Although satire is usually meant to be humorous, its great purpose is often constructive social criticism, using wit to draw attention to both particular and wider issues in society. ("Satire")

Including a Wikipedia quote in a scholarly essay on satire might itself be subject to satire, but this isn't that essay. Still, the difficulty is clear: satire is mean. Swift hated human beings, was disgusted by them. When the Houyhnhnms want to eliminate the human race, also known as Yahoos, most people read it as some sort of moral failing: I think it was Swift's fondest desire. Surely he would have been unmoved by Bernie Sanders or Elizabeth Warren:

> Let them, when they once get in
> Sell the Nation for a Pin;
> While they sit a picking Straws
> Let them rave of making Laws;

> While they never hold their Tongue,
> Let them dabble in their dung. (Swift, "The Legion Club")

"My goal," said Ed Dorn late in life, "is to make pain funny." We're not exactly oblivious these days to vices, follies and abuses, but seem to have conceded their transmission to headline news and late-night comics. Perhaps people think satire is unnecessary, or too dull a blade. But there are virtues to satire that people are overlooking. Here's the Dorn poem that started 14 years of a different voice in his writing:

> An Opinion on a Matter of Public Safety
>
> *Air Bag* sounds like eminent sickness
> This device should not be permitted
> General Motors was right to suppress it
> and wrong to have relented
> and Nader should stay out of it.
> Driving is based on alertness
> whether that be loose or tight
> Those who let their attention wander
> must not be encouraged to survive
> by a bag full of air.

I think it's fair to say that nobody knew what to do with this poem—or even questioned whether it was a poem—when it was published soon after *Gunslinger*; the same was true with the short satires that made up much of his work over the next 15 years. In one of his first interviews after these poems, he said he was going for a "flat" approach, and it's true that satire is seldom if ever "rounded," or complete in and of itself; it's always pointing to a larger world, not as an artifact but as a potential lifeline, a hand stretched imploringly out, which is always ignored. And here I have to quote from myself, in an essay I wrote about Dorn in 2004:

> Dorn is not a poet of causes.... In fact, he is suspicious of anyone who *favors* anything. In a letter to Amiri Baraka in 1961, Dorn pronounced himself "embarrassed at the poor prospect of fellow poets singing the praises of anything so venal as a State.... *Sides* are a bigassed drag. The biggest small-talk of all, like which one are you on? Motherfucker"

So here are a few other short Dorn poems that caught my eye on re-reading:

God Created Man?

There's no problem with
"God created Man."
Of course He did!
He just created
a lot of monkeys first,
for practice.

Weather Report

Golfball size hail
reported in Littleton.
There are those of us
who have been to Littleton,
and could wish
it'd been soccerball size.

Environmental Carcinogens

Environmental carcinogens
and large bowel cancer
go together like marble steps
and fancy dancers

That last one is relevant in the age of the coronavirus. But at the same time, the motivation is always aesthetic, never purely political:

Night Watchman, look to my flashlight

The common duty of the poet
in this era of massive dysfunction
& generalized onslaught upon alertness
is to maintain the plant
to the end that the mumbling horde
bestirs its prunéd tongue.

Finally, one more note about the etymology of the word "satire":

> The word is a specific application of *satura* medley; this general sense appears in the phrase *per saturum* in the lump, indiscriminately; according to the grammarians (??), this is elliptical for *lanx satura* which is alleged to have been used for a dish containing various kinds of fruit, and for food composed of many different ingredients.

I've known this etymology for some time, and never see a bowl of fruit without thinking about it. More optimistic practitioners counsel us to look at everyday life and find some hints of intelligent design, but it's just as easy to look around and find things that are unbearably fucked up. As the *I Ching* says: no blame. But mostly, etymology suggests that satire is a miscellany, a combination of different elements, so shouldn't be seen as just one writer attacking another, or another society. Indeed, the narrator of most satires is often satirizing him or herself, and there's always more than one "side" being espoused.

Likewise, many of Celan's poems are "miracles of perversity," prophetic expressions of radical negativity, expressions of an a-theology of the sort that he expresses in his poem, "Psalm":

> No one kneads us again out of earth and clay,
> no one incants our dust.
> No one.
> Blessed are thou, No One. (tr. Pierre Joris)

To address a negated God—apophatically to engage absence—is to assert a continuing dialogue of the sort that is thought to be distinctive of Jewish devotion. But the value of satire isn't just negative: it might be the only way we can recapture the real. Stephen Marche wrote a brilliant re-evaluation last year of David Shields' *Reality Hunger* in the *Los Angeles Review of Books:* "How do we find the truth," he asked, "in an age when technology and politics have rendered the line between fiction and nonfiction nearly impossible to distinguish? How do we write about the real world when reality itself is up for grabs?"

> We live in dangerous times and need dangerous writing. How many pieces do you read that feel dangerous? The stakes could not be higher. The loss of the possibility of sense is at stake. The

content of human connection is at stake. Logos, ethos, and pathos have been stirred into a hot sticky mess. The willingness to blur fact and fiction, in a world of fulminant identity-creation, turns out not to be revelatory at all. It turns out to be stupid—unimaginably stupid, profoundly willfully stupid. The fundamental question for writing today is how to make the world less stupid. That is also the fundamental political question of our time.

I want to close with the end of a Chana Block poem, "Hester Street, 1898":

Better and better.
This they believed, this they taught diligently
unto their children,
who taught it to me.
Whatever I give you, my sons,
I can't give you that.

Block isn't a satirist, but what a killer ending. It too is a clear-eyed look at the situation, and there's something bracing and true about copping to its essential negativity. "It's all in how you look at it." Right, and satirists believe we should look at it without illusions … and maybe with a little humor.

Poetry and Heresy:
The Secular as "Smooth Space"

"There must also be heresies among you," warned St. Paul (I Corinthians 11:19), recalling the close connection heresy has with orthodoxy; indeed, heresy can only exist when there's an orthodoxy to name it. Such naming kicked into overdrive in the eleventh and twelfth centuries CE, when the Church defined heresy as "disobedience [to Canon Law] rooted in pride," and as a result, hundreds of those disobedient people were burned at the stake. Dante was a good enough Catholic to consign heretics to Dis, the City of Pain, in the Sixth Circle of Hell.

For Dante, though, their great sin was believing the soul would die with the body, thereby denying God ... or, at least, the medieval Catholic god: in other words, heretics were heretics because they were secular. Today it might seem like a stretch to equate being secular with heresy, but there is a heretical streak in some secular contemporary poets, and the two notions are connected in interesting ways. There have always been poets who wrote against the grain of whatever maxims were ascendant at the time, but that's not what I'm talking about here. Edward Dorn's late poem "Languedoc Variorum: A Defense of Heresy & Heretics" comes a little closer—for one thing, his contempt for the Catholic Church is apparent throughout—but while I'll talk a bit about that remarkable work in this essay, it doesn't approach the supreme heresy of a figure like Marguerete Porete, the Beguine mystic burned at the stake on June 1, 1310 at the Place de la Grève in Paris (Dante had begun writing the *Commedia* two years before). "There are among us," complained a Franciscan friar in 1274, "women whom we have no idea what to call … because they live neither in the world nor out of it." He was talking about women like Porete, who inhabited an ambiguous location between the secular and the religious, and while many spiritual concerns have lost currency today, that location is still on the map: we can see it in the non-Euclidean reality Dorn's teacher Charles Olson wrote about in "Equal, That Is, to the Real Itself" (1958), and it also resembles the "smooth space" of philosophers Deleuze and Guattari. Medieval heretics like Porete (as well as her contemporary, Meister Eckhardt) were writing about a place—an attitude, a practice—where the visible and invisible can meet; then as now, the real heresy was experiencing the sacred while still alive.

Deleuze & Guattari introduce "smooth space"—and its opposite, striated space—in *1000 Plateaus* this way: "in the first case space is occupied without being counted, and in the second case, space is counted in order to be occupied."

> Conducive to rhizomatic growth and nomadic movement, smooth space consists of disorganized matter and tends to provoke a sensual or tactical response—haptic—rather than a starkly rational method of operation or a planned trajectory. (477)

This recalls Olson's description of the haptic universe of "Human Universe," where the Mayans "wear their flesh with that difference which the understanding that it is common leads to," and certainly Dorn's *Gunslinger* is one example of space being occupied without "a starkly rational method of operation" (and lest we forget, Slinger is the demigod of "impeccable personal smoothness"). The works I've mentioned constitute an expanded notion of the secular, one that contains its own transcendence and deserves the honorific of heresy.

* * *

In the summer of 1958, Olson published the essay "Equal, That Is, to the Real Itself." The occasion was ostensibly a review of a recent book about Melville, but he disposed of the review part quickly: "The idea on which this book is based, naturalism, is useless to cope with Melville." What he really wanted to talk about was the German mathematician Bernhard Riemann, especially his concept of two kinds of manifold, the discrete and the continuous. The continuous was a new concept in the 1850s, which, Olson writes, Melville had unconsciously exploited to write "the first art of space [*Moby Dick*] to arise from the redefinition of the real." Olson identified that art with congruence or "spatial intuition," the ability to fashion "elliptical and hyperbolic spaces" and "projective space." In doing so, he drew on quantity, one of the four arcs of study he had laid out to Ed Dorn in the bibliography addressed to him a few years back, but here called it "quantity as intensive" rather than extensive, which made it possible "to get God in the street ... the necessary secularization of His part in the world of things." This new art of space, Olson wrote, quoting a letter from Melville to Hawthorne, was a way to apprehend "the absolute condition of present things"; indeed, he calls the writing of *Moby Dick* "the only time in a lifetime in which Melville did manage to throw off the Semitic notion of transcendence."

A few years later, in "Proprioception," he described seven different "hinges of civilization" that could be seen by looking at human history through this "continuous" lens, and warned that if we didn't employ it, "the present will lose what America is the inheritor of: a secularization which not only loses nothing of the divine but by seeing process in reality redeems all idealism [from] theocracy or mobocracy." It's never wise to ignore Olson's religious side: the voluminous historical records of Gloucester he uncovers in *The Maximus Poems* are always in the service of the spiritual, whether Hesiod's Greek gods or Corbin's Angels. When those concerns are joined with his constant argument against the calcified and traditional academic notions he came across in his reading, it's certainly not a stretch to call him heretical.

I don't know whether the concept of heresy has ever been applied to the ideas of Deleuze and Guattari, but areas of their presentation resemble Olson's use of the "continuous," for example, "In striated space, lines or trajectories tend to be subordinated to points: one goes from one point to another. In the smooth, it is the opposite: the points are subordinated to the trajectory" (478). And just a few sentences later, there's this:

> In smooth space, the line is therefore a vector, a direction and not a dimension or metric determination. *It is a space constructed by local operations involving changes in direction.* (My italics) These changes in direction may be due to the nature of the journey itself, as with the nomads of the archipelagoes (a case of "directed" smooth space), but it is more likely to be due to the variability of the goal or point to be attained, as with the nomads of the desert who head toward local, temporary vegetation (a "nondirected" smooth space). Directed or not, and especially in the latter case, smooth space is directional rather than dimensional or metric. Smooth space is filled by events or haecceities far more than by formed and perceived things. It is a space of affects, more than one of properties. It is haptic rather than optical perception. Whereas the striated forms organize a matter, the smooth materials signal forces and serve as symptoms for them. It is an intensive rather than extensive space, one of distances, not of measures and properties. (478–79)

This is difficult stuff, but it's important to note the use of Olson's word "intensive"; also, reading the word "line" here as "poetic line" makes it a pretty close description of Projective Verse. Not only are striated and smooth synonyms for Olson's (and Riemann's) discrete and continuous, they also suggest a secular familiarity with the divine, as in Walter Benjamin's concept of "profane illumination." Indeed, the philosophers caution that the two spaces exist only in mixture: as the conclusion to this chapter states, "Even the most striated city gives rise to smooth spaces: to live in the city as a nomad or as a cave dweller. Movements, speed and slowness, are sometimes enough to reconstruct a smooth space" (499).

A parallel to these ideas can be found in one of our most talented readers of Olson, the poet Don Byrd; in his *Poetics of the Common Knowledge*, he writes that it's possible for people to live "autopoietic lives," propelled by "the proprioceptive equilibrium of their autonomy":

> When it is possible to survey an event in a statistically significant run, science will serve; when we have only one chance, as is always the case for a living being, poetry is required.... There is also, however, an otherness that cannot be appropriated, an otherness

on which we have no hold and that has no hold on us, an otherness that is not a phantom of our own psychic dynamism. Confronted with otherness as utterly alien, the problem of language in all of its originality appears. Discourse, the language that continues by its prearrangements, falls into silence: nothing is *ex*-pressed or *re*-presented. One is required to speak but has no idea what language might be. (337)

Olson had started "Equal, That Is, to the Real Itself" by remembering Keats' notion of negative capability, and this passage by Byrd not only remains in mysteries, uncertainties and doubts but echoes Olson's skepticism of mere "discourse" by invoking a visitation from the Muses (or the Outside, or God), in the face of which, "any *doctrine* [i.e., orthodoxy] must be subsumed by reason, egocentrism … The alternatives must issue in a *practice* that can be indicated in a series of injunctions having no authority but their own results" (342). A little later, he summarizes "The knowledge of nonstatistical probability, Whitehead said, represents 'the secularization of the concept of God's function in the world.' That is, the creation of the world is a secular, fine activity" (348).

* * *

The connection between this "enhanced secular" and heresy, though, might still be elusive. The word comes from the Greek *hairesis*, "a taking, choice," from the verb *hairein*, "to take." As I mentioned earlier, heresy, in its formal sense in Roman Catholic Canon Law and moral theology, refers to "a sin of one who, having been baptized and retaining the name of Christian, pertinaciously denies or doubts any of the truths that one is under obligation of divine and Catholic faith to believe" (Lester R. Kurtz, *The Politics of Heresy*, 3). For our purposes, it's necessary to remember what heresy meant to Dante:

> He meant an obduracy of the mind; a spiritual state which defied, consciously, a power "to which trust and obedience are due": an intellectual obstinacy. A heretic, strictly, was a man who knew what he was doing; he accepted the Church, but at the same time he preferred his own judgment to that of the Church. This would seem to be impossible, except that it is apt to happen in all of us after our manner. (125–26)

That's from one of the best books of Dante criticism that I know, Charles Williams' *The Figure of Beatrice*, first published in 1943, and he explains the essential strangeness of this idea in the next paragraph: Dante, he writes, "believed it to be less important that men should think for themselves than that they should think rightly. We later moderns, on the whole, believe that men had better think for themselves even if they think wrongly" (127).

Of course, the ability to define "thinking rightly" has always been a good gig, and was for the holy fathers. Kurtz identifies some of heresy's more important characteristics:

> First, heresy refers to an intense union of both nearness and remoteness. Heretics are within the circle, or within the institution; consequently, they are close enough to be threatening but distant enough to be considered in error.... The heretic is, furthermore, differentiated from the schismatic or infidel, who is outside the church. When the medieval scholastics developed catalogs of heresies, they were concerned not so much with abstract heresy as with guilty heretics, persons within the community who were defined as a threat to the faith and to the institution.... Heresy thus has an important social dimension: the heretic is a deviant insider. (3–4)

Edward Dorn has always been identified as a poet (i.e., "within the circle") but could as easily have been called a "deviant insider." Indeed, lots of people wondered about his late practice, and for good reason: he didn't always seem to show the greatest respect for the institution of poetry, as in the poem in *Hello, La Jolla* called "Inspection":

> Poetry is now mostly government product
> therefore we can dispense with the critical apparatus
> the grades assigned to beef will do nicely:
> Prime
> Choice
> Good
> Commercial
> Canners
> Utility

Gunslinger can also be called heretical in the sense that nobody had seen anything like it before; at the very least, it shares with heretics a suspicion of the accepted versions of reality. "Someone bumped by the Rational," says the Slinger at the beginning of "The Winterbook" in Book III, "could get on a plea / for unencumbered forward motion." That's mostly because we "are inattentive / and expect reason to Follow / as some future chain gang does / a well worn road" (Book 1). Reason may seem like "smooth space," but it's more like what Robart, the villain in this cosmic western, wants to enact in his "Cycle of Acquisition": the real battle, as I wrote in a review of its 50th anniversary publication (reprinted here as "Politics & Time")

> is between sensate beings, who "wander estranged / through the lanes of the Tenders / of Objects," and those ruled by calculation—those living in space-time or out of it—and that battle is waged, and won, throughout the poem. But it has to be fought again and again, or more precisely, we have to continually re-order our minds and senses and re-orient ourselves so as not to sink into stasis, because Rupert has "only named the game / you know, He AIN'T DELT YET" ("The Cycle," 101).

Avoiding Rupert's plan means to traverse a path where the company becomes "the guest of time / where the afterbirth of space hangs / in the mirror of rime / and where one place / is the center of all this terrific actualism." That passage is in "The Lawg," the short poem that begins the third book, and it rhymes with Deleuze and Guattari's ideas about "smooth space":

> There is no vacuum in sense
> connection is not by contact
> sense is the only pure time
> connection is a mechanical idea
> nothing touches, connection meant is
> Instant in extent a proposal of limit

For some, the work that came after *Slinger* was a diminution: "The political urgency of the later writing," wrote August Kleinzhaler in a review of *Way More West: New and Selected Poems*, "seems to overtake the poetry and, finally, to undermine it." It was certainly a poetry more based on flat statement than most readers of poetry were accustomed to; in a 1977 interview with Stephen Fredman, Dorn read a poem from *Hello La Jolla* and commented

> See, that's exhortatory and pontificatory, you hear that? I was trying for a tone to see how actually flat and rigorously final you could make a line. I think that kind of necessity is left over from a certain bounciness of *Gunslinger* motion. The tone came up as a natural consequence.

He went on to say that he thought he was "done with the La Jolla Book" and didn't feel he needed to follow that rigorous flat style anymore, but he was wrong about that: it was followed by *Yellow Lola* (a series of "outtakes" from *Hello La Jolla* plucked from Dorn's notebooks by Tom Clark in 1980) and *Abhorrences: A Chronicle of the Eighties* (1990), a period of time in which some people questioned whether he was writing poetry at all. He agreed:

> I've been told that an able-bodied person, otherwise in possession of their faculties, really shouldn't do such a childish thing as write poetry. It's hard to ignore that argument. That's why I don't think I write poetry. And increasingly, I make statements, & if they have the ring of poetry, that's OK: I don't mind.

One of those statements that had the ring of poetry in *Abhorrences* was "The Turk":

> Leading off with a statement
> like "I am Jesus Christ"
> was perhaps a bit strong.
> Nevertheless, if Jesus Christ
> were to return to Earth,
> he'd shoot the Pope.

Rather heretical, even if you don't remember that putative assassination plan in 1983. But after *Abhorrences* was published in 1990, Dorn did, I think, face the dilemma of what else was possible in verse given his predilections and habits of the past 15 years. One attempt was "Westward Haut," an unfinished poem featuring dogs speaking German on a plane, which didn't quite take off (!), but had some good moments. This is from "Ascending the Platte":

> High above the retiring Earth
> the final shadows are streaking
> the surface, strobing the stubborn tractors
> of the breadbasket, illuminating
> the resentful faces of their drivers, the groundless
> battalions of mechanical serfs in the airline zines
> Land Redistribution is copy long gone,
> never to be discussed in the greasy coach
> and stopped up toilets of the only venue where
> one can see it all from the still visible impression
> of the Oregon trail to the circle compasses, whereby
> they have mined the old, untouched waters of the Aquifer.

"You don't speak German," I said to him once after reading it, and he said "My dogs do." But another work of the nineties, "Languedoc Variorum" (originally called "Languedoc Around the Clock") is the obvious example of a poem sympathetic to heresy; its subtitle is "A Defense of Heresy & Heretics," and one of the first notes in the vertical middle section of the poem called "Subtexts & Nazdaks" reads "Looking back over the tyranny of Rome and Constantinople, heresy is the only honorable mode and response." There are two poems dedicated to the Japanese gas poisoner Shoko Asahara, who injured 5,500 people "in reprisal for the Americanization of Japan," and one for Ezra Pound, "The Greatest Poet of this expendable century / [who] was also its greatest, most public Heretic."

But "Languedoc Variorum" is also heretical in that it doesn't *look* like anything that came before it: its first 19 pages is made up of three alternating sections, the poems themselves at the top, the "subtexts"— which often give a contemporary gloss to the historical events of the poems—in the middle, and a chyron, or news feed, running across the bottom, which gives an entirely different perspective on "smooth speech." It looks like this:

NAZDAQ PLUNGES, LITERATURE FORCED INTO BANKRUPTCY—
BURGHERS OF THEORY REPLACE SAMURAIS OF LITERATURE—

MARKET VALUE OF NEW ISSUE NIL—SELL IT—FEAR AND LOAFING UP A NICKLE—WIDEN THE RUNWAY—GOOFBALLS STEADY—TAX SHELTER QUOTATION: INTIMIDATION BY WIELDING THE DEITY LONG TERM—BUY—GROS CHIEN UP HUIT MILLE FRANC—PIG HOCKS GLUT THE MARKET—GET OUT—BODY PIERCING UP A QUARTER—BACTERIA COUNT SHARP INCLINE—VIRUS BURST STEADY—HOLY VIRGIN UP A NICKLE—FRANCESCA DA RIMINI DOWN FOREVER—FEAR AND LOAFING UP A PESO

Smooth, maybe, but as Deleuze and Guattari write, "smooth spaces are not in themselves liberatory. But the struggle is changed or displaced in them, and life reconstitutes its stakes, confronts new obstacles, invents new paces, switches adversaries." (499–500) These chyrons at the bottom of this poem are a parody of the endless stream of capitalism, the North Atlantic Turbine that flows through all our interactions, and while some of them are screamingly funny— WESTWARD HAUT—I AM NO GREEK, QUOTED—THE BEARS YAWN— let's be clear: "Languedoc Variorum," despite its formal eccentricities and collision of language games, is a poem of immense rage. Dorn's contempt for the Inquisition and the corporations that have become its moral equivalent bleeds from every page. Not that this should be surprising: his work from the beginning scorned authority and championed the people crushed under it. Here's the first stanza of a poem from his first book, *The Newly Fallen*, called "Prayers for the People of the World":

> They were an exercise the ages go through
> smiling in the church one time
> banging and blowing in the street another
> where brother is a state very often of glue
> coming apart in the heat
> of British Guiana where
> the drainage and open canals
> make difficult the protection of the lower classes
> who have lands and moneys, food and shelter
> in the great escrow called Never

A brief story: in 1992, while he and his wife Jennifer were in Languedoc, they came to visit my wife and me in the Czech Republic, where we were temporarily living as Peace Corps volunteers (I had managed to get him a reading at the local university). One night in Prague, we met up with other Americans who wanted to eat at an expensive restaurant we couldn't afford, and told them so, but luckily a well-to-do elder diner picked up the check: that didn't prevent Ed's lecturing her on Aristotle's condemnation of usury across the dinner table. He was, as August Kleinzhaler put it, "the least endearing, domesticated or predictable of poets, always determined to go his own way, no matter what anyone thought."

But did any of this make him a *heretic*? It's true that his criticism of society is often so severe as to resemble the first heretics, the Gnostics, and their inclination to see the material world as evil. He was also a heretic of sorts in his disgust for official verse culture, his revulsion of mainstream media's "breaking news" and "gangrene crosstalk," and his disdain for anyone who took up a political position: any position.

And heresy was always a matter of politics. Before Luther, when it arose from religious disputes among Catholics, one of its determinants was social class: for example, Tyndale's translation of the Bible into English, or the lay Beguine movement in France (one of the apostolic groups in Lombardy later persecuted by inquisitorial forces was called The Poor). We know about Dante's association with the White Guelphs and subsequent exile when the Black Guelphs took power; he put his political enemies in his poem not only for reasons of personal spite but because he thought they were tearing the fabric of society—"the community of the faithful"—through their divisive politics. And in these days of insurrection asserted or ignored, it's eerie to re-read one of the epigraphs to "Languedoc Variorum" from Thomas Hobbes: "My country, some few years before the civil wars did rage, was boiling hot with questions concerning the rights of dominion and the obedience due from subjects, the true forerunners of an approaching war."

But I keep coming back to the value of that secular world, where, after all, Porete and other medieval mystics lived and advanced new and different conceptions of what it meant for the divine to meet the human, the state of mind and presence that I'm calling the original "enhanced secular." Here's what Dorn, in that 1977 interview with Fredman, said about the subject:

> There are certain Obligations of the Divine, whether those can be met or not. Part of the function is to be alert to Spirit, and not so much write poetry as to compose the poetry that's constantly written on air. What I've read and what I hear merge to make the field in which I compose.

We also might explore the etymological history of "secular." It's from the Old French *seculer*, from Latin *saeculum* "generation, age," and was used in Christian Latin to mean "the world" (as opposed to the Church). The word was just coming into common usage while Marguerete Porete was alive, c. 1300, and meant something like "living in the world, not belonging to a religious order," extended metaphorically to successive human generations as links in the chain of life.

I started this essay by mentioning Porete, so want to say a little more about her trial for heresy as I close. To the Holy Fathers of the Inquisition, Porete and others like her were "living in the world" a little too much. The main thing that bothered them was her assertion that religious people at a certain level—the fifth station out of seven—could ignore the stringent code of virtues: "a soul annihilated in the love of the creator," she wrote in her book *The Mirror of Simple Souls*, "could, and should, grant to nature all that it desires." But their hyperactive imaginations ignored her subsequent statement that nature "does not demand anything prohibited" of the liberated soul. As Jennifer Deane writes in *A History of Medieval Heresy and Inquisition*,

> Virtues, like sins, like will, like the self, are abandoned in the process, all remnants of the distracting and ultimately unreal material realm ... virtues are no longer necessary *because the liberated soul no longer needs such relatively artificial guides to reach God* (169, her italics).

So, as so often in the centuries of witch-burning to follow, Porete's persecution was a case of lifting passages out of context and interpreting highly metaphorical thought literally. But even though she could have easily defended herself, Porete never uttered a word of explanation or defense in her own behalf. Perhaps she understood, as Michael A. Sells writes in *Mystical Languages of Unsaying*, that "the unrepentant heretic was a defeat for the Inquisition" (141), but better to use her own words to describe "the souls annihilated in love": "They have no shame, no honor, no fear for what is to come. They are secure. Their doors are open. No one can harm them."

Edward Dorn also suffered a metaphorical burning at the stake in his treatment for pancreatic cancer, which he documented meticulously in his last book, *Chemo Sábe*: "Throat ripping / Ball torching / Fire balling / Gut trenching, war—/ The Iodine drift / In the trenches / The blasting of the seat / of the soul" he wrote in the poem "Iodine Fire." Nevertheless, as he wrote in another poem in that volume, "Tribe," "it would take more paper / Than I'll ever have to express how justified I feel."

OLSON

Letter to Olson

Published in *Letters for Olson*, edited by Ben Hollander, Spuyten Duyvil, 2017

When I was in graduate school in Boulder in the late '70s, I was sharing a house with two other creative writing students whom I miss and with whom I wish I were in touch (their names are Oscar and Randy). At one point while living in this quasi-suburban house, I remember throwing the *I Ching* (I always used the sticks, never the coins) and asking whether I should follow the "Olson philosophy" in my poetic life. I probably used other words when I was asking the question and wish I could reproduce them here, as one of the deals when consulting the *I Ching*—as I remember it—was getting one's question down to no more than eight words. Still, the answer was entirely positive. In fact, it was more than just "positive": it must have been insistent. So what was I really asking the oracle?

    I think it was whether I should follow mainstream poetics or whether I should be a "rebel." Perhaps that question, in all its infinite manifestations, is still an object of concern to people who write poetry today: I don't know. But the fact is that I hadn't even *heard* of Charles Olson until, in my junior year, I transferred to UC Santa Cruz, and had the great good fortune of taking a two-quarter class from Norman O. Brown, the first of which was on Pound's *Cantos* and the second on people who followed him, including Duncan and Olson. I don't think any of my professors at UCLA, where I spent my first two years, had ever heard of him: it was all Dylan Thomas and Sylvia Plath. Is he on the curriculum for undergraduates now? Probably not. And what does the word "mainstream" even mean these days? In the last

20 years, the AWP has assumed monumental status among creative writers, at least those attached to universities. I ignored them for a long time until I attended one of their annual conferences last year (I had finally published a book of poems and wanted to get other poets to read it). But how many people at this astonishingly huge conference, with hundreds of rows of small press publishers selling their wares, had been similarly influenced by Olson and the Black Mountain aesthetic? The answer, I suspect, is: not many.

Even Nobby (as all his students called him) said—half tongue in cheek—that Olson was a fraud because he didn't really know any Greek. "Let the young / educ the young" is what I remember in this context, and I just looked it up on Google and found it was actually in *Paterson*, a letter from Pound that Williams had reproduced ... and did Olson then put it in *Maximus?* Dunno. Anyway, that was the lineage for me: Pound and Williams leading to Olson. It's hard to reproduce the excitement of reading things like "Projective Verse" and "Human Universe" for the first time, but it was large. And then, in my second year of graduate school, Ed and Jenny Dorn came to Boulder.

I've written about the experience of being Ed's student and friend at *Cento* magazine (reprinted in this volume as "Once Upon a Time with West Ed"), and even though Ben Hollander wanted me to somehow adapt that story as a model for this one, I find that I can't, any more than I can somehow speak to Olson directly in a letter. But I can reproduce sections from another old piece, a review I wrote of two books by Dale Smith and Richard Blevins that wound up talking mostly about Olson. It turns out that, once formed, those bonds of "legacy" are hard to break: I'm still riding some of the ripples of that tremendous wave, coming back to Eric Havelock to write about the origins of written language, for example, for a textbook I'm writing. I said in a short letter to *House Organ* about the Heriberto Yepez flap that I didn't have the time to devote to that somewhat spurious issue (but I'm glad that Ken Warren and Ammiel Alcalay did, and have used it well). But this is what I did have time for, once upon a time, and still do.

from "What I See in Dale Smith's *American Rambler* and Richard Blevins' *Fogbow Bridge*"

Published in Charles Potts' magazine *The Temple*, Fall 2002

Anyone with more than a passing acquaintance with Charles Olson's work is familiar with the famous beginning of *Call Me Ishmael*—"I take SPACE to be the central fact to man born in America, from Folsom cave to now." Not as many, however, might know his literary formulation a few paragraphs later—after describing the Great Plains as "the fulcrum of America," he says "Some men ride on such space, others have to fasten themselves like a tent stake to survive. As I see it, Poe dug in and Melville mounted. They are the alternatives."

However accurate this proposition, the writers under review here have adopted the Melvillean alternative, "that travel/travail" as Richard Blevins has it in "Journey to the Source." It's implied in the titles of the books, *American Rambler* and *Fogbow Bridge*, and also, I think, in their methodology. Yet the poems also explore a corresponding stasis, a "rootedness" that can develop as a result of such travel, vertical as opposed to horizontal, inward as opposed to outward. These books, finally, give a sense of how what might be called the "Olson legacy" is being carried and transformed by various practitioners today, after twenty years or so of a quite different poetics being in the ascendant....

I had bought Richard Blevins' *Fogbow Bridge* largely because I saw Dorn had written a blurb for it and because Blevins had contributed a nice poem to a collection of tributes assembled by Ralph LaCharity, *A Wake for Ed Dorn*, but hadn't read it yet. So, in mid-June, feeling tentatively buoyant at the prospect of my first summer off from teaching in seven years, I started looking through it haphazardly, noting many references to Dorn and Olson and Haniel Long, a central personage in one of the many longer poems collected therein, "Court of the Half-King." At this point, the idea of combining reviews of both books in one essay dawned; I then came across a short poem by Blevins called "A Good Early Start," which begins

>   I don't teach again
>   til September
>   and today
>   is June thirteen.

Actually it was the fourteenth, but the coincidence was so sublime that I started making notes immediately! It's through connections like these, after all, that I came to poetry, and it's even possible that the writing I'm drawn to—including, very much, these two books—is about the possibility of such connection. Nothing else will (says Olson through Whitehead) do. Or as Dorn has it in *Slinger*, "Everything is prehensible / for from that which is not / we fall off"

> I don't think any of us should be talking if any of you haven't taken any one of the hallucinogens, because you really don't know, you're really just talking academically because you ought to have the experience, that's all.
>   —Charles Olson, "Under the Mushroom"

In addition to the content, the twisted, blunt, stacatto lines and line breaks here [in Smith's *American Rambler*] give a sense of the knotted and tangled nature of the experience, make these lyrics not, as Olson derisively calls lyric in general, "a block in the way of nature," but a passage/wormhole through *to* it; "it's not enough / to imagine it" Smith says, echoing Long's earlier insistence on the necessity of undergoing the experience—"only the whole body / knows what took place." And only through the whole body, one infers, can one attain those healing powers, the capacity to give paradoxically generated by having nothing to give....

> How to traverse is all.... This is a transit question: how far does any of us need to go to arrive? ... We don't know much about transit, why we will go from one place to another.
>   —Charles Olson, "Under the Mushroom"

So what is the "Olson legacy" anyway? Luckily, there are lots of people still around who knew him and will have, thus, their own particular senses. For me, Olson's admonitions to go to it are central: "This is eternity. This now. This foreshortened span." That's from "The Resistance," an early prose piece that was the first one collected in

Creeley's *Selected Writings of 1966* (I own the new, handsome *Collected Prose* but haven't had the heart to start using it), which might have been the first words of his I'd read. That is, no matter how learned or abstruse his references get, his insistence on putting them to *use*—to construct that "actual earth of value"—is what will always stay with me. When I consider the emphasis on (mere) text that's taken hold in the academies and elsewhere these last twenty years, I seem to be in a different world entirely. (In a way, the *project* of both of these books reminds me of the advice Olson had given Dorn in *A Bibliography on America* (1955), that what was important in terms of historical study is "how, as yourself as individual, you are acquiring & using same in acts of form").

Occasionally something he's said will still literally jump off the page. For example, in a panel discussion in Vancouver along with Duncan, Ginsberg, Creeley and Philip Whalen in 1963, he's expounding on his poem "Place; & Name" (a study of which helped immensely in the writing of this review), and he mentions a recent statement by then Secretary of Defense McNamara, to the effect that "nothing is going to happen to us in our lifetime."

> It isn't quite what he said, but as far as I can see it's just exactly a guarantee that really all our worries and fear and the danger has been really organized and set aside, so that there is nothing in our lifetime.... Like, McNamara does not support us in that remarkable projection, right? It just doesn't support us at all. In fact, on the contrary, it accomplishes the end of destruction, which is it destroys us sitting right here. It really just says we're all dreaming right through into some moment later, when this sort of thing will have gone away. It's—what is it?—it's wish-magic, brand new modern wish-magic. Just get rid of it. I think there's a deep split. ("On History," *Muthologos*, Volume 1)

No kidding! I leave it to wiser souls to ascertain to what degree this McNamarian vision has become "national missile defense." Later, in "A comprehension," this same "wish-magic" becomes "the new post-European concept of soul as *psyche*; ... the primary error of analogy as logic instead of image or actualness." The antidote to this poison was always the perception of and attention to minute particulars, "so that gesture and action, born of the earth, may in turn join heaven and hell" ("The Advantage of Literacy"), along with a new/old system of discourse in which "the words and actions reported are set down side by side in the order of their occurrence in nature, instead of by an order of discourse, or 'grammar,' as we have called it, the prior an actual resting on vulgar experience and event." ("Review of Eric Havelock's *Preface to Plato*").

But, you know, either this stuff gets you or it doesn't. It's possible that many practitioners today think Olson is an anachronism, even though there are, happily, others who are mining this rich ground, each in different ways. Enough, perhaps, to conclude with Olson's answer to the question he poses about transit at the beginning of this section, in the talk called "Under the Mushroom": "It's not some step that you take easily, or that even to take the step means anything more than you know without taking the step, if you stop to think about it. You're just who you are; what you do, if it's any good, is true; and you are capable of being alive because of love."

Charles Olson and Finding One's Place

A lecture given at the Gloucester Writers' Center, June 1, 2016
(podcast at https://gloucesterwriters.org/podcast/6795/)

"I'm a cosmopolitan," said my friend Jerry Rothenberg, when I told him the title of this lecture: "I'm not sure I want to find my place." I remember talking about the etymology of that word with Ed Dorn one day, its superiority to "metropolitan," the long view rather than the local. On the other hand, I've been reading Peter Anastas' novel *Decline of Fishes* while I've been here, which deals with the mostly unsuccessful struggles of the local fishing industry in Gloucester to preserve itself against encroaching gentrification, and yesterday had my first look at the Man at the Wheel Statue at the Fishermen's Memorial: "no difference," though, as Olson wrote, "when men come back."

And that's the story, isn't it? The local vs. the cosmos … or, as the writer we're talking about tonight had it, the local *as* the cosmos. But as the flyer for this lecture says, I've lived a lot of places, from Oklahoma City to Czechoslovakia to Encinitas, and if my wife Sara has anything to say about it (and of course she does), we'll be moving out of So Cal as soon as I retire in a few years. So I'm an unlikely candidate to tell anyone here about finding one's place, unless I can somehow usefully complicate our understanding of that word. Which I'll try to do, and then simplify things again. Because my real thesis is a line of Dr. Williams from *Paterson* that we all know, but forget every now and then: "The writing is nothing   the being in a position to write   that's where they get you." So finding one's place, for me, is being in a position to write. Or as Jack Hirschman had it in the recent *Letters to Olson*, Olson "is the one who most brightly shows the mind and heart how to / Begin. / The key word: Begin. / The essence of what poetry is." (181)

* * *

Written and published in 1960, "What I See in The Maximus Poems" has been called the first important critical evaluation of Olson's epic poem.

> you don't have a place just because you barge in on it as a literal physical reality, or want it to prosper because you live there. Instead go see the Grand Canyon, that's what it was made for. Place, you have to have a man bring it to you. You are *casual*. This is a really serious business, and *not* to be tampered with.

It's an argument, in one sense, for place *not* being local, at least not in the sense of parochial:

> I am certain, without ever having been there, I would be bored to sickness walking through Gloucester. Buildings as such are not important. The wash of the sea is not interesting in itself, that is luxuria, a degrading thing, people as they stand, must be created, it doesn't matter at all they have reflexes of their own, they are casual....

Dorn would always try to relativize simple location, most obviously in *Slinger* but also in his Olson Memorial Lecture in 1981 (published by Ammiel Alcalay in his Lost & Found series and also at https://media.sas.upenn.edu/pennsound/authors/Dorn/Dorn-Edward_Complete-Recording-1_Olson-Lectures_03-19-81.mp3): "[R]ealism precludes the occult, except on the coast. And the reason for that is that the coast is not the West, being infested with Orientalism" (about 25 minutes in). There are some funny shots about gods with eight arms and three faces in the "Maximus" essay; the thing about Ed was that his disdain was awe-inspiring, and to the extent that I got any spiritual instruction in Boulder, it wasn't from the Buddhists but from sitting around his dining room table with his wife Jenny and other friends who were passing through. It was great to hear his voice again in that lecture, because it reminded me that to truly understand him, you have to hear his intensely ironic, sarcastic, deadpan tone of voice. And it was Ed who got me on to the eighteenth century, about which more in a moment.

Anyway, here's some backup for his idea about east and west from an unlikely source, Deleuze and Guattari, who wrote in *Anti-Oedipus*: "But there is the rhizomatic West, with its Indians without ancestry, its ever-receding limit, its shifting and displaced frontiers. There is a whole American 'map' in the West, where even the trees form rhizomes. America reversed the directions: it put its Orient in the West, as if it were precisely in America that the earth came full circle; its West is the edge of the East."

* * *

I was reading the *New York Times* today about the NBA Playoffs and there was a note about Klay Thompson of the Golden State Warriors: "he thinks of the game as a process, describing himself as a 'continuous player.' Rather than dwell on individual possessions—the makes, the misses—he searches for his place within the game's broader rhythms." This is close to a zen-like saying about basketball that I like: let the game come to you. All this seems to be an argument for place being relative: just to include another local comment about the limitations of the local, the Boston NPR station this morning was interviewing a woman named Amy Cuddy, who said that people will never attain presence completely: "You can't 'Be Here Now' all the time." Speaking of spiritual instruction, I was glad to hear a reference to Ram Dass, one of my early influences.

* * *

Let's get back to the blurb on the flyer for this talk for a minute:

> So to start, it's one's literal place—the ground—that we're talking about, as Shakespeare wrote about his lover: "My mistress, when she walks, treads on the ground." But that place can also be inhabited in other ways, and has been by Olson and other writers like Geoffrey Chaucer—a place without hierarchy that exists without "displacing" other places—possible with "the attention, and / the care," even when "so few / have the polis / in their eye." That's the project.

Or at least, that was the project, because to be honest, I had no idea what "finding one's place" meant when I proposed the title to Henry (Ferrini) a few months ago. Of course, Olson's place was here, Gloucester, the city of Maximus, where the Maud/Olson library will open in a few weeks down the street. What else needs to be said? Well, perhaps that "such a precise location, as isolated as it is, now seems almost a luxury," Ammiel Alcalay asks, in his remarkable *a little history*:

> Has not the velocity of change and consumption, through some law of diminishing returns linked to depletion of the planet's life sustaining resources, overtaken our ability to stay in one place and allow ourselves the idleness local knowledge demands? (144–145)

Similarly, Michael Davidson, in an essay about Ed Dorn and his relation to Olson, writes that "'place,' as a strictly geographical term, no longer exists; it has been so totally mediated by entrepreneurial capital that one locale is the same as any other." So the ground might be here, but the only way we can make that ground an actual occasion, as Whitehead had it, or "the whole of the condition of space," as Jeremy Prynne had it, is if the lecture becomes a circular curve, "the condition of the cosmos where the cosmos becomes myth." By the way, that's a quote from a letter he sent to Dorn that Ed read in his Olson lectures.

So to that end, I'll announce tonight a new sub-title, namely, "My Special View of History." And that's because of what Olson wrote when he was preparing the materials for his own: "*a man's life is an act of giving form to the condition or state of reality at the exact moment of his birth*—So therefore error or truth in the execution of that imperative is the whole shot!" (11)

As it happens, I was born on April 4, 1953, which turns out to be the exact day Olson, at Black Mountain, received in the mail Vincent Ferrini's magazine *Four Winds*, later the occasion for *Maximus* Letter 5; indeed, that week in 1953, a run of *Maximus* poems were started (thanks to the scholarship of Tom Clark and George Butterick here) including Letter 6, from which the quotes to the flyer Henry made were taken. So, in context:

> Eyes,
> & polis,
> fishermen,
> & poets
> > or in every human head I've known is
> > busy
> both:
> the attention, and
> the care
> > however much each of us
> > chooses our own
> > kin and
> > concentration

and a few lines later

> so few
> have the polis
> in their eye

So these are the poems by Olson that were written the week I was born, which is slightly mind-boggling, at least for me! But as for the actual content of "Letter 5," I have to go back to Ammiel's *a little history*, in which he makes clear that Olson depended on Vincent and his wife Mary as "the one brother and sister that I have" and that the so-called "slam" against Ferrini and *Four Winds* has been taken out of context:

> One of the things that Olson is trying to say here is—if you're going to have an independent society, which is this magazine— an independent community—then it has to be as good as any other endeavor. I think at some point he compares it to a fishing vessel where everybody on your crew would have to be tested, you wouldn't want to have somebody on that boat, on your crew, just because you heard they were good. That could be very dangerous. So Olson engages Ferrini. (103–04)

I'll always be grateful that I was engaged in that way in my education, first by Norman O. Brown at UC Santa Cruz and then at the University of Colorado with Ed, in very much the same form as Robert Duncan says, when he talked about "the force of Charles and his use of the school":

> He saw education as spiritual attack. On the first level we can take it as to attack a subject. There also was a kind of spiritual attack, it seems to me, on students frequently. He wanted things to happen in them. I don't mean he wanted things to happen in his classes. He wanted things to happen in them spiritually.... Charles wanted to produce a new and redeemed man. This is actually Charles' alchemy. (qtd. in Charters 11)

* * *

In a way, this lecture started three weeks ago, when I picked up a few books about Olson at the Encinitas library (Encinitas is the town I live in in Southern California, my current "place," at least geographically, which I've written about in my book *Coastal Zone*).

But it really started earlier than that, when Robert Duncan, in a panel discussion in Vancouver in 1963—where Olson read his poem "Place; & Name"—also used the words of the blurb on the flyer: "Someone here asked a question about care and attention. And we did get that the only place you have any care or attention is right where you are, right where you are in the poem or right where you are in the event."

> a place as term in the order of creation
> & thus useful as a function of that equation
> example, that the "Place Where the Horse-Sacrificers Go"
> of the Brihadaranyaka Upanishad is worth more than
> a metropolis—or, for that matter, any moral
> concept, even a metaphysical one ("Place; & Names")

Robert Creeley was quoted in Ann Charters' introduction to *The Special View* that Olson was "trying to break the habit of history as some discrete ordering apart from what energies or active forces were the case," and that "the only place they [the materials of history] could obviously be was where you were, if they were to be there at all" (6). So bearing in mind Slinger's caution that "All is transhistorical, functions / Have no date," let me throw out a few other dates that make up this particular special view: I've already mentioned 1960 and 1981 and 1953: then there are 1390, 1742, 1847, and, again, this week.

And by the way, it's not a literary inheritance I'm tracing—it has more to do with orality and visuality than literacy—but I do want to bring in other writers who have inhabited this ground, and talk about how they got there, most of them not usually mentioned in the same breath as Olson: I'm thinking of Geoffrey Chaucer and Henry Fielding. That's partly because I've been teaching British Literature over the last four months while I've been writing and not writing this lecture, and the two activities sometimes became confused, but it's also because the nature of that confusion is very much what "finding one's place" is all about for me. So here are the next parts of this lecture:

1. 1390–1399: Chaucer gives up his court duties and composes *The Canterbury Tales*
2. 1742: Henry Fielding publishes Joseph Andrews
3. 1847: Emily Dickinson writes a letter

Gerrit [Lansing] took us to see Jack Hammond's medieval castle yesterday, where he used to live, and one of the things I found out while teaching this Brit Lit class was my special connection with Chaucer's *Canterbury Tales*; that is, I told you that my birthday is on April 4, and that's, it turns out, when the poem begins: "and the Yonge sonne / Hath in the Ram his halfe cours y-ronne" … that is, when the sun is halfway through Aries.

Anyway, the first tale had been told by the noble if somewhat inarticulate Knight, and the narrator wants a monk to go next, following the order of the medieval social hierarchy. But the drunken Miller interrupts and insists that he be the next to tell his story (a recording of the prologue can be found at https://www.youtube.com/watch?v=bGVDeafmsco, this section about 40 seconds in):

> "Now telleth ye, sire Monk, if that ye conne,
> Somwhat to quite with the Knightes tale."
> The Millere, that for drunken was al pale,
> So that unnethe upon his hors he sat,
> He tolde avalen neither hood ne hat,
> Ne abiden no man for his curteisye,
> But in Pilates vois he gan to crye,
> And swoor, "By armes and by blood and bones,

> I can a noble tale for the nones,
> With which I wol now quite the Knightes tale."
>   Oure Hoste sawgh that he was dronke of ale,
> And saide, "Abide, Robin, leve brother,
> Som better man shal telle us first another.
> Abide, and lat us werken thriftily."
>   "By Goddes soule," quod he, "that wol nat I,
> For I wol speke or ells go my way."
>   Oure Host answered, "Tel on, a devele way!
> Thou art a fool; thy wit is overcome." (10–27)

In other words, "There are no hierarchies, no infinite, no such many as mass, there are only / eyes in all heads, / to be looked out of" ("Letter 6"). The Miller then goes on to deliver an obscene parody of the impossibly romantic and mostly mangled Knight's Tale, and if you've read it, you know its comic pleasures. Of course, this isn't the only time in the history of poetry when a large man under the influence of alcohol has assumed the stage and held forth to an audience, some of whom found his lecture unwelcome:

> "Now herneth," quod the Miller, "alle and some!
>   But first I make a protestacioun
>   That I am dronke, I knowe it by my soun.
>   And therefor, if that I misspoke or seye,
>   Wyte it to the ale of Southwerk, I you pray." (28–32)

But the point, or one of them, is this: when Chaucer is introducing the various characters in the Prologue, the last group includes the so-called untrustworthy servants, including the Miller, but also "A somnour, and a pardoner also, / A maunciple, and myself—there were namo." In other words, he includes himself among the rogues, and by so doing, makes a pretty funny reference to the beginning of Dante's *Divine Comedy*, when Dante meets the famous poets of Limbo and includes himself among them. And he does so not because he's a thief or some kind of untrustworthy servant himself. Rather,

> by beginning *The Canterbury Tales* with the Knight and Miller, Chaucer makes a clear statement that he is writing no longer from within the world in which he had for all his life served. On the

contrary, he is now standing outside that world as an independent, and by no means uncritical, observer. He is not an untrustworthy servant—like the Miller, Reeve, Manciple, Summoner, and Pardoner. But his position is even more radical: he is a servant no more. (Patterson 14)

As Olson with the Democratic Party, so Chaucer with the court of Richard II. The radical act, the break between this and his poetry that was, to some extent, "commissioned," has to be recognized: finding one's place is to move from slavery to freedom.

But there's more: "[Chaucer] shows us a world in which our view of hierarchy depends on our own position in the world, not on an absolute standpoint" (Mann 26). The pilgrims in Chaucer's tales are grouped on how they work and what they do, not on ideas of chivalry or any other ideal conception. Written in then still-rare vernacular English, his is a purely comic and narrative art. The Miller's Tale

> finds the physical world enough—its plenitude, its charm, its energy, its rules ... an idea of order sufficient to man's needs ... a world temporarily—by an act of imaginative exclusion—unshadowed by Last Things (Kolve 92).... Characters in such stories live, for the most part, as though no moral imperatives existed beyond those intrinsic to the moment. They inhabit a world of cause and effect, pragmatic error and pragmatic punishment, that admits no goals beyond self-gratification, revenge or social laughter. (70)

To be secular is to exist in a place where no moral qualifiers are allowed to exist: "an animal world in which instinct takes the place that reason holds for man, a world in which instinct and necessity are one" (79). "the HEART, by way of the BREATH, to the LINE." "It's the secular I don't think is going to go out of our bones yet," wrote Olson in "Bill Snow," who later in that essay has a rather startling prediction of the War on Terror:

> by which courage is suddenly a new word in the dictionary, that we are surrounded by enemies and must stay fit. It sounds like athleticism to me, and when all that is is only demonstrated by self-consciousness of that it is, games are being played. I'd go

straight from Nature to the World. If form ever did lie in tales and on short stretches of distance between personally known towns already the Collector of Port Duties on Wool in the city of London in 1390 had it.

* * *

Another time Olson refers to Chaucer is at the beginning of "Proprioception," after detailing the old "psychology" of feeling, desire, sympathy and courage being linked to the heart, liver, bowels and kidneys, which he calls "(Stasis—or as in Chaucer only, spoofed). Today: movement, at any cost."

So let's move on to 1742, when another comic writer, Henry Fielding, is trying to make a case for his novel *Joseph Andrews*, one of the first novels in English, and he's having a rough time trying to classify it: "it may not be improper to premise a few Words concerning this kind of Writing, which I do not remember to have seen hitherto attempted in our Language" (3). One of the great things about the eighteenth-century novel in England was that people were just making it up as they went along, because there wasn't a tradition of fictional prose and there were no conventions to follow—think of *Tristram Shandy* a few years later—so he settles on "a comic Epic-poem in prose."

It is very funny—I'll read you an example—but comedy, as we saw with Chaucer, also involves social realism. "And perhaps there is one Reason," Fielding writes in the Preface, "why a Comic Writer should of all others be the least excused for deviating from Nature, since it may not be always so easy for a serious Poet to meet with the Great and the Admirable; but Life every where furnishes an accurate Observer with the Ridiculous" (5).

This was actually Fielding's second attempt to respond to the success of Samuel Richardson's *Pamela, or Virtue Rewarded* two years earlier, a novel of an innocent young girl who's rewarded for her chastity by a marriage proposal from the Squire who had been trying to seduce her: Fielding couldn't believe that such a story had gotten popular. So he first tried to undermine its success with a novella called *Shamela* in 1741, where Pamela is re-imagined as a very different character—

duplicitous and carnal—and then decided to write a much longer novel in which Joseph Andrews is Pamela's brother, a male version of Richardson's character, a virtuous and innocent young lad. Besides putting other fictional characters in his story, he also puts in real people and establishments: "within four Hours, he reached a famous House of Hospitality well known to the Western Traveler. It presents you a Lion on the Sign-Post: and the Master, who was christened Timotheus, is commonly called plain Tim" (53). That was an actual place outside London: as Olson says in the *Special View,* "the dimension of fact" was the story: there was no separation between fact and fancy, the real and the imagined.

So there's humor—constant improvisations and spinnings and intrusions into his own novel—but this is also a novel that charts a period before the stratification of social classes, when rich and poor mingle throughout in what today would be called a revolutionary social democracy: like Chaucer in his *Tales,* he includes all the characters of his society and has them clash verbally with each other. And that decision to represent revolutionary society—one of absolute equity—necessitates revolutionary form:

> She [Lady Booby] resolved to preserve all the Dignity of the Woman of Fashion to her Servant, and to indulge herself in her last View of Joseph (for that she was most certainly resolved it should be) at his own Expence, by first insulting, and then discarding him. O Love, what monstrous Tricks does thou play with thy Votaries of both Sexes! How dost thou deceive them, and make them deceive themselves! Their Follies are thy Delight. Their Sighs make thee laugh, and their Pangs are thy Merriment! … Thou puttest our our Eyes, stoppest up our Ears, and takest away the power of our Nostrils; so that we can neither see the largest Object, hear the loudest Noise, nor smell the most poignant Perfume.… If there be any one who doubts all this, let him read the next Chapter. (41)

That's from a chapter called "Sayings of wise Men. A Dialogue between the Lady and her Maid; and a Panegyric, or rather Satire on the Passion of Love, in the sublime Style"; the next chapter is called

"In which, after some very fine Writing, the History goes on." It's also probably relevant to say that this was a novel that was published in stages, so that there was always a sense of beginning again, as if for the first time.

But let's get back to the social realism and the politics of the situation:

> Traditionally, there is a tendency to see literature and the other arts as having a tenuous connection to politics at most. The aesthetic, the argument goes, is above the political, meaning not only "better than" but "beyond" and having little to do with the political. In this model, the critic tends to look at the organization and appeal of the formal attributes of the poem, often pointing to its representation of universal themes. (Lee Morrissey)

I don't have to point out the silliness of this argument to anyone here tonight, but would point out that this is still very much the model in academia, despite our so-called liberation from the new critics, the new new critics and most college and university literature programs. But it's not just literature and politics that were melded together in this writing, it was all branches of knowledge:

> Today, literature has come to be associated generally with the "literary" or the aesthetic use of words, and it is often thought to be separate from many other fields. During the Restoration and the 18th century, however, literature was a very capacious field, and could include drama, history, natural philosophy (which we would today call "science"), political philosophy and poetry.

This reminds me a lot of Olson's attempts to re-make the curriculum at Black Mountain and Jack Clarke's Curriculum of the Soul. And while we can find this capaciousness in Dryden and Swift and Pope—and certainly in Milton, perhaps the most politically radical of all English poets and whose most famous works were written in this time period—where we find it most is the 18th century novel. And it's an international world: that is, "cosmopolitan." Just as Chaucer traveled to France and Italy as a diplomat and absorbed the work of Dante and Boccacio, "the major 18th-century novels are often engaged globally, rather than domestically," writes Lee Morrissey, who's making a contrast between them and the more familiar and domestic 19th-century novels:

> [T]he most famous 18th-century novels are populated by world explorers such as Robinson Crusoe and Lemuel Gulliver.... the landscape of the Restoration and 18th-century novel is the *terra incognita* of colonial locations, the New World that Britain was increasingly engaging. (255)

Of course, "the New World that Britain was increasingly engaging" also included the colonies, as the plaque at Stage Fort Park we saw yesterday testifies. Interestingly enough, it was Ed Dorn who got me interested again in the eighteenth century; as an undergraduate, I had leaned, naturally enough, to the Romantics, and thought that Pope and Dryden were a little too arch and contentious. And Ed, as he did every once in a while, told me I was full of it: "They're us!" One of his favorite books at the time was Samuel Johnson's *The Life of Richard Savage*, and I'm here to tell you that it's an amazing piece of work.

There's one more thing I want to say, though, about Fielding's narrative style, constantly correcting itself and elaborating on previous points, as in "Letter 15": "It goes to show you. It was not the 'Eppie Sawyer.'" And 'You go all around the subject.' And I sd, 'I didn't know it was a subject.'" This is from Curtis White's book called *The Middle Mind*:

> Art is most itself, is "true" art, when it makes itself not through the conventions of the universal ... but, as Adorno thought, "by virtue of its own elaborations, through its own immanent process." Lawrence Sterne understood this ... as the only true law of the novel: the novel is "the art of digression." This is why, ultimately, craft has little to do with whether or not a work is a successful piece of art. The most powerful and sinister gambit of what Adorno calls "administered society" is to promise the freedom of individuality while simultaneously prohibiting it.... Art is a response to this repression. (52–53)

And here's where Deleuze and Guattari come in again: "Unlike the graphic arts, drawing, or photography, unlike tracings, the rhizome pertains to a map that must be produced, constructed, a map that is always detachable, connectable, reversible, modifiable, and has multiple entryways and exits and its own lines of flight. It is tracings that must be put on the map, not the opposite."

Mapping the ground we walk: On First Looking Through Juan de la Cosa's Eyes. It's what the AWP, in its all-consuming ambition to institutionalize poetry, never does. And it's what comparison and classification don't do, in their attempt to mute the active displays of knowledge, what's said and what's seen.

* * *

Creeley, Vancouver, 1963: "I would like to center on the question of context, i.e., in what context does language operate, in terms of what is the ground that you walk on, in no metaphoric sense, but actually. Because I think the first day we were here the poems were still isolated from quote 'actual events' unquote, and I'd like to take it not so much into the whole business of what you can do with a poem, where you can put it or hang it on the wall, but where—what is 'history'?"

So the last thing I'd like to mention tonight is that other word that follows from the polis—not Donald Trump, whom I still believe will self-destruct any day now—but, for example, Peter Anastas' *Decline of Fishes*, an example of Gloucester politics. And again, Ammiel's book, on which I've leaned so heavily:

> it's almost unimaginable but extremely valuable for our understanding, to understand what dissent can mean and what assertiveness can mean and how it can be tied, how political thought, action, and what placing the body, literally, in line, can mean and how that can be tied to the imagination, to the imaginative faculties, to the creative possibilities and how constrained we are, how constrained things have become in so many ways.

I mentioned that Gerrit had given us a tour of Gloucester yesterday; after we'd dropped him back at his place, Sara and I followed a mail truck to make sure to get our mail-in ballots posted on time for next week's California primary (because, you know, our two votes are going to put Bernie over the top). And I remembered our book club in Bolinas in the late '80s—Sara, Bob Grenier, John (Shao) Thorpe, Joanne Kyger, others—reading *Maximus III* and wondering whether Olson would note Kennedy's assassination somewhere, since the poems were mostly arranged in chronological order around that time. At Vancouver that year Olson said that we have to get back to the etymology of history and politics: "Otherwise we're simply getting caught in the event either of the society, which is one form of what's boringly called history, or the event of ourselves, which is also that damn boring thing called personal history" (*Muthologus* 1). Last week I saw this old letter from another Massachusetts poet: "Wont you please tell me when you answer my letter who the candidate for President is?" she wrote her brother Austin in the fall of 1847, when she was sixteen.

> I have been trying to find out ever since I came here & have not yet succeeded.... Has the Mexican war terminated yet & how? Are we beat? Do you know of any nation about to besiege South Hadley? If so, do inform me of it, for I would be glad of a chance to escape, if we are to be stormed. I suppose Miss Lyon would furnish us all with daggers & order us to fight for our lives, in case such perils should befall us.

Olson took national politics a bit more seriously than Emily Dickinson—at least for awhile—but there was a time when he gave it all up, to find a more central place in which to construct a republic, in gloom or otherwise: "a place as term in the order of creation." So I think it's instructive to compare him with possibly the most apolitical poet we have. This is from a reprint of a *New York Review of Books* article by Christopher Benfey (1999):

> Scholars have combed her verse and prose for mention of the Civil War, which coincided with her greatest outpouring of verse. But her inspiration during those years seems to have been resistance to high rhetoric.... Edmund Wilson may well be right in claiming that she never referred to the Civil War in her poetry. Her father's commitment to the Whig values of compromise—he had served a term in Congress and campaigned for Zachary Taylor and Henry Clay—may have tempered her response. While Julia Ward Howe

was writing her saber-rattling "Battle Hymn of the Republic," and Whitman his "Drum-Taps," Dickinson was quietly demolishing myths of heroic pomposity:

> Finding is the first Act
> The second, loss,
> Third, Expedition for the "Golden Fleece"
> Fourth, no Discovery—
> Fifth, no Crew—
> Finally, no Golden Fleece—
> Jason, sham, too—

I think that's just an amazing poem, and I'd never seen it before. Benfey goes on: "Dickinson's language, oblique and sharply objective, can be seen as one response to the degraded verbiage of the Civil War era, and the Gilded Age pieties that followed.... a voice raised against the pompous posturing of both sides. She once mentioned to Higginson her adamant resolution to 'never try to lift the words which I cannot hold.'"

As with Olson's cautions against "hypostasizing" in "Special View" and in Maximus V. III.11:

> I am a ward
> And precinct
> Man myself and hate
> Universalization, believe
> It only feeds into a class of deteriorated
> Personal lives anyway, giving them
> What they can buy, a cheap
> Belief. The corner magazine store
> (O'Connell's, at Prospect and Washington)
> has more essential room in it than
>   programs.

* * *

About three weeks ago, Sara—who's here in Gloucester this week with me giving a workshop on poetry and food—offered to read a draft of the lecture while I was writing it, and I said it was still in a nascent state. We argued—as we do, occasionally—about the pronunciation of that word, but the next day I realized that the lecture had to end in a nascent state as well (and I don't mean the "nascent capitalism" of *Maximus* 23).

That is, "finding one's place" is finding a place where one can move freely—can act—without any restraints but those self-imposed, as limits are what any one of us are inside of. "Every place, according to Olson, is an opening place," writes Shahar Bram, who wrote the Olson and Whitehead book, "and can serve as a gate inward that can be used to return outward, after further growth." We don't exist until we act: it's the kinesis of the thing. "that no event // is not penetrated, in intersection or collision with, an eternal / event" ("A Later Note on Letter #15). Or, rather, the local *contains* the eternal: "finding one's place" is a constant action, a means of travel without necessarily going anywhere, because "one's place" is always being invented, and might be another's as well, plus the space between. Just find a place to make your stand, and take it easy. This is eternity: this now. "The writing is nothing / the being in a position to write / that's where they get you"

Projective Verse, Space-Time, and Attention

A talk given at the Louisville Conference on Literature and Culture
February 22, 2020

I want to start this morning by reading the abstract I sent to be on this panel, which has changed about a dozen times since I sent it in a few months ago, including this Tuesday. So today (!), I see "Projective Verse" as one battle in the eternal war between motion and stasis in which, briefly, motion gained the advantage. This has been stated in more philosophical terms by Heidegger and Whitehead,[1] but what's important is that this particular motion, in the spirit of space-time, goes both forwards and back. "Reality was without interruption," wrote Olson in "Equal, That Is, To The Real Itself" (1958) and in his "Letter to Elaine Feinstein" a year later he added "Thus one is equal across history forward and back": a state brought about, one could say, through warps in the fabric of space-time. These proclamations enlarged the "stance toward reality outside a poem" that he outlined in the second part of Projective Verse, which has proved as important as the narrower technical matters of the first part in the ideas and poetics of our own time. This paper seeks to resume acquaintance with that stance, other elements of which are teased out in "The Special View of History" (1956)—an addendum to which was recently published in

---

1. "To retrieve the ontological priority of temporality, of process, over Being or Form in the circle of understanding and a notion of truth, not as spatializing and distancing correspondence, but as *aletheia*, the always 'going-on' (Heidegger's phrase) of truth as concealment/unconcealment, which is the measure of being-in-the-world" (Spanos).

Dispatches from the Poetry Wars—and the rest of the Feinstein letter. It was a view of reality that never fundamentally altered throughout Olson's wide-ranging explorations across space-time even though always dependent on chance and circumstance: indeed, chance and circumstance, plus genetic inheritance and idiosyncratic creative agency, are all factors that allow us to see our actions on the earth in new ways. The paradox of celebrating the essay seventy years after its publication at a conference on literature is that it was never meant to be literary, but, rather, an instruction manual on how to ascertain and transmit what Robert Duncan called "the depths of the Immediate" or, as Olson had it, "the absolute condition of present things." This involves "prehension," to use Whitehead's term, which depends on active and informed observation rather than the lazier intellectual activities of comparison or classification: the content that results empowers poets to "do more form than how form got set" ("Letter to Feinstein").

* * *

It's easy to read the second part of "Projective Verse" as if it were an extension of the first because it also seems to deal with aesthetic matters, specifically, the altered subject matter that might attend the usage of projective techniques. But it also looks ahead to its genetic cousins "The Special View of History" and the "Letter to Elaine Feinstein," which develop that new "stance towards reality" in more explicit ways, some of which borrow from Einstein's theories of relativity.

That is, one of the main tenets of space-time is that the way we experience the universe is dependent on our motion through it, and that motion makes simple space and simple time malleable: that much was clear from Einstein's formulation of special relativity in the early years of the twentieth century. In 1915, though, came a new wrinkle; Brian Greene, in his book *The Elegant Universe*, used that word advisedly, as general relativity posited that space and time can warp and curve in response to the presence of matter or energy. As he had it, they "can no longer be thought of as an inert backdrop on which the events of the universe play themselves out; rather … they are intimate players in the events themselves."

Olson's lecture notes about these theories in "The Special View of History" sometimes make one wonder if he understood them completely; even if he didn't, of course, he'd be part of the great tradition of how mistakes and misunderstandings lead to illumination, as with Pound and Fenollosa's Chinese written characters. As Olson prepped, "the Mysteries, Alchemy, Gnosticism & now Einsteinian physics—Energy & Matter, the General Field Theory, that only in *the exchange* of each is the real: *process* is reality." And later, "we are not Ionians. We are Einsteinians. We can know thermodynamics, and get our hands in. It is a crazy time."[2]

Anyway, my specialty isn't physics, and I won't spend a lot of time with the intricacies of relativity. But Olson referred to space-time early and often, so I want to tease it out a bit here. One of the earliest instances is the "Bibliography on America for Ed Dorn," where he's at first tentative, in his discussion on millennia, about employing "light years" as a measure of time, but then reverts to classic Olson-ism, giving an intimidating definition of attention, namely "the intimate connection between person-as-continuation-of-millennia-by-acts-of-imagination-as-arising-directly-from-fierce-penetration-of-all-past-persons, places, things, and actions-as-data (objects)." This is nothing less than a saturation job, finding out everything worth knowing about whatever particular subject is under review ... "as though," he writes, "there were any other 'like' than an attention which has completely saturated or circumvented the object." But what's important about that attention is that it opens up space-time for exploration. And equally as important is what it's not: "not by fiction to fiction: our own 'life' is too serious a concern for us to be parlayed forward by literary antecedence. In other words, 'culture,' no matter how great."

I'll want to return to the limitations of culture and literature, at least as he saw them (unless you really care about T. S. Eliot's love

---

2. When I read this supplement to *The Special View of History*, I wondered—not for the first time—what it was like to be in one of his classes. They were "especially inhospitable for women," Ben Friedlander writes, but as Miriam Nichols says in her great book *Radical Affections*, criticizing Olson for machismo is a little like criticizing Dante for being Catholic.

letters), but if space and time are malleable, it means, as he says at the end of the Bibliography, that "the littlest is the same as very big if you look at it." It then becomes possible, as Ammiel Alcalay writes in his essential book *a little history*, "to shift the tides of human motion in relation to our known past and all means of recording and preserving that past." It led, Alcalay says in an interview (part of which I'll play you in a minute), to "poetry that had the force of ancient texts, that was of a different order than how poetry had been." For example, here's Jeremy Prynne, a year after Olson died:

> Maximus looks out to sea. He looks through the sea, down into the sea, out into the cosmos, we have the whole of Okeanos, we have the whole of the void, we have the whole of the circular curve. We have the whole of the condition of space. The circular curve is an important condition of the lyric, because the cosmos, in Olson's sense, comprises the rearward time vector, back to the past, and all the space vectors extended until they go circular, that is to say, until you reach the ultimate curvature of the whole, so that they solve themselves as myth…. So that at once the curvature is reached, the lyric concludes, what takes over is the condition of myth.

Max Raphael defines the concave-convex curve as the basic formal element of Franco-Cantabrian cave painting; one finds no "geometrization" into a sine curve or a straight line, because "the curve is not a sequence of points that obey a rigid and always identical course, but a motion caused by an elemental force (mana) whose rhythm it follows" (Raphael, p. 20). And just as "the shape of space *responds* to objects in the environment," writes Brian Greene, changing as our attention changes, "time is warped if its rate of passage differs from one location to another." Topology is of course a word of great importance for Olson, so it might be interesting to know, as Miriam Nichols writes, that it's now a branch of mathematics, "which has as its object the study of the properties of space as these are preserved under deformation. Homeomorphisms, or functions that stretch space, are of particular interest" (31). No kidding.[3]

---

3. Any supposed influence of quantum physics on Olson has to also take into consideration his statement "I am an anti-Einsteinian," in the *Paris Review* interview conducted by Gerard Malanga (in *Muthologos* II).

"This is eternity. This now. This foreshortened span" is the first line of the first essay in Creeley's edition of Olson's *Selected Writings*, and it's also the first thing I ever read by Olson in 1973 and to which what I'm saying this morning offers an extended gloss. So for those of you willing to take a yoga breath at this point, please do. "Indian Yoga," wrote Olson in that supplement to "The Special View of History," assumes that "the sympathetic nervous system can be as known and used as the central nervous system," and a little later in that piece, he calls the "in breath" Psyche and the "out breath" Pneuma, offering another biological analogue to the skin of "Human Universe" as a boundary between inside and outside. Breathing as a function of being alive, a direct connection to one's physicality … I read somewhere, but can't cite, an account that Olson in his last days said that the one thing he regretted, and which could have kept him alive a little longer, was not breathing deeply more often. "Projective Verse," in that sense, is a fundamental acknowledgment of breath, rhythm, and cadence in articulation.

"[b]eing a poet," said Ammiel Alcalay in a video I'll show you a little of now, "means knowing how to breathe" [https://www.youtube.com/watch?v=4mWo9OPPOS8: the whole thing is worth watching, but the relevant portions for the purposes of this paper are from 4:10 to 7:30]. The first person you'll see is Hettie Jones, who published, along with the then Leroi Jones, one of the first editions of "Projective Verse."

At one point in Alcalay's *a little history*, he has occasion to recall one of Olson's earliest published pieces, a reflection on Ezra Pound's incarceration at St. Elizabeth's called "This Is Yeats Speaking," in which Olson asks "What have you to help you hold in a single thought, reality and justice?" Projective Verse was one of his first answers to that question; by extension, the forms that arise from projective techniques are analogies with the hoped-for form of a reunited world, "an actual earth of value." So when Alcalay says about Projective Verse that its intent has been misunderstood and also that "a certain ossification of its meaning has set in," so that "on the one hand too much is made of it and on the other not enough is made of it," I think what he means is that instead of seeing it as yet another literary movement, we might think of it as as a way to generate "poetry that had the force of ancient texts, that was of a different order than how poetry had been":

> He attempts to go across time, through place, by going to the Yucatan. He begins to research, and conceive of, culture in a holistic way, something that's begun to return more recently, connecting archaeology and astronomy, anthropology, ecology, neurology, biology and linguistics, relating these and looking at production and culture as being of a piece, as humanly connected.

Alcalay says that this focus "anticipates the most advanced contemporary thought," but interestingly enough, in the spirit of space-time, it also recalls the past. One of the sourcebooks I used for my classes in English Literature has this to say about the concept of "Literature" in the eighteenth century:

> Today, literature has come to be associated generally with the "literary" or the aesthetic use of words, and it is often thought to be separate from many other fields. During the Restoration and the eighteenth century, however, literature was a very capacious field, and could include drama, history, natural philosophy (which we would today call "science"), political philosophy and poetry, to take but a few examples.

This, of course, is what Olson always thought, and it's also a hint to think more generously about the Enlightenment and the eighteenth century than as just repositories for rational thought.

I want to touch now on some of the specific ideas of the second part of Projective Verse and also, later, the letter to Feinstein. Perhaps its central idea is "Objectism," which involves "treating the poem as an object among other objects, by seeing its life interfused with other made things, and by granting it the freedom to explore its own limits." At least, that's how Michael Davidson put it in an essay on Olson and Edward Dorn some 40 years ago. Achieving this meant shedding a few things like the ego:

> getting rid of the lyrical interference of the individual as ego, of the 'subject' and his soul, that peculiar presumption by which western man has interposed himself between what he is as a creature of nature (with certain instructions to carry out) and those other creations of nature which we may, with no derogation, call objects.

This doesn't really have anything to do with Zukofsky's Objectivism; Olson was never interested in a purely objective or factual poetry. What he was interested in was messing with a sense of time that was strictly linear and creating an energized map where historical events, always, affected the present. Making those events become part of the process—a synthesis of history and artistic practice—was what Olson meant by methodology. Olson's advice to Dorn in the "Bibliography on America" was to "... dig one thing or place or man until you yourself know more abt that then is possible to any other man. It doesn't matter whether it's Barbed Wire or Pemmican or Paterson or Iowa. But exhaust it. Saturate it. Beat it." And he warned against the strict treatment of history as events; the results of historical study are not "how much one knows but in what field of context it is retained and used." Interestingly enough, he wasn't the first American writer who wanted to implicate the poet/historian in the moment:

> The student is to read history actively and not passively to esteem his own life the text, and books the commentary. Thus compelled, the Muse of history will utter oracles, as never to those who do not respect themselves. I have no expectation that any man will read history aright who thinks that what was done in any remote age, by men whose names have resounded far, has any deeper sense than what he is doing today.

And that, as some of you know or might guess, was Ralph Waldo Emerson.

If there's one thing I want to stress this morning, though, it's that MOVEMENT between the past and the future is the missing third term between body and soul, inside and outside, interior and projective: it's the feedback loop. A lot of things become possible if we accept this conception of space-time: for example, "poetic lineage" can as easily go backwards as forwards: Olson at his most Blakean (in some parts of "The Special View") can make us re-think *The Four Zoas* and then send us back to Jack Clarke, whose work tried to blend them.

Another writer I want to mention here, and a little later, is Jack Spicer; he wrote a letter to Graham Mackintosh in 1954, which included this passage: "There's a big difference between talking as a teacher, which is easy, and talking as a poet, which is heartbreakingly difficult if you want to talk honestly." And Ed Dorn, in an interview conducted by Stephen Fredman in 1976 called "Roadtesting the Language,"

> There must be something in "being a poet," and it's demonstrably not material, so I therefore suspect it must be divine. The obligations would be self-evident. It's *divining* like science is divining.

Or like a divining stick: Dorn was talking about what he called "The Obligations of the Divine," part of which were "to be alert to Spirit, and not so much write poetry as to compose the poetry that's constantly written on air."

Such a practice may or may not be "literary": it involves figuring out where to get information, and how. But speaking of literature, here's part of Iain Sinclair's review of Ed Dorn's *Collected Poems*:

> Olson was an inconvenient guest ... Sunset to sunrise, Olson would rumble, thump, burn, growl; whaling his chain of Camels, as Dorn said, in one gulp.... [He] remembered, "those were amazing times. Jeremy Prynne came over from Cambridge. Olson turned our house into a kind of salon. Those were beautiful active times. I mean not literary active, but more expanded. It was never literary with Charles. He liked the literary, but that was a small role for him."

Davidson wrote that Olson "had no use for the generalized cultural despair of a Joyce or an Eliot," but it's important to understand how far that went. Most of us are probably familiar with Olson's condemnation of "the universe of discourse," which he says started with Socrates and Plato, but here's an example of what he's talking about, a famous critic named Meyer Abrams, who's attempting to summarize all of Western literature:

> the nostalgia for lost origins pervading form in the Western literary tradition beginning with Aristotle's logocentric apotheosis of plot as the "end and purpose of ... tragedy" and Virgil's "construction" of Homer's eccentric narrative into a technique of prophecy/fulfillment, through Dante's understanding of narrative as cosmic

vision from God's eye, to Wordsworth's definition of poetry as "emotion recollected in tranquility," Proust's conception of fictional form as a circular recherche du temps perdu and T. S. Eliot's affirmation of the "mythical method" as a "way of controlling, of ordering, of giving a shape and a significance to the immense panorama of futility and anarchy which is contemporary history."

Yikes! I hope it's clear that the poetics of Olson and Creeley set out in a completely different direction.

I've already mentioned Miriam Nichols a few times, and as she's very much one of the muses of this talk, I want to quote her here and a little later about why Olson fell out of favor in what she calls "the theory decades":

> the popularity of continental theory in North American academies, just as projective verse had begun to attract serious critical attention, had the general effect of cramping [its] propositional content and methodological potential rather than opening it up … the visionary cosmicity and politics of the New Americans seemed too utopian, too out of touch with the social realities of the times. As Adorno warns, art that celebrates creative agency where the real potential for such is limited becomes a travesty. What was needed at the end of the 1960s, it seemed, were poetries oriented to emerging globalization and to the ideology critique of social relations that were increasingly occulted by a changing economy—the elephant in the room.

So much for the *Obligations of the Divine*. She's talking about poems that recognize the post-modern condition, where everything is mediated and nothing is true. But Olson believed in truth! (with an exclamation point, as in the letter to Feinstein), and dismissed such theories, in the "Bibliography on America," as "sociology": "that dreadfull beast," "without exception a lot of shit." Here, I think we have to see him as totally un-ironic. The goal was to attain agency in space-time, or as Nichols has it, develop techniques that will "maintain our balance on the slippery earth." It's not that Olson's writings aren't "literary" in the sense that other works discussed at this conference are, but he was serious about the possibility that projective verse would usher in a new literature and a new ethos, which involves living on the earth in a different way, among human beings and the non-human as well: just to take one example, if we had accepted his ideas, catastrophic climate change might not be as threatening as it is now.

But as Nichols implies, there hasn't been a shortage of critics. One writes "Olson naively assumes that a vocabulary and syntax oriented to speech and sense perception rather than the rhetorical tradition can yield a world that is more authentic and less mediated than that of the tradition he rejects." Also, "American romanticism, in Ahmad's view, settles for the oracular and transcendental rather than rooting down in real social relations; its radicalism is consequently limited to the idealist tradition that seeks change through the transformation of consciousness rather than by changing the material conditions of life." (The language in that last one is particularly unfortunate: what's wrong with a transformation of consciousness?) Nichols summarizes these critics this way:

> Olson famously appealed to perceptual experience as a means of renewing poetic language and restoring the "familiar"—intimacy with nature and the body—to the human species. In the 1970s and 80s, however, it was precisely perception that fell under Jacques Derrida's poststructuralist critique of phenomenology.... Lacan's was another discourse that consigned experience to the imaginary realm of *méconnaisance*, a space to be exposed by the analyst and deconstructed by the aware critic as 'always already' mediated by the unconscious and the symbolic order. These philosophies focus on the production of experience through the socialization process: whatever counts for reality at a given moment is to be regarded as a heavily mediated sociolinguistic construct rather than a spontaneous experience.... [BUT] Olson and others of his company were interested not in how experience is produced, but in *how the human species might be redefined and repositioned in relation to planetary life*. In the theory decades, however, the vocabulary of projective poetics, steeped as it is in *mythopoesis*, seemed naïve in its situating of humanity in a cosmos "outside" the mind, when psychology and postmodern philosophies had so firmly moved everything in.

It was bracing to read this, because it's something I've thought for a long time—from taking a class in *The Cantos* from Norman O. Brown in 1973 to this morning—but never articulated quite as well. It also spotlights the value of this work and the others for environmentalism. For example, here's an important section from Part II of *Projective Verse*:

> If he sprawl, he shall find little to sing but himself, and shall sing, nature has such paradoxical ways, by way of artificial forms outside himself. [At this point on the page I had scrawled in the margin "He's talking about Lowell, Berryman and Schwartz" … god knows what I was thinking]. But if he stays inside himself, if he is contained within his nature as he is participant in the larger force, he will be able to listen, and his hearing through himself will give him secrets objects share.

William Spanos glosses this addendum to "By ear he sd": "Listening can attend to the invisible, whether that be 'other minds' or persons who fail to disclose themselves in their 'inner' invisibility, or the Gods who remain hidden, or my own self, which constantly eludes a simple visual appearance." Similarly, Nichols:

> War, murder and torture have become the wallpaper of the evening news and the clichés of documentaries. Homeless people, casualties of decades of neoliberal public policy, line the streets of the world's major cities, and ordinary well-meaning people pass them by because what might have once been perceived as urgent has become commonplace and finally barely perceptible. To these social examples might be added the killing off or brutalization of nonhuman species, environmental degradation, and the prospect of catastrophic climate change. At issue is more than a precept for which a poet is hardly needed; it is the possibility of imagining a different relationship with the planet. Relational thinking is pre-religious imaginative ground that needs to be cultivated if we are to even dream of an "actual earth of value." The situated mind, actively engaged with the multiple dimensions of its world, is a mind capable of holding the world as shape. (63)

"It follows," she says earlier, "that the new and the particular come about through the way the organism selects and redeploys the past it inherits as it responds to the contingencies of its environment; it is a route, a path—a *Tao*—rather than a static substance" (29). In other words, *the feedback is the stance*. Interestingly enough, Walter Benjamin, whom you'll hear about in other panels at this conference, had a similar take. As Richard Wolin writes in *An Aesthetic of Redemption*:

> Benjamin takes his stand ... in the midst of profane life. And from his lowly station in the fallen historical world, he sifts through the ruins of bygone ages for traces of redeemed life in the hope that if these traces can be renewed for the present, the link between the Messianic era ... and the present era, however godforsaken it may appear, can be, if not guaranteed, at least prevented from falling into oblivion. (107)

Hannah Arendt, in her introduction to *Illuminations*, glosses this ambition:

> he concluded that he had to discover new ways of dealing with the past ... the transmissibility of the past had been replaced by its citability and that in place of its authority there had arisen a strange power to settle down, piecemeal, in the present and to deprive it of peace of mind.... [he wrote] "quotations in my works are like robbers by the roadside who make an armed attack and relieve an idler of his convictions"[4]

I'd said I wanted to talk about Spicer in this context; this "experiential" focus, as Miriam Nichols says often, is the opposite of Spicer's pessimism. His second "Imaginary Elegy" posits that "The moon is God's big yellow eye," and she glosses: "This eye of God is the virtual past—the past that in the differently oriented poetics of Olson and Duncan is the fertile ground of the future (i.e., space-time), the raw material of the cosmic *combinatoire*. In Spicer's poem, however, the eye suggests a knowing that is an effect of the Word-machine" (153). In his last lecture in 1965, Spicer called Olson one of the "bosses" of poetry that one would do best to ignore. Although he shared with Olson the desire to capture the real, they used opposite methods,

---

4. More from Arendt on Benjamin: "without being a poet, he *thought poetically* and therefore was bound to regard the metaphor as the greatest gift of language. Linguistic 'transference' enables us to give material form to the invisible—'A mighty fortress is our God'—and thus to render it capable of being experienced."

and Spicer's discovery of the outside mainly convinced him that the inside wouldn't do. That is, Spicer points to the real, but doesn't see any way to bring it forward: even the Martians' messages are important only to poets.

Part of the "business" is to write poems incorporating (or summoning, or recognizing) the real world, and not just weave patterns of language. Although "one significant form" in Olson's poetics "is his attack on syntax" (Nichols 59), the attack is meant to conjure what lies beyond it, the real. So to speak in terms of that spurious term "influence," one thing Projective Verse *didn't* lead to was Language Poetry: it's much deeper and more inclusive than that. Spicer said in his last lecture that the politics of the poet were never the politics of the time, and that poetry was useless as a vehicle of social change. That's SIMILAR, but not at all where Olson was going, which was, as William Spanos had it—remembering the phrase from "The Gate and the Center," "living oral law to be discovered in speech as directly as it is in our mouths"—much more hopeful: "Olson is attempting to retrieve for the present a phenomenological understanding of language as the act of its occasion, as a process of discovering." Or as Adorno remarked, "the essay does not aim at a closed, deductive or inductive edifice. It revolts especially against the doctrine, which has taken root since Plato, that the changing and ephemeral would be unworthy of philosophy; against that old injustice to the transient."

So coming to the end here, if I were to use my various sources this morning to summarize Olson's poetics, it might look something like this:

> the view that the world we perceive as an array of disparate things
> is actually a Whole, variously inflected by the entities that
> compose it ...
> subjects and objects are local *modes* of the universe
> rather than essentially discrete entities, and as such they are tied
> to the cosmic totality as figures on a ground
> to which they are neither separate nor identical
> AND/OR
> dualisms of matter and mind, content and form,
> the sensible and the intelligible, the finite and infinite
> are better understood as zones of varying intensity

> in an ever-evolving, heterogeneous continuum
> stretching from a grain of sand to the depths of space
> AND/OR
> a new way to imagine being in the world;
> the search for a world view and stance
> that might issue in a new ethos.

I want to stress that part of Olson's greatness, for me, is his rescue of spontaneity, of luck and chance being essential factors in poetry, or as he has it in "The Special View," "life is the chance success of a play of creative accidents." My presence at this conference participating in a panel sponsored by "The Charles Olson Society" with Dale Smith and the sadly infirm Jeff Davis is one such accident, as was meeting Gerrit Lansing a few years ago and being a writer-in-residence at the Gloucester Writing Center, as was meeting Don Byrd for the first time just a few months ago in Brooklyn, where he took me on his famous walking-tour, as is having Olson scholars like Chuck Stein at the conference.

And then there are the friends one encounters along the way: Ed Dorn, Tom Clark, and John Daley, and then, in Bolinas, Joanne Kyger, Bill Berkson, and Duncan McNaughton. The real "special view" is that history is happening all the time, which is the reason a new "stance towards reality" is necessary: it allows us to see the world as one act, one recognition. "I have stayed with that care because it is necessary and important," wrote Dorn about the publishers of his work in his first *Collected Poems*. No generalization or idealization will cut it; as Olson had it, "what Socrates did was to isolate the value and thus raise and isolate the man-time from space-time. What he performed was a removal from the particular." Or as Mississippi Fred McDowell sang, "You got to move you got to move." If the poem is energy to the reader, it also obligates the reader to give back to the poem: as the motto of *Rolling Stock* said, "If it moves, print it."

It's a great privilege to talk about Olson among people who have spent a good deal of their lives with him, and that's part of the special view of history I draw on here.

Charles Olson & Brooks Adams

If people know anything about Brooks Adams, they know that he was the descendant of two presidents, John Adams and John Quincy Adams, and the younger brother of the more famous Henry Adams; they may not know that this distinguished family was always a huge burden for him. Although this essay is mainly about his book *The New Empire* (as that was what Olson mentioned most often), another interesting piece of his is "The Heritage of Henry Adams," the introduction to a book of Henry's later essays called *The Degradation of the Democratic Dogma*. In it, it's clear that Brooks identifies with what he calls the failures of his great-grandfather and grandfather, and cheerily predicts, with Henry, that thought will have reached the end of its possibilities in 1925, followed by chaos, massacres, and the end of the world. So before we talk about his attraction to Olson, it's important to understand one big difference: the Adams brothers always saw entropy on the horizon—they *believed* in the second law of thermodynamics—while Olson, as I read him, is one of the greatest practitioners of negentropy in our literature.

Brooks' relationship with his brother was his most important intellectual influence, and they shared many ideas. "A change of phase," writes Henry in his late essay "The Rule of Phase as Applied to History," "was to be recognized by a change of Form; that is, by a change of Direction; and was caused by Acceleration, and increase of Volume or Concentration." If we substitute those terms from physics for precious metals and economics, we have a pretty good summary of *The New Empire*, so it's fairly amusing that, around the time it was written, Henry had bought a small colored print by the French artist Jean-François Raffaelli, "because the two small donkeys are wonderfully like me and my brother Brooks ... Brooks looking sideways as though preparing to kick, while I look straight at you, patient and resigned."

Brooks Adams was a difficult man. In a long essay on his work and thought in 1948, Daniel Aaron called him "unusable." "There are still many people in Boston and Cambridge who remember this eccentric and arrogant man," that essay begins, and proceeds to mention his "gruff manner and his penchant for saying shocking things at dinner parties" ("The Unusable Man"). Other troublesome qualities included imperialism, anti-feminism and anti-Semitism—the latter partly because of his lifelong hostility to "the bankers" or "gold bugs"—and when we recall the famous motto of Teddy Roosevelt's presidency, "Speak Softly but Carry a Big Stick," we might remember that the stick was Brooks Adams' idea.

To his credit, he was aware of how he came across to others. Here's what he wrote about himself in "Heritage":

> That same summer I came home and married, explaining to the woman who consented to share my fortunes, which were likely to be none of the most brilliant ... that I was eccentric almost to madness, and that, if she married me, she must do so on her own responsibility and at her own risk.... [s]he seemed to regard this as a kind of poor joke, but, in the end, she found it serious enough.

This seems like accurate self-analysis. Just how serious his wife took it isn't immediately apparent in this letter she sent from their trip to Venice in 1894:

> Brooks is reading all sorts of abstruse works in their original. I enjoy the gondola & making no exertion. Brooks enjoys going miles & miles out of town astride a bicycle, & also learns to row the gondola rather than sit in it at rest. I don't think I can keep him contented here much longer, and then we shall roam through the Black Forest & learn German.

"And as I wandered," Adams wrote in "Heritage," "and looked at the remains of the past and considered the topography of the lands

I had visited, ideas came to me as wide as the poles from what I had previously supposed such ideas could be." Here we start to get at one of the reasons he was so attractive to Olson, not so much for his specific ideas (although some of those will surface in surprising ways in *The Maximus Poems*), but because of his method. In 1895 he confessed "I can't masquerade as a scholar seeking truth at the bottom of a well. I am dealing with all the burning questions of our time." A year later, he describes his earlier book *The Law of Civilization and Decay*:

> I never read the book through consecutively till I read it in Rome, and then I read it with the utmost astonishment. I had no conception that it would be what it is. In other words it was automatic, and was the work of some second self—a self who must be very active, but who does not come to the surface.

Which isn't projective verse, but it'll do in a pinch. Adams also shared with Olson a penchant for dividing history into broad periods of time, but rather than static categorizations like Golden, Silver and Bronze or Classic, Medieval and Renaissance, his involved movement, as in this self-blurb from *The New Empire*:

> Maps ordinarily represent repose, but I have tried to suggest motion by colored lines drawn from fixed bases to an ever-changing seat of empire. In civilization nothing is at rest, least of all the circulation, and the arteries through which that circulation flows vary in direction from generation to generation.

In his review of *The New Empire* in 1954, Olson wrote that "history before [Adams] had been repose," and six months later the book showed up in the "Bibliography on America for Ed Dorn," where, quoting Whitehead, Olson wrote "we should start from the notion of actuality as in its essence a process." I've always had a special fondness for the Bibliography (delivered to Dorn's window at Black Mountain one night in January of 1955), because I studied with Ed and read many of the works that Olson had suggested. *The New Empire* was on the list under "Millennia," one of the four axes (or the "double ax") he developed to siphon energy and attention away from "the local," which, he wrote— along with "the sentimental"—"is how humanism comes home to roost in America." Millennia was different than "time as history," and seeing the local through its lens can change it into something intensely active and alive rather than a "crutch of ambience." As I'll suggest at the end, that's a central concern of *The Maximus Poems*.

Right after the chart of the double-axe is the important phrase "Applying all four of these at once (which is what I mean by *attention*)...." Attention is a key concept for Olson. I like the way Don Byrd, one of our finest readers of Olson, puts it in his *Poetics of the Common Knowledge*: "we are now faced with the task of recalling the organism from historical time, where it had been placed in a domain of scaleless abstraction, to somatic time, where it can begin once again to deal responsibly with its environment" (313). The Critical Art Ensemble puts it this way: "First, organic being in the world must be re-established as the locus of reality, placing the virtual back in its proper place as simulacra" (Ammiel Alcalay, *a little history*, 178). Back in 1965, Olson closed "The Vinland Map Review" with a reminder: "The care anyway, in any of this, is to improve, or re-gain an attention, which off-hand would seem to be lost ... certainly decisively by 1250."

Another way to get at this improvement is implied by the title of the presentations (to the American Literature Association) today and tomorrow, "Outside the Western Box"; it comes from another book recommendation (in Olson's *Mayan Letters*) for Pound's *Guide to Kulchur*, with the qualification that Pound stays "inside the Western Box, Gemisto, 1429 AD and up." In the "Bibliography" Olson calls this "the trap of history as time," or as he writes in "The Vinland Map Review," "History as Usual—renaissancy (modern) mindness." Likewise, Brooks Adams didn't much like "History" as a term for what he was doing: "It sounds like Harvard" (I guess we can call that a "special view" of history). He would also never allow himself to be put inside a box, Western or otherwise, as a few examples of his machete-like prose might testify:

> The Romans were rigid, and the massacres which attended their readjustments are memorable. The slaughter of the Gracchi, the proscriptions of Marius and Sulla, and the lists of the Triumvirs are examples. On the other hand, Caesar miscarried because of

too high intelligence. He measured circumstances accurately, and because he did so, he misjudged others. Had he comprehended the stupidity of Brutus, he would have killed him. (*The New Empire*, xiii)

And here's his view about religion in medieval times:

> The medieval cleric was a powerful necromancer. Nuns and monks worked day and night to ensure intercession with the supernatural. By 450 the miracle rose in value, and the Church grew wealthy enough to begin the monastic movement. (qtd. in Beringuase 119)

This no-nonsense style is one reason he warns, in his introduction to *The New Empire*, that "ideals would probably suffer," an echo of Olson's preference for Melville's "physicality," his "ability to go *inside* a thing, and from its motion and his to know, not its essence alone (this was mostly the gift of ideality) … but its *dimension*, that part of a thing which ideality … tended to diminish" ("Materials and Weights of Herman Melville").

So a focus on millennia brings in more gritty and particular detail, which any reader of Olson will be familiar with, a brake against any kind of universalizing tendency. His speculations about different locations—the Yucatan Peninsula, Tyre and Cyprus, the Scandinavian countries of "The Vinland Map Review"—are all related in a general way: "so that gesture and action, born of the earth, may in turn join heaven and hell." "One wants phenomenology in place," he writes, "in order that event may re-arise" ("The Advantage of Literacy is that Words Can Be on the Page"). In other words, he wants "to get as graphic as the earth is," which Adams achieved by "going below all the laws" ("Brooks Adams' *The New* Empire"). He also found similarities between Adams and other historical exemplars, like John Smith:

> Why I sing John Smith is this, that the *geographic*, the sudden *land* of the place, is in there, not described, not local, not represented—like all advertisements, all the shit now pours out, the American Road, the filthiness, of graphic words, Mo-dess ("Captain John Smith").

Or as Adams had it, in the preface of The New Empire:

> All my observations lead to the conclusion that geographical conditions have exercised a great, possibly a preponderating, influence over man's destiny. I am convinced that neither history nor economics can be intelligently studied without a constant reference to the geographical surroundings which have affected different nations.

So movement, and ideals, and geography, and a few more things: in "A Further Note" about the advantages of Eric Havelock, Olson concludes "(1), that the gods and heroes of mythology are *metaphors;* and (2), that both gods and heroes are *conspicuous* and *public.*" Adams, for his part, calls attention to Jason bringing back the golden fleece from Colchis and Hercules "who sought, in the garden of the Hesperides, those golden apples which were to be plucked in Spain" (TNE, 21) as predecessors to the miners whose gold from Potosí propped up the European economy in the early sixteenth century and whose gold from Sacramento and the Yukon propped up the American economy in the nineteenth and twentieth. Movement in these cases was engineered by trade, especially trade for metals: people needed them to make superior tools, and power and money followed their most efficient extraction. Olson quotes Adams as saying March 1897 was the month where "consolidation at Pittsburg undersold the world in steel," thus beginning the "new empire" of the United States. Adams lays out the stakes at the end of his preface:

> Nature has cast the United States into the vortex of the fiercest struggle which the world has ever known. She has become the heart of the economic system of the age, and she must maintain her supremacy by wit and by force or share the fate of the discarded. What that fate is the following pages tell.

For Adams, this consolidation was inevitable and necessary, how civilizations and empires were formed and maintained with swift, ruthless administration … in the face of which, democracy didn't stand a chance. In this he agreed with his brother Henry. And in Letter 15 of *The Maximus Poems,* right after he refers to Pound and Gemisto and 1429, Olson says that "The American epos, 19- / 02 (or when did Barton Barton Barton Barton and Barton?" 1902 was the publication date of *The New Empire*.

By the way, there was a story in the *NY Times* a few weeks ago (summer, 2021) that the steel industry is enjoying boom times again, partly because of the Trump tariffs; however, the economic competition now, mostly with China, is focused on other metals, the kind that have to be mined for green energy, "a group of metals, known as rare earth elements ... used in the production of magnets and batteries, which makes them of interest to renewable energy companies and other hi-tech concerns.... They can be very costly to mine" (Tom Stevenson, *Times Literary Supplement*, 5–14). So the empire moves on, "a metal hot from boiling waters."

I want to close with some thoughts about how a millennial focus infuses *The Maximus Poems*. In an untitled essay written March 14 1965, Olson wrote

> the "hero" of my poem (Maximus of Gloucester) is in truth Maximus of Tyre. And thus, whether I liked it or not, at a very early point, in fact in the very first letter addressed to Gloucester, the position off-shore of Maximus is indeed an enormous expropriation of the other side of the Atlantic, the other side all the way back to man's first leaving the massive land continent of "Asia" for Cyprus, the 1st "island" in that Tonly made into a peninsula when Alexander, to reduce her, for the first time in history—as late as 333 bc—built the mole.

The mole is a highway that connected Tyre to the mainland, just as Gloucester is connected to the mainland by Highway 128. So Gloucester isn't Tyre, exactly—and Maximus isn't Maximus of Tyre, exactly—"it's not a reference," he says in a note among his papers, October 1969, "it's an inner inherence." And Tyre, of course, was the chief city of the Phoenicians, about whom Adams writes "The Phoenicians were the greatest navigators and metallurgists of antiquity. They penetrated every inlet and prospected in every land ... and as the sphere of Phoenician enterprise expanded, the lines of communication changed to correspond" (TNE 14). In an echo, George Butterick wrote:

"Olson chose Maximus before he had a fully developed sense of Tyre as being an Old World analogue for Gloucester—the chief port of the Phoenicians the same way Gloucester was a center of the American fishing industry, and the last holdout against Alexander the Great's 'universalism.'" I have Jeff Davis to thank for that link to Butterick's annotations, but let Olson say it, in a tape he made at Goddard College:

> the only thing in the world that confronted the universalization that Alexander proposed—which I think is the great complement to the present—was Tyre. It so refused to be knocked down by this Macedonian athlete that it was the sole place in the world which bucked him, and it took Alexander … was it three or four years to reduce Tyre, and in order to get at her he built a mole from the mainland.

In a note from February 10, 1960 among his papers, Olson would write:

> The interest is not in the local at all as such—any local; & the choice of Gloucester is particular—that is the point of the interest, particularism itself; to reveal it, in all possible ways and force, against the "loss" of value of the universal … Tyre as (with Gaza) the only city which resisted Alexander's universalization.

That last line, of course, has some resonance today.

So one last collage of Olson's unpublished notes and we're home:
- **1952:** it is necessary "to invert totality—to oppose it—by discovering the totality of any—every—single one of us."
- **January 1960:** Quickly, the poem is a man "Maximus" addressing a city "Gloucester" to induce its people, himself among them, to see and take life in and be a scale of which they, and their "fishing," say, are better examples than any outside or "universal" reference; that the relevance lies in what is nearest, and most familiar, that the smallest or least can be lived in
- *Muthologos* II, 161–162: I regard Gloucester as the final movement of the earth's people, the great migratory thing … migration ended in Gloucester … the motion of man upon the earth has a line, an oblique, northwest-tending line, and

Gloucester was the last shore in that sense. The fact that the continent and the series of such developments as have followed, have occupied three hundred and some-odd years, doesn't take away that primacy or originatory nature that I'm speaking of. I think it's a very important fact. And I of course use it as a bridge to Venice and back from Venice to Tyre, because of the departure from the old static land mass of man which was the ice, cave, Pleistocene man and early agricultural man, until he got moving, until he got towns. So that the last polis or city is Gloucester.

And here we have not just a millennial focus, but (remembering Dante) metaphorical, analogical and anagogical as well: "a fourfold vision is given to me."

Brooks Adams, then, offered Olson another way out of the static categories of history and politics that prevented the kinds of perception so essential to his theories. The one qualification Olson offered about Adams' work was his greed, an "analogical reasoning for nature as machine" in the "Bibliography on America for Ed Dorn," which Dorn said many years later in a private conversation should probably be disregarded. From that Bibliography to "The Vinland Map Review" ten years later to one of his last essays, "Continuing Attempt to Pull the Taffy off the Roof of the Mouth" in 1969, Brooks Adams was one of the touchstones for Olson's thought, so I thought it might be useful to find out why.

Charles Olson and the Bolinas Nexus: Avant-Pastoral?

A talk given to the Louisville Conference on Literature and Culture
Louisville, KY, February 25, 2022

The poets who lived in Bolinas, CA, in the 1970s and 1980s never achieved recognition as a particular school having its own poetic; rather, they embraced or were sympathetic to several of the familiar twentieth-century groups that were laid out in Don Allen's *The New American Poetry*. But it's worth remembering that Allen lived in Bolinas for a time, and his press the Four Seasons Foundation—and, later, Grey Fox—were based there.

I've been corresponding for a while with the prose writer Dale Herd, whose work some of you might know, and he told me this story last month:

> The first person I met in Bolinas was Don Allen and, at the same time, Robert Creeley, who later rented me a small cabin in back of his and Bobbie's farmhouse where I worked on *Dreamland Court* and *Wild Cherries*. Bob and Don and I took a walk that day along the bluff and down below on the beach a group of young guys saw us up there and began waving. "Who're those guys?" I asked. "Oh, a bunch of would-be poets," Bob said, "hoping to be recognized." I remember Don smiling a very tiny smile. We continued the walk.[1]

So who were those poets hoping to be recognized? In the *New American Poetry*, they included members of the New York School,

---

1. A little later I read, in the *Times Literary Supplement*, a fitting description of this phenomenon: "a serious outbreak of poets."

including Tom Clark, Bill Berkson, and for a short time in 1971, Ted Berrigan and Alice Notley (although to be fair, most of the New Yorkers wound up hating it). Bob Creeley was there, some years after Black Mountain, and his ex-wife Bobbie Louise Hawkins taught at Naropa along with frequent visitor to Bolinas Anselm Hollo; Language Poetry was represented with Bob Grenier and Stephen Ratcliffe (who still lives and surfs there), and early on, the Beats, the Spicer Workshop and the rest of the San Francisco Renaissance were just an hour down Highway One. But such groupings, as Kevin Opstedal writes in his monograph *Dreaming as One*, are just shorthand for the uninitiated: poets like Joanne Kyger, Lewis McAdams, Duncan McNaughton and John Thorpe, longtime Bolinas residents, had many and numerous worldwide influences and could have been included in these groups or others, but were also intimately familiar with the work and thought of Charles Olson and adapted it, in various different ways, in their own work.

I'll talk about some of those correspondences here—including that all of those poets wrote sections in Jack Clarke's *Curriculum of the Soul*, a project first envisioned by Olson, which Mike Boughn will talk a little about today—but any paper detailing a particular place in relation to Olson brings up the subject of Gloucester, a "working-class town," writes Joshua Corey in his essay "'Tansy City': Charles Olson and the Prospects for Avant-Pastoral," "dominated by the fishing industry, on the margins of an increasingly urbanized society, [forming] the model for Olson's ideal city or 'polis,' even as he saw it under threat from the forces of postwar capitalism and 'pejoro-cracy.'" He also says it was "marked by otherness and resistance to imperial 'smoothing,'" and that it wasn't "brow-beaten into any provincial 'localism'" … or as Olson had it, "not localism, not that mu-sick."

Bolinas is similar in many of those particulars, but it was far from an ideal. Likewise, Gloucester, wrote Ammiel Alcalay *in a little history*, "now seems almost a luxury"

> as isolated as it is. Has not the velocity of change and consumption, through some law of diminishing returns linked to depletion of the planet's life-sustaining resources, overtaken our ability to

stay in one place and allow ourselves the idleness local knowledge demands?

One can understand Alcalay's concern and yet realize that Bolinas, on a different coast, always prospered from both local knowledge and idleness. But finally, I'm not talking about places, Bolinas or Gloucester, but a more general sense of permission. As Duncan McNaughton had it,

> It hasn't anything to do with sentiment or agreement in values. It has to do with sympathetic coexistence in a single human fabric.... We were, many of us, living together, and that makes some deeper human sympathies possible. *There was no agreement at all, except the one of permission.* That is a very subtle matter and asks a thoughtful inspection.

Vagaries of Regionalism

A quick survey of some contemporary poets about the concept of regionalism doesn't exactly put the notion in high regard. "The San Francisco Renaissance is a good case in point," said Brooklyn poet Mark Weiss; "except for three or four of those now included in it, and who made a point of the geographical identification, most were migratory." A recent interview with the Seattle surrealist poet John Olson by Giorgia Pavlidou yielded a similar sentiment. When asked whether place mattered when he was called to writing, he replied

> No, not at all. That said, I can't really speak for other people, especially those for whom place—city, region, neighborhood, orbit—is inspirational. Poets like Theodore Roethke—who lived many years in the northwest and devoted much of his attention to the rain and mushrooms and ferns which characterize this region—come to mind.

Olson did allow that even if regionality was of little importance to one's overall practice, "one way or another it will find itself in your work" (giving the example of *The Maximus Poems*), but he went on to say that even those poems "were more directly inspired by Pound's *Cantos* … [so] could've been produced in any region." Gertrude Stein was more of an influence for him, he confessed, and wondered whether language could be called a region: "English is deeply polyvalent, polyglottal and tropical. It's a wilderness of howls, millipedes and funky trails leading to enchanted wells."

Similarly, Michael Davidson, in an essay about Ed Dorn and his relation to Olson, writes that "'place,' as a strictly geographical term, no longer exists; it has been so totally mediated by entrepreneurial capital that one locale is the same as any other." This skepticism aligns well with Dorn's early essay "What I See in the Maximus Poems," where he wrote

> ... you don't have a place just because you barge in on it as a literal physical reality or want it to prosper because you live there. Instead go see the Grand Canyon, that's what it was made for. Place, you have to have a man bring it to you. You are *casual*. This is a really serious business, and *not* to be tampered with.

As the word "casual" has seldom seemed so menacing, I wanted to read you one more paragraph from that 1960 essay, an argument for place not being local or parochial:

> I am certain, without ever having been there, I would be bored to sickness walking through Gloucester. Buildings as such are not important. The wash of the sea is not interesting in itself, that is luxuria, a degrading thing, people as they stand, must be created, it doesn't matter at all they have reflexes of their own, they are casual ...

An interview of Dorn in 1977 by Stephen Fredman went into a bit more detail:

> I've moved around because, as I said, once you leave a place like I came from, you've left. If you're a poet, you have to swallow the whole assignment: you can't elect a piece of it. Like your Locale, for instance. I'm not a localist at all, and I don't take much interest in Locality by any definition, and certainly not a small display of rings like the solar system.

The idea that regionalism is really in the imagination, like Shakespeare's "seacoast of Bohemia" or Jack Spicer's California, might be contrary to most people's expectations or habits. We've tended to identify poets with geographical regions at least as far back as the Lake Poets in England, and possibly even the Ionians in Greece. On our shores, there were the Fugitives or Southern Agrarians, and more recently, the New York Poets and the Black Mountain poets. But Corey in his essay calls such associations "nostalgic," calling Wendell Berry's work "Virgilian pastoral," which "insists on a mystical community or consonance between the traditional values of the poem (its rhythm, its capacity for narrative) and the traditional values of the land: a fundamentally religious idea, based on the idea that 'the existence of the world is rooted in mystery and in sanctity.'"

Bolinas Poets

In January of 1988, I published John (Shao) Thorpe's essay "'Regionalism': All Chiefs & No Indians?" in a magazine I edited called *Peninsula*. That first issue featured writers who were currently living in Bolinas, but the end notes contained a warning: "this isn't the West Marin Chamber of Commerce, and tourists of any persuasion are cautioned. The place implied in the title isn't a 'simple location,' and no merely local fascination with geography is being claimed." Thorpe (always and forever known as Shao, which I recently learned meant "young" or "new" in Chinese), was called by some "the true poet of Bolinas," but his essay shows how complex any notion of "regional literature" can be. Walt Whitman, in "From Blue Ontario's Shores," prophesized "Land of lands and bards to cooperate!" but that cooperation entails different forms, relations, and even mutations: as Charles Olson posited in 1966, we might think we're going out into space, but what's actually happening is that space is coming back in to occupy us.

If you had to fit Thorpe's essay onto a postcard, you could do worse than say "Place, yes: regionalism, no." Place, he writes, is for the poets he knows "a romance with primary or primordial things," most assuredly not a movement or school eligible for literary patronage; for one thing, it's imperfect, fallible, and makeshift, as open systems tend to be. "Otherwise poetry," he writes, "becomes a mockery of real estate." Shao traced the etymology of "region" back to the words "Rajah," "Rex" and eventually our word "king." The regal metaphor continues, he wrote, with terms like the "majestic" Rockies and "national" defense, and the entire legacy—monotheistic, Titanic, finally imageless—he called "the Jefe complex." This is a short essay, but it's very dense, so I need to give a longish quote for you to see exactly what Shao is up to here:

> On this peninsula, we have parks, ocean, villages, and not too distant cities, each with their inputs and outputs, under the mighty flow, night and day, from the celestial world. Great extents meet in a relatively slim zone of moist scum yin and contortionistic prana, where the mammal brain still isn't on top of it, and the outlying world can be hid in a moment by tent-covers of watery air meandering over the bunching emaciated leaf cups of mesa shrubbery.... From towers, past cows, secure in purple, the town cried a nonsense of swan warts and corn tin. I tried to befriend it variously by bird-watching, long walks, tootling on shakuhachi and autoharp and tambourine, wearing odd-colored tank tops, squatting in caves, and otherwise being a dismal and passionate courtier. This is by the Ocean which rushes and eats a thousand Miltons for breakfast. Everything seen—twisty buckbrush shapes in rain; and heard, like quail rah-coo-coo; and devoured, like succulent rockfish—seemed to have an old harpoon shivering in it—blended from sunrise to sunset by a cloud-rubbing gong—the truest mystery of pitch, rhythm, and colors I've known.... In no sense has it been local. From the intimacies with shapes I felt an immense *distant* scale, something uncontained and independent of its own independence.

Earlier in the essay, Thorpe wrote "there are a hundred million microbes in a gram of topsoil, and the forms within hemoglobin are apt to be as complex, and the community (and communities) of these even more so," which chimes perfectly with Andrew Schelling's introduction to Joanne Kyger's "ecological" chapbook, *Lo and Behold*: "The only poetry that can be a voice from the American land will be one that enacts an ecology. One that feels as biologically complex as a cubic inch of our underfoot soil." What he's learned from Kyger's poetry, he writes, "is that when a poem is open, and begins to look like an ecosystem, unexpected creatures just show up." As in her poem "1990":

> The spirit has no accidents.
> By now the land has turned very green.
> A neighbor sells me a little studio he has dismantled. Don and friends rebuild it here. Then the house is rewired, and electricity brought out to the studio, from which I write, at this moment.
> The smell that skunk let go about two hours ago is still really strong, really strong.
> "Enjoy things by giving them up."
> "A lot of religious baloney, that's what it is."

I'm mostly a fan of Seamus Heaney, and I particularly like his poem "The Skunk," but it can't be denied that the skunk in that poem screams "symbol" from miles away, whether de-mythologized or not. In Joanne's poems, skunks appear because their smell does. One might also note the prosaic fact of her new writing studio keeping company with the "poetry"—the kinship of land and spirit—and that, even though she's often identified as a Buddhist, she criticizes the dogma as much as follows it, perhaps because (as she writes a few lines later) "Fortunately when we 'find' our voice, we have many voices. / Every phenomena becomes an inspiration to 'sing.'" Even pain: here are some lines from the next poem in that chapbook, "1991":

> Don definitely has a herniated disc. Pain. A souvenir from Mexico.
> Here's a chunk of rainbow, about four inches long, left of the sun
>   in the silver-misty sky. That's hope.
> Forty sparrows on the table eating seeds. Tremendous admiration
>   for the folding Purepecha stool. Then sixteen quail arrive.
> Cold Alaska winds blows south. That's where we are, south.
> Bush's "New World Order." What does it mean, besides the arrogance of his people.
> The "commonplace" versus the "corporate."
> "We" killed people of Iraq in the desert. The whole thing was phony …
> Don "up" for an hour this morning.
> After nine weeks Don walks about.
> Thousands and thousands of wild iris on the green slopes above the reef.…
> "Magic is the total appreciation of chance." It's all so brief.

No need to dress it up as beauty.
Will I ever write anything but notations again?

If you read enough these days, you can still see the tired divisions that poetry has always been subject to, whether political poems or lyric poems or narrative poems or even an epic or two, so it comes as a great relief to read Joanne's work and understand all of them working together. She's also a master of the immediate; her contribution to *Curriculum of the Soul* was called "Phenomenological," full of particular details of a trip to the Yucatan in 1984, and recalling Olson's antipathy for any sort of generalization.

I'd be remiss not to feature some snippets from the great interview of Joanne conducted by Shao and another old friend, Diana Middleton-McQuaid, called "Congratulatory Poetics." Shao started by asking Joanne about Homer, and she responded with what many of us feel when we first read Homer, the romance and adventure. "But also," she asked herself, "how could you feel inside this California landscape, how would you find your affinities? Well, I found Homer, and then I finally called it the Homer Dome. So Homer grew up like this great kind of dome over my head inside writing" ... which is certainly an extension of what anyone might mean by regionalism. Here's the end of the interview:

> I want to see how you live in your environment or in your compassion for place. One thing I realized teaching at Naropa Institute this summer, as the class was reading Jaime de Angulo, was that I was really trying to get people over to this space where they have some animal spirit connection. To realize that the tree is in a simultaneous breath with ourselves, and it's not a *difference* of consciousness. The tree is talking directly to me, rather than the tree is a likeness like some other metaphorical likeness.

As for her question at the end of "1991," "Will I ever write anything but notations again?", it's answered, in a poetic way, at the end of the four-page poem "1992," the last poem in that book: "See? There's enough room here." As the title to one of my favorite books explains, we have "All This Every Day." Here's part of that book's last poem:

> What we commonly
> know in the air, in our dreams, what chooses
> continually & continually to grow, the obvious
> under our notes, is this life. Yearning is blind-
> ness. The weed has a name, is quite proud of it-
> self, builds a community with other weeds, birds
> hop through. The imported domestic is a labor
> of love, but a labor, such a labor. At home here,
> no single thought is my thought. It whispers
> through the air in sweet misty fog,
> in bright sky blue.

And what, exactly, was "all this"? Some few months after Olson died, in January of 1971, millions of gallons of oil washed up on the Bolinas lagoon; in connection with "an actual earth of value / to construct one," the community spirit that formed around that event generated a book—*The Town that Fought to Save Itself*—and the eventual construction of the sewer farms, a massive septic system which severed Bolinas from the main sewer line from Stinson Beach and helped make it what it was: a fiercely independent and unincorporated village that guarded its privacy jealously. If people know anything at all about Bolinas, they know the stories of the Bolinas Border Patrol, a group of local patriots who took down the signs on Highway One that led to the town whenever they appeared: a strict anti-tourist mentality was always in force. It was a quiet, rural outpost that—between 1965 and 1980—became home to, as Kevin Opstedal had it,

> a varied group of psychedelic refugees, radical representatives of the sixties counterculture, artists, writers and visionaries. Together they created a community that was as unique and eclectic as were these individuals themselves. *Members of the counterculture believed their way of life should express their political and social beliefs.*

I imagine that most graduates of today's MFAs and poetry workshops would find that last sentiment (with my italics) strange, besides the point of awards or magazine publications. But the richness of an unincorporated community—Anne Waldman called Bolinas "a site of Outrider survival"—has some connections to Olson's poetics and with the writers who identified with them: for one thing, it takes work. And "nothing is possible without / doing it."

A lot of inspiration and perspiration in creating the sewer farms was the work and thought of Lewis MacAdams, whose work resembles Olson's in a few important ways, most notably in its ecological and community consciousness, the inclusion of public talk and politics, and being unashamed of naming poetic influences and friends in the work itself: "backwaters and broken concrete," writes Gary Snyder in a blurb for Lewis' Selected Poems *Dear Oxygen*, "bird and fish knowledge, hydrology and community hearings." Lewis' late muse was the Los Angeles River, which was never more than a sewer drain when I was growing up there, and his great poem "The River" speaks of his poetic and political relationship to that now thriving body of water. Here's an earlier poem titled with a line by Dr. Williams, "If politics were the science of humanity," that speaks to those ideas:

> Dear American people, I've just got
> to talk to you about your government.
> You are the government,
> the way we are the earth and sky, the way
> we are the blood and the government
> the branches of the tree. You and I
> are the government and we need
> no more amateur presidents, please.
> Once again, if you and I are the suit,
> the government's the tie we wear into the world.
> America, *we* are the fabric; and to knit that tie together
> takes *state*craft. Is it too much to ask ourselves
> to pay attention?
> To make of government a proper tool?
> To make of governing a skill and craft to
> steer the ship of earth into the daylight?

The last Bolinas poet I'll touch on here is Duncan McNaughton. In his "Perspective" on the poetics program at New College, he takes a capacious view of poetics: "whatever in the world, or out of it, the poet needs for poetry." Similarly, in "Tres," the first poem of his book *Sumeriana*

(Tombouctou, 1977) dedicated to Joanne Kyger, we encounter the proposition that

> the United States of America is the best place for the gradualisms
> of social recreation, the free-est place
> allowance, a place
> to be, large and open for movement and inquisitiveness

which concludes "as / long as you have the money." A motif in Duncan's work, it seems to me, is a tangle of different rhetorics, with the smart-ass and sardonic voice never far from the surface:

> "Full moon and
> empty arms": Bolinas
> that's not really true of me here
> but the words are, and I know what they mean

Another theme is a rueful appreciation and even nostalgia for old linguistic ideals, not the "totally false romanticism" that's generated from the equation of suffering and creativity but "the actualization of imagination's needs," for which some "basic schoolwork" is necessary ("Perspective"). Here's part of another poem, "Realities of Intellect":

> Robin
> is going to Delphi
> next month, to live
> that's what I like about 'gentle Robin'
> it was likely the glass of retsina at Bill Berkson's
> led to these Grecian sunsets,
> μελωδια of the sea
> th' evening's dark sky
> an impossible moment
> when, as hoped for, one steps into vision
> over a mountain, and
> the ache of eternity settles on
> Stinson Beach

Anyone who's spent some time in Stinson Beach knows the enormity of that fall ... "whether in the world, or out of it"

So while Bolinas and environs appear often—in the form of

McNaughton's friends and neighbors and land forms, familiar figures sliding through the dream, those moments just before waking fully—it mostly gives his learnedness an everyday feel, constantly testing its value.

Olson and Bolinas

In the notes for "West," an unfinished project of the late 1940s and early 1950s, Olson mentioned "the oppression of human singularity" by various Ahabs (conquistadores and Salem judges, eventually leading to the empire of American business). These were vertical men usurping the horizontal, contra naturum, what he called in those notes "the black fruit of ego & will over nature," and he offered Lao Tze as an example of the latter, water seeking its own level. Similarly, Duncan McNaughton, in conversation, told me that the West wasn't subject to the "ghosts" of the east coast: it was fresh ground, native, also very old, and demanded a different sensibility, like that of the Plains Indians.

Much later, in the third volume of *The Maximus Poems*, Olson adopted a fable from Henri Corbin between the angels who dictate and those who write (501). He usually gave precedence to the second group, the ones who write and act: they listen to the dictation, even though "it is almost impossible" to obey, because "nothing is possible without / doing it." As with his favorite etymology (*historin*, finding out for one's self), it's the *evidence* of what is said that he was after, more shout than discrimination or measurement, and thus a more mythic-holistic perspective than one that emphasized science or discourse. He returned to that doubleness in his important essay on Melville, "Equal, That Is, to the Real Itself":

> man in the nineteenth century was suddenly possessed or repossessed of a character of being, a thing among things, which I shall call his physicality. It made a re-entry of or to the universe. Reality was without interruption, and we are still in the business of finding out how all action, and thought, have to be refounded.

That missing twin of discourse was what Olson calls in this essay "the continuous," and inasmuch as Bolinas poets had any sort of common poetics, it might be that "writing of the continuous" ... again, not an ideal, but a place for discovery, or shout, as against discrimination. Aram Saroyan said that Bolinas provided "the psychic X-factor ... exactly the sort of lightning one waits to be struck by"; it taught him to expand his artistic attentions from the strictly artistic creation of one-word "objects" to a sense of being a poet, attuned to artistic opportunities, but at the same time "tuned to a wavelength where art is secondary to life." "I began speaking as a citizen," he wrote in the Afterword to his book *Day & Night: Bolinas Poems,* "about all the things that were important to me: my wife, child, family, friends, and community." As Opstedal wrote in *Dreaming as One,*

> The hallmarks of Bolinas poetry include an engagement with everyday mystery, with social critique and transcendence set against the imagery of the place, within the context of the community, as factors in a very "human universe" and along those lines confronting the place, in particular and general, and where that leads one, inside and out, is a direct offshoot from Olson's teachings.

"So much vibrated out from Bolinas," to quote Anne Waldman again; it was "the most intense collection of poets in one place not around an academic or university scene—so therefore more visionary, 'utopian.'" "These poets taught me that psychology, magic, history, and dailiness could exist in poetry in equal measure," wrote Lewis Warsh in the introduction to *The Angel Hair Anthology.* "It was a way of life," said Duncan McNaughton; "one was on duty all the time."

That's also what Bolinas felt like to me when I moved there in 1983, 40 years ago now. One of the first images that come to mind is sitting on a bench at the end of Wharf Road with Bobbie Louise Hawkins, talking about *Zephyr,* the magazine I was then editing: "What are your INTENTIONS?" she asked. My intentions here were to remember a few poets who used to live in Bolinas, old friends whose work and thought often remind me of Charles Olson, and who once welcomed me among them.

But regionalism, finally, seems a problematic notion, as informed as much by one's reading and writing practice as the ground beneath us. The work of the writers I've talked about here is constructed mainly from the eccentric nature of their perceptions and attentions: John Thorpe, Joanne Kyger, Lewis MacAdams and Duncan McNaughton, like all the writers who lived in Bolinas or spent some time there, shared a place and a sensitivity to it, but they saw that place mainly as a reservoir of open possibilities. "The writing is nothing" wrote Dr. Williams, "the being in a position to write   that's where they get you." Being in a position to write is a poetic place, but it's not on the map until it is.

*A*LCALAY

Unmasquing a Whole Hole Chapbook

A Masque in the Form of a Cento, composed by Ammiel Alcalay
from the writings of Anne Bradstreet, John Bunyan, Daniel Defoe,
John Dryden, Andrew Marvell, Alexander Pope and Jonathan Swift
Hole Chapbooks, Calgary/Philadelphia/Vancouver, 2000.
Available from: Rob Manery, 2664 William Street, Vancouver, BC, Canada V5K 2Y5.

From 1977 through 1981, a show called *Meeting of Minds* was shown on public television in the United States. The project, developed by comedian Steve Allen over a period of eighteen years, brought together actors who portrayed historical figures such as Plato, Francis Bacon, Marie Antoinette, and Galileo and sat them around a table to mildly assert the theories for which they were most generally known. It was also in 1977 that Ammiel Alcalay composed *Masque in the Form of a Cento*, the characters of which Daniel Defoe, Jonathan Swift, Alexander Pope and John Dryden (with cameos by Bunyon, Bradstreet and Marvell) proclaim various samplings of their published work on a stage divided into three sections; there are also spoken parts given to a narrator and the foils Lisideius, Crites and Neander.

First things first: while a *masque* is indeed related to "masquerade," the term as English majors know and love it is more accurately defined (by the OED) as "a dramatic composition ... originally consisting of dancing and acting in dumb show ... afterwards including dialogue (usually poetical) and song." And the Latin word *cento* is a "garment of patchwork, also the title of a poem made up of various verses"; thus, "a composition formed by joining scraps from other authors." It's completely accurate, then, to use the words "composed by" with the author's name; in a note at the end of the masque, he says that he has long striven to "level the playing field" by allowing different roles (poet, translator, scholar, editor, critic, journalist, teacher, reader, person) to dictate working priorities back to him. One of the first steps in allowing this to happen, for him, has been the experience of immersion into the words of others and the use of himself as conduit or channeler of those words (1).

In providing these definitions and notes, however, I hardly want to make this work seem less strange, and thus provide "any facile assimilation of [it] within familiar categories or uninformed cultural and historical assumptions" (2). Indeed, if there's a word that would not apply to Alcalay, it's "uninformed"; among the roles he mentions above, he's perhaps best well-known as a Middle Eastern scholar, one whose pioneering book *After Jews and Arabs* sought to redefine and refocus the conflict between these peoples as a Middle Eastern or Mediterranean mosaic. Inasmuch as we're inclined to see Israel as a "western" country surrounded by "Eastern" enemies, Alcalay directs us to the common Semitic roots between the peoples, in the process helping to uncover a shared *mizrahi* and Sephardic culture in the region that had been almost completely ignored. He takes us back to the "golden age" of Levantine culture, from the ninth century when much that was Jewish was actually written in Arabic and when the two peoples had close interpenetration and commerce to the expulsion of Jews and Arabs from Spain (and, incidentally, the JudeoArabic culture from European culture) in the fifteenth. By implication, he mourns the artificial divisions of statehood that have obscured that fact, and that history (3).

Thus, a central concern for Alcalay has been the recovery of memory that's been obliterated by exclusionary and exclusivist histories imposed by "religious fanaticism and retrograde nationalism," as Spanish writer Juan Goytisolo has it in the preface to Alcalay's recent book of essays *Memories of Our Future* (4). In one of those essays, a review of Goytisolo's own poetics, Alcalay recalls Cervantes' "ability to create a completely new reality by freeing a remarkably diverse range of existing characters from the strictures of their history and generic circumstances" (5). Later in the same essay, he comes even closer to describing the masque at hand, quoting the Guyanese novelist Wilson Harris, who speaks of an "imaginary constellation" where you can steep yourself in a theater, so to speak, of plural masks that bear on the travail of humanity; in an orchestration of ancient and modern histories and characterizations and imageries as well revolving, so to speak, around a transitive principle or musical chord (6).

So to speak. And what is that "chord" around which the various characters "revolve" in this masque? It has something to do with the clash of certain triumphal states of mind with the more ground level journalistic observations of the writer/characters. Defoe, for example, is given privilege of place and time, the only character stage left who both opens and closes the proceedings. On a mattress in "a garret or attic room," he reads (from *A Journal of the Plague Year*) about those who "perished in the streets and fields for mere want, or dropped down by the raging violence of the fever upon them." This dispassionate recital is followed by a disembodied but cheery narrator (lights on, stage center) giving more "official" history: "It was that memorable day, in the first summer of the late war, when ... the two most mighty and best appointed fleets which any age had ever seen, disputed the command of the greater half of the globe." Then Defoe again, indirectly refuting this rather smug and opportunistic propaganda: "So in the plague it came at last to such violence that people sat still looking at one another, and seemed quite abandoned to despair."

When Swift comes onto the scene (on a small rowboat away from the other boats stage center), he disputes the view of Crites that "almost a new nature has been revealed to us" with the observations of a character in *Gulliver's Travels*, namely, "that the historical account I gave him of our affairs during the last Century ... was all only an heap of conspiracies, Rebellions, Murders, Massacres, Revolutions, Banishments; the very worst effects that Avarice, Faction, Hypocrisy, Perfidiousness, Cruelty, Rage, Madness, Hatred, Envy, Lust, Malice and Ambitions could produce."

So there. This isn't just a contest between competing versions of history, though; the familiar phrase "history is written by the winners" doesn't take into account the death and destruction that allows that history to be written. Swift is here indicting not just the English, but a universal cast of mind that assumes one standard of belief or judgement (or, for that matter, aesthetics or politics) that will serve for all: "I hate and detest that animal called man," Swift says later, evoking the misanthropy with which many of these writers are popularly associated, "although I heartily love John, Peter, Thomas and so forth."

Similarly, Alcalay brings into counterpoint one Neander, who finds it convenient to "pronounce of our present poets, that they have far surpassed all the ancients, and the modern writers of other countries" with Pope, who ridiculed a similar view expounded by "Martinus Scriblerus" in *The Art of Sinking in Poetry*, and whose lines from Book IV of *The Dunciad* "There marched the bard and blockhead, side by side, / who rhymed for hire, and patronized for pride" find inclusion here, as do Dryden's "When tragedy was done / Satire and humour the same fate have run / And comedy is sunk to trick and pun." These rather severe judgments were made partly because most of the poets with whom these writers were familiar had "learn'd to please, and not to wound." As Pope writes, in lines included here:

> Those who cannot write, and those who can
> All rhyme, and scrawl, and scribble, to a man.
> Newborn nonsense first is taught to cry,
> Maggots half formed in rhyme exactly meet
> And learn to crawl upon poetic feet.

How *mean!*, some of us might say. Indeed, although the writers here included are all honored subjects of study in Jack Spicer's English Department of the Soul, and thus seemingly not the victims of historical destruction, it's also true that their popularity has waned more than waxed in recent years; as Alcalay says in his note, in 1977 they "couldn't have been more unfashionable or, apparently, distant from what I supposedly thought my concerns were." Edward Dorn, in another interview in 1980, had this to say about the eighteenth century's reputation: "People were willing to insult each other in that century. All the time. It was a total century of insult. And it was a brilliant century. It invented the modern.... I mean, it's now looked back on as unsanitary.

It's now looked back on as arch, in this kind of pernicious way" (7).

Rather than arch, then, we can also look back on these writers as public commentators, for whom there was no separation between their art and their political sensibilities; in fact, they were models of the "public literary activism" which Alcalay says inspires his writing. "What's more," says James Scully in a slightly different context, "their aesthetic achievement is *because of* their politics, not in spite.... It is a poetry that talks back, that would act as part of the world, not simply as a mirror of it"(8). Pope's *Dunciad* began as a typical Scriblerus literary prank, yet by Book IV, 15 years later, the ridicule of certain of Pope's contemporaries evolved into a fullscale assault against a cosmic principle of dullness that was overtaking the world:

> *Wit* shoots in vain its momentary fires,
> The meteor drops, and in a flash expires....
> Nor *public* Flame, nor *private*, dares to shine;
> Nor *human* spark is left, nor Glimpse *divine!*
> Lo! thy dread Empire, CHAOS! is restored;
> Light dies before thy uncreating word:
> Thy hand, great Anarch! lets the curtain fall;
> And universal Darkness buries All (9).

This century hasn't shown us, as yet, an apocalypse, but we have had the chance to preside, over the years in which this masque was composed and now published, over the deaths and destructions of various smaller "worlds," from Beirut and Sarajevo to Srebenica and Rwanda. Is it really true, Alcalay asks rhetorically in an interview collected in *Memories of Our Future*, that the example of a multiethnic community in the Bosnian fashion, including mixed marriages, tolerance, and mutual respect, might actually turn out to be contagious and pose a real threat to the sterility of dead ended politics, and the further concentration of power and capital? (10)

In other words, the current enemy isn't a lot different than Swift's or Dryden's; globalization, and a "greater concentration of capital now in fewer and fewer hands" (11) has aesthetic consequences as well as political ones. Similarly, if the history of Jewish/Arab contact in the Mediterranean can be seen to stretch back to the ninth century (not merely to 1948) is our sense of "literature" really not large enough to include these enlightenment writers of the eighteenth century? Everyone who has written in, or been translated into, English is potentially at least part of our inheritance; as Alcalay says in his concluding note, "the past remains open before us, waiting to be mined."

Strictly from a writer's standpoint, it's fascinating how, as more than a few people have said, we all write (or compose!) the same poem over and over. As noted, this masque was composed in 1977, long before the Levantine studies and travels that have made Alcalay's primary reputation, yet as I've tried to show here, it's not finally very different from his current concerns. Defoe closes the masque with remarks that might as well apply to Bosnia, or Lebanon, or Toledo and Granada in the Golden Age: "neither shall I say anything more of it but that it remains to be lamented."

End Notes

1. Edward Dorn, in a 1976 interview responding to a question about the function of the poet, had similar thoughts about process: "Part of the function is to be alert to Spirit, and not so much write poetry as to compose the poetry that's constantly written on air. What I've read and what I hear merge to make the field in which I compose." Edward Dorn, *Interviews* (Bolinas: Four Seasons Foundation, 1980), p. 66.
2. Ammiel Alcalay, *Memories of Our Future* (San Francisco: City Lights Books, 1999), p. 148 (speaking of the work of Juan Goytisolo).
3. Somewhat ironically, this review is being written just after a two-week "summit" between the Israeli government and Palestinian representatives at Camp David which concluded without a peace agreement (although both sides are being careful to accentuate the positive aspects and new talks are scheduled).
4. Op cit., p. xxi.
5. Ibid., p. 151.
6. Ibid., p. 151. These comments are reminiscent of Charles Olson's comment on Pound's cantos: "Ez's epic solves problem by his ego: his single emotion breaks all down to his equals or inferiors.... Which assumption, that there are intelligent men whom he can outtalk, is beautiful because it destroys historical time, and / thus creates the methodology of the Cantos, viz, a

spacefield where, by inversion, though the material is all time material, he has driven through it so sharply by the beak of his ego that, *he has turned time into what we must now have, space & its live air*" (my italics). *Selected Writings of Charles Olson* (New York: New Directions, 1966), p. 182.
7. Edward Dorn, *Views* (San Francisco: Four Seasons Foundation, 1980), p. 22.
8. James Scully, *Line Break: Poetry as Social Practice* (Seattle: Bay Press, 1988), p. 56.
9. Alexander Pope, *Selected Poetry & Prose* (New York: Holt, Rinehart and Winston, Inc., 1972), pp. 513‑514.
10. Ammiel Alcalay, *Memories of Our Future* (San Francisco: City Lights Books, 1999), p. 261.
11. Ibid., p. 261.

FROM THE WARRING FACTIONS

Ammiel Alcalay. *from the warring factions.*
Los Angeles: Beyond Baroque Books, 2002. 212 pp. $12

In "Theses on the Philosophy of History" (his last published essay), Walter Benjamin wrote that "only a redeemed mankind receives the fullness of its past—which is to say, only for a redeemed mankind has its past become citable in all its moments." In *from the warring factions,* Ammiel Alcalay seeks to bring about such a redemption. This assemblage of poems, songs, novels, scholarly work, gossip magazines, letters from friends, interviews, and film scripts presents what Alcalay (in a useful interview with Benjamin Hollander that concludes the book) calls the "limitlessness of historical specificity"— superior, he says, to the "fatalism, cynicism and sentimentality" that accompanied the widespread dissemination of the early Auden poem "9/1/39" after September 11, 2001 (198). The point, and the approach to history it entails, is worth stressing. Rather than circulate such "idealist" poems, "as if they could sum up or even relate to the experience we had just witnessed," Alcalay suggests instead a "poetry that might have something to say to the matters at hand, that might have reverberated with the worlds these attacks demanded we pay attention to" (199). *from the warring factions* is both a presentation of such worlds and a plea to attend to them.

One example of his method appears in the final section of the book, with a quotation from an Islamic novel called *Zabibah and the King*. After Zabibah is dragged into a forest and raped by her estranged husband, she says to herself, "Rape is the most serious of crimes, whether it is a man raping a woman or invading armies raping the homeland" (143). The king, enraged at the fate of his confidant, launches a war of revenge, which results in the deaths of both Zabibah and her husband. At this point in Alcalay's text, we've been informed only that this novel "is 'by its author'" (141), but a note at the end identifies the novelist as Saddam Hussein.

Saddam also appears in the book's first section, "Old Bridge":

> posters of Saddam whirl and spin
> stealth bombers drop TVs
> over Baghdad books
> burn in Sarajevo
> babies choke in clouds
> of evaporated milk (8)

Yet some of these lines are themselves from an earlier source, Alcalay's *The Cairo Notebooks* (1993). And in that book, says Alcalay to Hollander,

> I pillaged my own writing, some of it dating back to the 1970s. I felt that it was important not to jettison parts of other, older selves … going back in time in a personal way but also interrogating the materials of political, cultural and human encounters rooted in specific places and times. (177)

So it's clear that Alcalay's writing in this book "includes history," as Pound famously defined the epic, but it's a special kind, akin perhaps to what Charles Olson was describing as "The Special View of History" at Black Mountain in 1956. "I cannot begin to indicate what history is," Olson said in those lectures,

> if the dimension of fact as the place of the cluster of belief isn't understood to be the heart of it…. And it has been the immense task of the last century and a half to get man back to what he knows. I repeat that phrase: *to what he knows*. For it turns out to coincide exactly with that other phrase: *to what he does*. (*The Special View of History*, Berkeley: Oyez, 1970, 21, 29)

Robert Creeley has explained that Olson was "trying to break the habit of history as some discrete ordering apart from what energies or active forces were the case," and was intrigued with "Pound's ability to pick up materials of history so they're all coincident and contemporary. You weren't transforming them, but the only place they could obviously be was where you were, if they were to be there at all."

In a recent talk at Cornell, Alcalay cited a letter from Olson to Ruth Benedict that also bears upon the techniques of *from the warring factions*: "In New History," Olson wrote, "the act of the observer, if his personality is of count, is before, in the collection of the material.... I think if you burn the facts long and hard enough in yourself as crucible, you'll come to the few facts that matter, and then fact can be fable again." Similarly, Alcalay wants to bring "knowledge and history back in ... in a form that questions various conventions and fixed ideas" (203). The time span ranges from the ancient Near East to last night's transmissions from the "embedded" journalists of the corporate mass media:

> (as when a broadcast, tightly controlled by
> conquering censors, begins transmission, word
> for word the listener battles each instinct to reach
> for reason and intellect, to fend off the impending
> enclosures that occupy seeing or hearing all images
> of division cut along the lines of any other fabric) (21)

Alcalay's own writing in this book is "embedded" in a different way. Following a method of both Pound and Olson, the overwhelming majority of the material here is from other sources, composed and arranged in "historical jump-cuts" that seek "to disrupt accepted patterns of doing things" and "disturb [the] deadly slumber" of insular American cultural life (183–184). This process, Alcalay writes, is "far from experimental"; he compares it to "the Arabic *al-iktibas*—'The lighting of a flame from a fire already blazing'" (192). It's an unorthodox geographical practice as well. The book ranges over vast expanses—the former Yugoslavia, Baghdad, Rome, Iran, Palestine, and Lebanon, all sites of wars undertaken for empire, large or small—but it's never further away than the Native American ground under our feet: "I was not writing," says Alcalay, "about something that happened 'over there'" (186).

Similarly, Edward Dorn, in an interview with Roy K. Okada in 1973, said he was interested in a "mystical sense" of geography, one that would obligate him to "get out of that kind of soft dependency on the description" and allow "the narrative to operate by itself, if possible"—separate from any control of the narrative ego, which is "pretty obviously dead." Alcalay, too, felt as if he needed to "confound the whole notion of a narrator, or single self" (186). He does so, partly, in passages like this:

> "mica"
> "volcanic glass"
> "chalcedony"
> "conch shells"
> "shark teeth"
> "copper" (99)

and

> a kind of paradise of Walnut or Cedar
> or Chestnut "& stones to strike fire" "fish and fur,
> oaken ship timbers, spars and masts of white pine,
> iron made from ore raked from the floors of coal
> bogs" "the Wildernesse" "a cleere resemblance of
> this world" (104)

Such collocations "war" against each other, slowing down the narrative pace and forcing us to evaluate their conflicting claims—they're "something not completely palatable" "like earth and dirt" (103). One of the most harrowing is a description of the uniforms of some Serbian irregulars:

> tigers falcons hawks scorpions grey wolves black swans
> yellow ants white eagles horses of fire autumn rain alley
> soot dusan the great green legion red berets jokers knights …
> lilies scarves olive fatigues beards and green berets black
> clothing with a round unit patch on the sleeve a black
> swan penetrating a woman lying on her back Special Unit
> in white letters above the picture and underneath in black
> letters the words Black Swans no insignia except a metal
> plate on the shoulder bearing the name Captain Dragan (78)

I've suggested some parallels and analogs to the work of some prestigious forebearers in an attempt to explore some of the parameters of this book, but I'm in no way trying to underestimate its difficulty. Alcalay's characterization of these materials as resembling the "very relaxed, kind of disheveled atmosphere" he found at the Grolier bookstore he frequented as a youth in Boston might be true enough, but many readers will find the kind of "eccentric space" (179) that results a bit daunting. *from the warring factions* might be better seen as the literary equivalent of antiwar demonstrations in which protestors seek to disrupt "business as usual." That is, although there's been no shortage of poetry against the U.S. invasion of Iraq, factions isn't just reactive—an attempt to respond to a particular event—but projective, wanting to disrupt "accepted patterns of doing things" (184). Alcalay is disturbed, for example, that "you can read a lot of innovative poetry from the last decade without even getting a hint that two genocides took place in the world" (178) and wants to return to the "ancient sense" that art "shouldn't primarily be about beauty but about pain and suffering" (177). At its haunted best, *factions* is a tour through the killing fields of history, the skulls, dead bodies, and documentary materials all showing different aspects of the grief, sorrow, treachery, and barbarity, "the slaughter we live by trying to remember" (112). "The issue was not to 'say something' or impose an order upon the world," he says; "I had to let events read themselves back into the texts" (187).

Adorno famously asked whether there was any use for poetry after the Holocaust: *from the warring factions* is one possible answer. What William Carlos Williams wrote in his preface to *The Wedge* (1944)—"The war is the first and only thing in the world today. The arts generally are not, nor is this writing a diversion from that for relief, a turning away. It is the war, or part of it, merely a different sector of the field."—would also make sense affixed to this book. As Benjamin wrote, in the essay with which I began, "Only that historian will have the gift of fanning the spark of hope in the past who is firmly convinced that *even the dead* will not be safe from the enemy if he wins" (255). Alcalay, a poet/historian/scholar in the front lines of that particular struggle, is trying to rekindle those fires.

Resurrection of the Ancillary & Ghost Talk

A Bibliography for After Jews and Arabs (Punctum Books, 2021)
Ghost Talk (Pinsapo Press, 2021)

Whoever does not fight against visible evil loses the protection of the invisible.
—Paul Celan, Microliths

The first thing one encounters in Ammiel Alcalay's *A Bibliography for After Jews and Arabs* is an unusual note from the publishers: "Before you start to read this book, take this moment to think about making a donation to punctum books, an independent non-profit press, at https://punctumbooks.com/support/" (you might feel free to take that moment as well). A little further on we're introduced to their tagline—*spontaneous acts of scholarly combustion*—and the particular imprint of Punctum Books that produced the book, The babel Working Group: "a collective and desiring assemblage of scholar-gypsies with no leaders or followers, no top and no bottom, and only a middle." babel, write the members, "roams and stalks the ruins of the post-historical university as a multiplicity, a pack, looking for other roaming packs with which to cohabit and build temporary shelters for intellectual vagabonds. We also take in strays."

Whether Alcalay is a stray or one of the original pack, it's in this context that we might take the book itself, and not just because (as he mentions twice in the various essays this book contains) he hasn't published another book with a university press since *After Jews and*

Arabs appeared in 1993. There's a story behind that, and part of it is contained in the 1999 essay "Behind the Scenes: Before *After Jews and Arabs*" reprinted here, a salvage into the shipwreck of the academic publishing industry. But more positively, this volume focuses attention on those parts of books often dismissed with the word "ancillary" (prefaces, forewords, introductions, epigraphs, notes, references, afterwords, bibliographies), providing vagabond insight into how they can both provoke writing and perpetuate it. As such, the book celebrates what's becoming more and more mysterious: old-fashioned scholarly methodology, as dependent on chance and good fortune and networks of friends as meticulous research habits.

I use the word "mysterious" advisedly, because for some time now Alcalay has focused on bringing hidden things to light, whether forgotten or deliberately obscured: that's true most visibly with his essential *Lost & Found: The CUNY Poetics Document Initiative* (https://centerforthehumanities.org/lost-and-found) but also in his previous works and a volume of poems, *Ghost Talk* (Pinsapo Press), being published concurrently with the *Bibliography*. The 40+ projects in the *Archive*—which grad students under his direction have undertaken since 2009, and which, he said in a talk at Kelly Writers House last year, "involve a higher set of skills than the standard dissertation"— have brought back into print works from important writers like Muriel Rukeyser, Diane Di Prima and Langston Hughes, but also published tributes to musicians like Cecil Taylor: an early event was a 100th anniversary celebration for Sun Ra. The focus is on extra-literary pursuits (letters, journals, lecture notes, photos, old magazines) because the best thought among writers of the 1950s and 1960s, as he said at the Writers House, was in communication with each other: thus, the archive looks not just to preserve the work but to try to re-enact the conditions under which it was produced.

As Alcalay says in another context, "there were ways back to forgotten melodies one never knew" (26). Those goals are part of this book as well: by letting us see "a little history" of *After Jews and Arabs*—the missing bibliography, anonymous old reader reports at presses where it was rejected, and a thoughtful essay on the "poetics of bibliography"—Alcalay has discovered in the *Bibliography* another way of preserving the disappeared past and ensuring its continued power.

* * *

After Jews and Arabs is a wildly ambitious book covering vast stretches of space and time, from the Abbasid Dynasty and the glories of Al-Andalus culture in Muslim Spain to current conditions of Jews and Arabs in Israel and Palestine (a period of more than a millennium) and from one end of the Mediterranean to the other, and some found it a little too ambitious. In the "Behind the Scenes" essay, Alcalay reproduces two anonymous reader reports from presses where the book was rejected; through them, he detects a form of academic censorship "technical, technocratic, and professionalized" in nature (20)—if not racist—and "largely in service of state power and imperialist policies" (24). It should probably be obvious that the politics of a book entitled *After Jews and Arabs* wouldn't be identity politics, and Alcalay has some scathing rhetoric about the current state of affairs in those precincts:

> State resources and propaganda mechanisms steered the necessary undertaking of identity formation ... toward the very divisive free-for-all that identity politics now seems to have become ... forcing people to divide along various lines of identity through disinformation campaigns and institutionalized forms of treatment according to category of person. (27)

This isn't an environment in which it's possible to achieve common ground. At one point in his account, Alcalay meets "Moroccan and Iraqi-born Jewish Black Panthers in Jerusalem" (28): one way to grasp the spaces the book opened is to ponder the cognitive dissonance of that phrase. In an uncharacteristically optimistic mode, Alcalay writes that "certain prior and prevailing assumptions, often racist and exclusionary at core, no longer have footing, or at least no longer pass uncontested" (19). One can hope.

Another consequence of the book's ambition was that a vast number of sources needed to be consulted: the bibliography, finished in 1992 and first published here, is 50 pages long and divided into seven different categories, notable because "The world I set out to investigate had no label, no category connecting to the present or tying various pasts together" (28). But it's not just the amount but the *kinds* of sources that are important:

> from architectural accounts of the creation of new cities like Fustat and Baghdad, to fragments of early medieval bills of lading and letters written by merchants drawn from the Cairo genizah; from covert Judeo-Spanish translations during the Inquisition, to accounts of the destruction of Palestinian villages in 1948; from contemporary acts of resistance to cultural assimilation by Jews writing in Arabic, to the revolutionary context of the first Palestinian intifadah. (17-18)

All of these sources were refracted through Alcalay's personal experience living in Jerusalem for eight years in the 1980s, and that combination, he writes, demanded a methodology capable of accessing and collecting the information, perhaps no longer possible with today's digital-only research. In this way, the "poetics of bibliography" start to reveal themselves.

That is, one of the goals in publishing these 30-year-old materials is to create "a form of world-making, an offering that provides an example of how materials from the past can be arranged to perforate the caul too often obscuring our vision, preventing us from seeing a ground we can actually stand on" (21). It's true that the bibliography is arranged in standard MLA format, a bit inconvenient for world-making and not at all like Charles Olson's *A Bibliography on America for Ed Dorn*, which Alcalay quotes with justified enthusiasm. As such, it might be difficult to understand why it would need resurrection, especially considering the detailed and often provocative original notes that were published with the book: as he admits elsewhere, it's "an artifact of an earlier era, curious, possibly useful, but very difficult to fully decode" (32). But he's also anticipated such an objection:

> Mine was a bibliography largely composed through card catalogues; open stacks; smaller, more manageable collections; and used or antiquarian bookshops, as well as through a large network of informants based in different languages, geo-graphical sites, and particular human and political experience. Unquestionably,

more than some of that residue remains in the very choice and organization of the items included. (19)

In other words, "old scholarship," research methodologies that might uncover a medieval bill of lading, is disappearing. And as scholars, Alcalay writes, we "need to throw out wider nets to our students and readers to provide guidance for how some of this older experience can be assessed and transmitted" (20). In that sense, the bibliography is "a constituent element, a creative act penetrating the fog to make available the ground upon which other realities can be imagined and enacted" (30). Ed Dorn, in his memorial lecture for Charles Olson in 1981 published by Lost & Found, would seem to agree:

> The value of a working instructional bibliography lies in its net of connections. It isn't concerned with the latest so-called "corrections" and insights of the latest worker, or the latest hot number. The value for a student in a well-conceived bibliography is not in the bibliography's comprehension, but in the engagement of certain of its genes.

Alcalay insists that he doesn't want to "rarify" the pre-digital age, but does bemoan one unintended consequence of research in the digital world, namely that

> while it's much easier to find something already identified in particular, it has become that much harder to find something one *isn't* looking for. Chance encounters leading down unknown paths have become exceedingly hard to experience. (32)

Be that as it may, while working on this review, I discovered a book by Geoff Huth called *The Anarchivist: History, Memory and Archives*, which offers some apposite reflections. "Archives," he writes, "are the evidence of the past, proof the past occurred, and an imperfect explanation of how it happened." Conversation around archives usually presumes solid buildings or vaults that will last forever, but all buildings will be destroyed eventually: in his introduction, Alcalay mentions "the precarious nature of archives and of various living repositories of cultural memory" (xiv), while Huth, reflecting on the interplay between history, archives, and memory in how we imagine facts and truth into being, speaks of the necessity to "[hold] the text up to the light to see through it into the past … we must take this disarrayed past and give it structure, we have to divine the connections between events." For Alcalay, such divination lies, as Olson writes, "in the collection of the materials":

> this process hearkens back to all kinds of different material situations: open stack libraries, antiquarian bookshops, personal collections, all of which must be physically looked at in markedly different circumstances rather than in solitary reception through a screen. (32)

* * *

In Alcalay's *Ghost Talk* (his first published poetry since 2011), he explores the invisible in a different mode, "more song than talk," as an introductory note by Peter Blegvad has it. It's a lament for a lost love, much in the vein of Villon's "Mais où sont les neiges d'antan?"

> How many times had she walked barefoot down the path and through the grass until her feet touched sand and she dug her toes in below the heat to get the cooler part? No matter how the song was sung, her heart was heavy. (7)

One of the things poetry does is return us to our senses, the body, its sensations, but also its doubts, sorrows, confusions. Formally, *Ghost Talk* is a mix of prose and poetry, and while the poetry often seems like fragments of conversation or wisps of thought, with large gaps in between, one aspect of the prose is that the last two lines of most paragraphs are shorter, like poetry: a signal that the impetus behind the thought is receding and something else coming into view. For all the activation of the past that the *Bibliography* counsels, *Ghost Talk* is a reminder that recollection is always a mixed pleasure: "The poet knocks on silence," writes Blegvad, "an open door":

> a dirge,
> a cup, a stone —
> merge, then pause —
> unsung, some reminded
> of a melody, one on
> bones, another strings (27)

while another page announces

THE SURFACE IS AS SHOCKING AS THE DEPTH (14)

The visible and the invisible, memory and imagination, always embracing: "It makes no sense at all because it is the eternal breaking in on the temporal," wrote Marilynne Robinson about love. That seems about right.

*　*　*

Speaking of ancillary materials, part of the Preface to Ed Dorn's first volume of *Collected Poems* (1956–1974, published in 1975 from Don Allen's Four Seasons Foundation in Bolinas, one of the presses Alcalay praises here) has always stayed with me:

> Throughout this period I have published through persons, and except for two cases not represented here, not with houses. I have stayed with that care because it is accurate and important. Important equally for those who have published me. From near the beginning I have known my work to be theoretical in nature and poetic by virtue of its inherent tone. My true readers have known exactly what I have assumed.

Ancillary, from the Latin *ancilla*, a female servant. Or ghost.
all our
dead floating around us
hovering among and
between us stuck here
on the ground (29)

As the title of one of my favorite Sun Ra songs says, "There Are Other Worlds (They Have Not Told You Of)"; in these two recent books, in very different modes, Alcalay announces his continuing exploration of them.

SATIRE & ROMANCE

Notes on *A Modern Dunciad* by Richard Nason (Part I)

I've been asked by the editors of *Dispatches from the Poetry Wars* to write a series of introductory notes for their serialization of this important book, first published by The Smith in New York in 1978, and I'm happy to do so. Perhaps the best way to begin is to go back to the original *Dunciad*, the final lines of which commemorate the triumph of the Goddess of Dullness, and which I can rarely read without shivering:

> See Mystery to Mathematics fly!
> In vain! they gaze, turn giddy, rave, and die.
> Religion blushing veils her sacred fires,
> And unawares Morality expires.
> Nor public flame, nor private, dares to shine;
> Nor human spark is left, nor glimpse divine!
> Lo! thy dread Empire, CHAOS! Is restored;
> Light dies before thy uncreating word:
> Thy hand, great Anarch! Lets the curtain fall;
> And Universal Darkness buries All. (Book IV, l. 647–656)

I'd guess few practitioners today, when looking for inspiration or information from writers of the past, would choose Alexander Pope, nor any of his stable mates. The eighteenth century is too arch, too contentious, for most tastes today, and besides, there are all those rhymed couplets in iambic pentameter, which have been out of style for a hundred years or so.

But the music is one thing—and Pope, working on that limited palette, is masterful—and the matter another. I'm talking about a kind of verse and prose that flourished in his time and which has only intermittently flashed a pale light through the fog since, the art of satire. Today we think of satire as Alec Baldwin doing Trump on *Saturday Night Live,* with perhaps a passing nod to Stephen Colbert. English majors among us will be quick to hold up Pope's friend Jonathan Swift's "A Modest Proposal" as exemplary, but what else? If I had to think of a fairly recent work, published about ten years after *A Modern Dunciad,* it would be Ed Dorn's *Abhorrences.* Today those poems would get trigger warnings on syllabi and sanctioned safe spaces. He might even have been fired from Breitbart.

But Nason went all the way back to the master, and though he's modest about it—the second line of the prologue mentions "Popeless couplets, noteless lays"—his music in this semi-archaic form is pretty strong and consistent throughout. These are some of my favorite lines from Book I:

> Indeed, our Goddess seems immune to harm,
> And packs on added poundage with each bomb!
> In any case, her boundaries exceed by far
> The frailties of Pope's and Queen Anne's War.
> As man fans forward in his strange parade,
> We find her plastic banners bright arrayed;
> Though Gardist poets are her darlings still,
> Their empty doings leave her time to kill:
> In every human effort, as you name it,
> Where worthy impulse might arise, she'll tame it;
> Where Grossness needs a prophet or a messenger,
> You'll find her busier than Henry Kissinger.

Pope named names, and so does Nason. I suppose the sections of his poem that will attract the most attention—and, in some quarters, outrage—are when he wittily calls to account most of the poets of the late twentieth century, many of whom are still alive. But we need to remember the tradition he's channeling: "For Pope," reads his first footnote (and the poem is heavily footnoted, as was the original), "the greatest of the Dunces were the appointed Laureates of his day. Only Wit could negate the powers of Dullness, and satire was used to keep the Dunces at bay." Actually, that reminds me of the work of another contemporary poet—one of the editors of this publication—who's been employing this ancient art for two decades now.

"There are some occasions," I remember the crime novelist Carl Hiassen saying, "when satire is entirely unnecessary." I suspect we might be living in one of them, and I'm still holding out hope that the string theorists are right and that we've wandered through a porthole into an alternate universe. But if that's not true, we need to challenge this "new normal" with all the intelligence, wit and outrage at our command, and could do a lot worse than to see how it was done in this forgotten masterpiece. I'll have more to say about it, and satire, in forthcoming segments.

Permanent Revolution: The Value of Bitterness

Notes on *A Modern Dunciad* by Richard Nason (Part II)

The first installment of these notes on satire—which accompanied a scan of the prologue and Book I *A Modern Dunciad* (first published in 1976 by The Smith)—was published in *Dispatches* three months ago, on March 27. As it happens, I had clicked on another link earlier that same day, one of an occasional series of quasi-philosophical columns in the *New York Times* called "The Stone," this one entitled "Our Delight in Destruction" by one Costica Bradatan. Editor Boughn had some reservations after I posted that link on Facebook, but I've just re-read it and think it made some points that are relevant to this discussion, one of which was that the reason everyone was so sucker-punched by Trump is that we still imagine ourselves living in an Enlightenment universe.

Some eighteenth-century writers like Swift knew better, but most of them, including Dryden and Pope (at least until the very end of his life), celebrated an Augustan ideal of divinely instituted order. This order didn't exist above or beyond nature: it was us, our real human nature, and all we needed was a little training to see it and realize it. Pope even published the execrable "Essay on Man," which has these forgettable lines:

> All Nature is but art, unknown to thee;
> All chance, direction, which thou canst not see;
> All discord, harmony not understood;
> All partial evil, universal good.

> And spite of Pride, in erring reason's spite,
> One truth is clear: Whatever is, is RIGHT. (lines 289–294)

I don't think six more disgusting lines exist in English poetry. His buddy Voltaire, who had mercilessly satirized this Deist idea of intelligent design in *Candide*, calling it Pangloss' "best of all possible worlds," probably choked on his croque monsieur; it may also have been why Swift wrote "almost obsessively about dirt and shit, as a breathless insistence that the contrary was true" (John Stubbs, *Jonathan Swift: The Reluctant Rebel*, p. 171). But as I said, near the end of his life, Pope went back to a poem he thought he had finished ten years before, *The Dunciad*, and added an apocalyptic fourth book to the previous three. By that time, he probably realized that the ideal he had served all his writing life wasn't going to show up any time soon.

And it's mostly that last book that inspired Nason in his modern re-enactment of this poem. Near the end of Book One (in the previous installment), we find these lines:

> The thrust of all the Goddess saw and heard
> Lay in corruption of the Written Word;
> For being Greek she needs no other brief:
> All Form is webbed within the Poet's leaf;
> Society, to fall in every part,
> Must wither first within the Poet's heart!
> Now this she had achieved to some degree,
> Else how account for what we are, and see?

How indeed? Walter Benjamin famously wrote, in "Theses on the Philosophy of History," that "there is no document of civilization that is not at the same time a document of barbarism," and Horkheimer and Adorno, who were heavily influenced by that idea, wrote in the preface to their *Dialectics of Enlightenment* they had set out to do "nothing less than to explain why humanity, instead of entering a truly human state, is sinking into a new kind of barbarism." Speaking of barbarism, let's see what Wikipedia has to say:

> **Satire** is a genre of literature, and sometimes graphic and performing arts, in which vices, follies, abuses, and shortcomings

are held up to ridicule, ideally with the intent of shaming individuals, corporations, government, or society itself into improvement. Although satire is usually meant to be humorous, its greater purpose is often constructive social criticism, using wit to draw attention to both particular and wider issues in society.

Including a Wikipedia quote in a scholarly essay on satire might itself be subject to satire, but this isn't that essay: I have too much self-respect to be an academic (I got that quote from the show *Billions* on Showtime). Still, the difficulty is clear. Satire traffics in *shaming*—fat shaming, slut shaming—it's hard to defend a practice like that, let alone anyone being held up to ridicule. After all, satire is *mean!* Why should we pay it any attention whatsoever? Not to mention that one person's vice is another's kink, and we've become notoriously shy about inhabiting any high moral ground. "Homo sum, humani nihil a me alienum puto" (I am human, and think nothing human alien to men). Such a remark—from Terence, as in Houseman's "Terence, This is Stupid Stuff"—shows the vast difference between satirists and well-meaning humanists. Swift hated human beings, was disgusted by them. When the Houyhnhnms want to eliminate the human race, also known as Yahoos, most people read it as some sort of moral failing: I think it was Swift's fondest desire. Surely he would have been unmoved by Elizabeth Warren or Bernie Sanders:

> Let them, when they once get in
> Sell the Nation for a Pin;
> While they sit a picking Straws
> Let them rave of making Laws;
> While they never hold their Tongue,
> Let them dabble in their dung.

Satire, of course, has a long history, and it's true that not all of it is vicious. The Romans gave us Horace, known for clever mockery, playful criticism, light-hearted humor: smiles rather than anger, folly rather than evil. Everybody loves Horace, a real mensch. Here are some more adjectives for him: comfortable, avuncular, diverting, delicate, equable, compassionate, supporter of the status quo. He was the Billy Collins of ancient Rome, never malicious or morose: think *The Simpsons*, *The*

Rape of the Lock, Gilbert and Sullivan, *Saturday Night Live*. But of course, like Virgil, he had imperial sanction, and only became famous after Octavius had killed Antony and Cleopatra in the savage wars of the Triumvirate. "Rome's propagandists," wrote Howard Weinbrot in his book *Eighteenth Century Satire*, "depicted a city and a literature changing from brick to marble":

> Their Harps with flattering Sounds repay'd
>   Th'Imperial Patron's skillful Cost;
> But whilst th'applauded Artists play'd,
>   The Roman liberty was lost.

That's from a Mr. Wickstead (Weinbrot was unable to find out his first name), a poet of 1717. But there was an alternative, the blunter tones of Juvenal, more contemptuous and abrasive than Horace, whose satires feature active attacks, exaggeration, parody, scorn, outrage, and savage ridicule: he made his victims seem ridiculous. Think *A Modest Proposal, Abhorrences, Black Mirror, American Psycho* … to which we can add the final book of Pope's *Dunciad* and, I think, *A Modern Dunciad*. Or perhaps you think these lines about the Goddess of Dullness choosing John Ashbery for her chosen poet in Book III are avuncular:

> That name, however she might push or shove,
> Was like a magnet to the joint above,
> And wouldn't let her move it up or down,
> Until she pledged 'Ashbery, John' the crown!
> How right she was to let the Fates prevail:
> A Harvard grad who won a Prize at Yale!
> Who felt that Verse so badly failed the age
> Because it had not put the sound of Cage,
> With all the force of calligraphs by Kline,
> Into a kind of Audenesque address,
> That doubles back with Stevens-like finesse,
> And by a subtle overlay of optics,
> Is shattered as the shuttered gaze of Coptics,
> To give our age a dazzling sense of Self
> That might compete with Prufrock on the shelf!

> "Now this," he told O'Hara, "we should do,
> If for no other reason than it's new!
> Then once it's done, the future could be spent
> In asking people what we really meant!"

I can hear some people objecting to these lines: why pick on Ashbery (which Nason continues to do in this Book, going through all his published work at the time this poem was published)? He's a "great poet," after all. Aren't there better, more important targets? Dryden, in one of the first essays in English on satire, warned against the lampoon, calling it "a dangerous sort of weapon, and for the most part unlawful. We have no moral right on the reputation of other men; it is taking from them what we cannot restore to them." Aren't these lines what Dryden called a lampoon, and not true satire?

William Blake would respond "Poetry fettered fetters the human race." And besides, it's *funny!* Can't you count the poems that have made you laugh out loud on one hand? I can. They include these lines, from Book II below, when Nason writes that "Academia"

> Keeps thin all forms, makes substance only seem,
> The notion of Narcissus on a stream,
> A wan, reflected face, a rippling gloss,
> Bewitching *The New Yorker*'s Howard Moss!

"Until all Excellence depart the air / And only nonsense reach the dullard ear," or, to name names yet again: "By turning 'Standards' to position 'Off,' / She brings banality, embossed, from Knopf!" And laughter is serious business: in 1698, Joseph Addison wrote that there "has been long a Dispute among the Learned, whether that Keenness and Bitterness of ... JUVENAL ... or HORACE's more jocose *Lampoons* are most agreeable to the End of Satire ... in the one shines the *Ridicule*, in the other the *Severe*." (Either I never knew or never noticed this ancient technique of printing authors' names in small caps, MICHAEL BOUGHN and KENT JOHNSON, but tentatively think it has some advantages.)

Let's go to the book: **satire** [F, fr. L. *satira*, *satura*, a poetic medley, fr. *satura*, a dish filled with various fruits, a medley, fr. *satur* full of food, sated.] 1. A poem or prose work holding up human vices, follies, etc.

to ridicule or scorn. 2. Trenchant wit, irony, or sarcasm, used for the purpose of exposing and discrediting vice or folly. My 1961 uses the Oxford comma, whereas the *OED* itself, interestingly enough, seems sparing of them:

> in early use a discursive composition in verse treating of a variety of subjects; in classical use a poem in which prevalent follies or vices are assailed with ridicule or with serious denunciation. The word is a specific application of *satura* medley; this general sense appears in the phrase *per saturum* in the lump, indiscriminately; according to the grammarians (??) this is elliptical for *lanx satura* (lit. "full dish"); *lanx* dish, *satura*, fem. of *satur* full, related to *satis* enough), which is alleged to have been used for a dish containing various kinds of fruit, and for food composed of many different ingredients.

"Enough! Or too much." I've known about this etymology for some time, actually, and never see a bowl of fruit without thinking about it. More optimistic practitioners counsel us to look at everyday life and find some hints of intelligent design, but it's just as easy to look around and find things that are unbearably fucked up. As the *I Ching* says: no blame. But mostly, etymology suggests that satire is a miscellany, a combination of different elements, so shouldn't be seen as just one writer attacking another. Indeed, the narrator of most satires is often satirized himself or herself, and there's always more than one "side" being espoused.

And here I have to quote from myself, in an essay I wrote about Ed Dorn in 2004: (reprinted in this volume as "Ed Dorn and the Politics of Love")

> Dorn is not a poet of causes," agrees Donald Wesling, in his essay on Dorn in *Internal Resistances*. "In fact, he is suspicious of anyone who *favors* anything" (35). In a letter to Amiri Baraka (then Leroi Jones) in 1961, Dorn pronounced himself "embarrassed at the poor prospect of fellow poets singing the praises of any thing so venal as a State.... *Sides* are a bigassed drag. The biggest small-talk of all, like which one are you on? Motherfucker" (quoted in von Hallberg 58).

And in the Fredman interview, he adds:

> There are some people who have power and a certain kind of means at their disposal who are trying to get the society to think in a certain way, to do a certain set of things, and so forth. I think any responsible writer is never that. No writer is ever trying to get anybody to *do* something; what they're trying to create is a cognizance in the society of itself, to furnish the means—through clarity of language—for a self-appraisal and self-evaluation.

Because really, what's the advantage in seeing human nature as basically good, or some other Romantic nonsense? Nobody's immune, least of all cretin politicians, but nobody else either. Yes, I'm talking about US ... the well-meaning, vaguely liberal, vaguely tolerant, vaguely intelligent "counter-culture." What lets us off the hook? Why does what Adorno called "the culture industry" get a free pass? This is the big question about the two books of Nason's poem reprinted below, and what's so hard for many people to appreciate. People ask: why spend so much time criticizing *other poets*? Why shouldn't Nason be seen as someone who couldn't find a publisher for his own verse because people like Ashbery were sucking up all the oxygen? How evil is the AWP? Aren't we all on the same side, sorta kinda?

Well, no. For one thing, there's Blake's line above about being fettered. Who's to say that every young poet who writes a line these days doesn't become inhibited by the unseen and unspoken aesthetic wafting across the land: the necessity to be lyrical but apolitical, imagistic but equable, and for whatever reason, never mention actual people in one's verse? In that sense, isn't it possible that the enemy has already won?

So here, at the end of this installment, are my thesis statements:

1. Satire isn't just another category or genre; rather, it's a part of all poetry, whether its object is other people or social practices or language or the satirist herself, and there's some evidence that its origin is before written language, in oral curse poems. (Archilochus, the second poet of the Western World after Homer but the first satirist, is thought in some accounts to have caused the death of his almost father-in-law and almost-

wife by the power of his iambs, something that Wally Stevens probably wasn't thinking about when he wrote, about poetry, "It can kill a man").
2. The best satire combines cruelty and humor; it's never solemn or earnest.
3. A society or culture that doesn't value satire, for any reason, is in trouble. And before we start patting ourselves on the backs, Alec Baldwin and Melissa McCarthy are NOT really satire; Jon Stewart and Steven Colbert are NOT really satire. Rather, they're mild entertainment—human valium pills—and exist to make us accept the status quo and nod off to sleep, thinking there are still some people who "get it." Good luck with that.

Or, as Ed Dorn had it in *Yellow Lola*,

> The common duty of the poet
> in this era of massive dysfunction
> & generalized onslaught upon alertness is to maintain the plant
> to the end that the mumbling horde bestirs its prunéd tongue. (63)

Notes to Richard Nason's *A Modern Dunciad* (Part III)

In the epilogue to Richard Nason's *A Modern Dunciad* (reprinted elsewhere in this journal) are the following lines:

> It may be more than deadlines that we meet;
> Her Armageddon that we go to greet!
> If Pope could warn "She comes, she comes!" O, fear!
> May we not say at last, "She's here, she's here!"

It's an attempt to remind his readers that the book has a serious intent: to prevent the Goddess of Dullness from destroying the world. Of course, readers might have forgotten that purpose after reading these lines from Book IV, the results of an imaginary baking contest, in which many poets active in 1978 competed:

> The contest over, Koch's "Raisin Snack"
> Was given to the poor, who gave it back;
> Joel Oppenheimer early lost the race,
> As lofty cakes collapsed to lower case;
> Giorno's "pounder" weighed much more than pound,
> Because it held a heavy boot he'd "found";
> H. Nemerov, adept at prankster jolts,
> Had baked in his a box of nuts and bolts;
> Saroyan proved an overeager "also ran,"
> By using just an inch or two of pan;
> While Justice took defeat with solemn air,
> Both held and ate his cake, a perfect square;

> The Goddess gave MacLeish a grateful nudge
> For sticking to his guns and making fudge;
> And Alistair Reid, a "limey" awf'ly "in,"
> Brought down the house by lacing his with gin;
> Bright Corso eyed the prize but could not nab it,
> Not with those "potted brownies" baked from habit;
> At last, poor Moss engaged in great harangue
> When Brinnin was dismissed for pure meringue;
> King John, of course, as always, justly won:
> His entry: empty pan entitled "Bun"!

The King is the recently deceased John Ashbery, for whom you might have read a recent obituary or two; if Nason were still alive, he probably wouldn't have been asked for his reaction. "It's too soon to talk about that," as Second Amendment proponents say.

I've covered in previous installments why this verse, an imitation not only of Pope's *Dunciad* but of the eighteenth-century heroic couplets in which he wrote, will probably seem foreign to today's poetic tastes. But those who think it's somehow disrespectful to mention other living poets in one's verse clearly don't have a historical sense of the art. For example, Byron found some room in his masterpiece, *Don Juan*, to comment on some poets who were still alive:

> 90
> Young Juan wander'd by the glassy brooks
> Thinking unutterable things: he threw
> Himself at length within the leafy nooks
> Where the wild branch of the cork forest grew:
> There poets find materials for their books,
> And every now and then we read them through;
> So that their plan and prosody are eligible,
> Unless, like Wordsworth, they prove unintelligible.
>
> 91
> He, Juan (and not Wordsworth) so pursued
> His self-communion with his own high soul,
> Until his mighty heart, in its great mood,
> Had mitigated part, though not the whole

> Of its disease: he did the best he could
> With things not very subject to his control,
> And turn'd, without perceiving his condition,
> Like Coleridge, into a metaphysician.

I found out recently that Thomas Love Peacock, with whose work I was never familiar, was also a satirist ... and if any literary period ever needed satire, the painful and angst-ridden Romantics might be at the top of the list. A recent article by Pamela Clemit in *The Times Literary Supplement* reviewed two of Peacock's re-issued novels: *Nightmare Abbey*, she wrote, "is now perhaps his most popular on account of its well-turned caricatures of leading Romantic poets ... a send-up of the inward-looking, obscurantist Germanic trend in contemporary literature." The cast of characters included Scythrop Glowry (Shelley), Mr. Flosky (Coleridge) and Mr. Cypress (Byron). By all reports, the satirized took it in good humor, with Shelley writing "I know not how to praise sufficiently the lightness, chastity & strength of the language of the whole." One wonders if they thought the same about Byron:

> Thou shalt believe in Milton, Dryden, Pope;
> Thou shalt not set up Wordsworth, Coleridge, Southey;
> Because the first is crazed beyond all hope,
> The second drunk, the third so quaint and mouthy. (from stanza 205)

And satire goes much further back, of course, all the way to Archilochus, whom Guy Davenport called "the second poet of the West" after Homer. Here's another criticism of the inward-looking trend:

> Like Odysseus under the ram
> You have clung under your lovers
> And under your love of lust,
> Seeing nothing else for this mist,
> Dark of heart, dark of mind.

Archilochus, says Davenport,

> was both poet and mercenary.... There is a tradition that wasps hover around his grave. To the ancient, both Greek and Roman,

he was The Satirist.... 'Hasten on, Wayfarer,' Archilochus' tomb bore for inscription, 'lest you stir up the hornets.' To mock, a Greek proverb goes, is to thumb through Archilochus.

The high-minded Spartans banned Archilochus' poems for their mockery of uncritical bravery, to which he might have responded:

> I prefer to have, after all,
> Only what pleases me.
> Are you so deep in misery
> That you think me fallen?
> You say I'm lazy; I'm not,
> Nor any of my kin-people.
> I know how to love those
> Who love me, how to hate.

Well, "The tigers of wrath are wiser than the horses of instruction," as Blake said, who wasn't above a little satire himself, especially in the neglected early "An Island in the Moon," with the immortal lines:

> Lo the Bat with Leathern wing,
> Winking & blinking,
> Winking & blinking,
> Winking & blinking,
> Like Doctor Johnson.

Perhaps satire is just alien to the American mind, with our naïve and idealistic aspirations. We don't want to accept the basic truth, that our values aren't things like self-reliance, independence and toughness, but "success, promoting deception and the fast con, easy cash, hustling and the love of money." Neil Gabler was writing in *Truthdig* last July:

> Americans take it for granted that "everyone's got an angle," except maybe themselves. This idea, that you succeed through grift and guile, has made many Americans more cynical than idealistic, more Barnum than Alger, and, yes, more Trump than Obama. Barnum understood the financial implications of the swindle. He was a brilliant self-promoter and ballyhoo artist who sold an unsuspecting public on things like seeing George Washington's 160-year-old nurse, or an "authentic" stuffed mermaid, and then

made additional money by exposing his own frauds, realizing that people actually liked being fooled.

Of course, this was written before the magic paper towels were thrown to suffering Puerto Ricans. Anyway, the theory is that this was what the Trump-voters saw in him, and what the Democrats, too virtuous for their own good, will never understand. They prefer affirmations,

> those cheery slogans intended to lift the user's mood by repeating them: "I am a lovable person!" "My life is filled with joy!" Psychologists at the University of Waterloo concluded that such statements make people with low self-esteem feel worse—not least because telling yourself you're lovable is liable to provoke the grouchy internal counterargument that, really, you're not.

That's from a useful article entitled "The Power of Negative Thinking" by Oliver Burkeman from the NY Times, who also writes

> Ancient philosophers and spiritual teachers understood the need to balance the positive with the negative, optimism with pessimism, a striving for success and security with an openness to failure and uncertainty. The Stoics recommended "the premeditation of evils," or deliberately visualizing the worst-case scenario. This tends to reduce anxiety about the future: when you soberly picture how badly things could go in reality, you usually conclude that you could cope. Besides, they noted, imagining that you might lose the relationships and possessions you currently enjoy increases your gratitude for having them now. Positive thinking, by contrast, always leans into the future, ignoring present pleasures.

This seems clear enough to me, which is why it's hard to imagine anyone denying themselves the pleasure of these Nason lines, inveighing against some poets' proclivity for getting grant money:

> The hottest beds of interest, now as then,
> Find Moss and Ginsberg bucking up their men,
> And cudgeling both Institute and Fund
> To give their proteges the cummerbund,
> To Corso, say, as some belated "beat,"

> Or Merrill for his cold aesthetic feat,
> While Hornick and the zombies she espouses
> With private cash bring plague on both their houses!

I'm sorry Nason wrote this poem before the advent of LangPo: he would have had a blast ... "not," writes Burkeman, "by ignoring unpleasant sensations, or refusing to feel them, but by turning nonjudgmentally toward them":

> From this perspective, the relentless cheer of positive thinking begins to seem less like an expression of joy and more like a stressful effort to stamp out any trace of negativity.... The social critic Barbara Ehrenreich has persuasively argued that the all-positive approach, with its rejection of the possibility of failure, helped bring on our present financial crises. The psychological evidence, backed by ancient wisdom, certainly suggests that it is not the recipe for success that it purports to be.

But the value of satire isn't just negative: it might be the only way we can recapture the real. Stephen Marche wrote a brilliant re-evaluation this summer of David Shields' *Reality Hunger* in the *Los Angeles Review of Books*: "How do we find the truth," he asked, "in an age when technology and politics have rendered the line between fiction and nonfiction nearly impossible to distinguish? How do we write about the real world when reality itself is up for grabs?"

> The question is what to do now that the very categories of relevant and irrelevant, meaningful and meaningless, are slipping away from lived experience. What is the role of those who make meaning in a world of its slippage? What does it mean to write post- fact?...
>
> A whole new range of literary problems has emerged that no one could have imagined even five years ago. "My task [...] is by the power of the written word to make you hear, to make you feel—it is, before all, to make you see." That's how Joseph Conrad defined literature. First you have to see. Then you have to share what you've seen. Then you have to be willing to see what others see. Every step in that equation is now up for grabs. The essay as a genre will have to be reimagined from the ground up....

We live in dangerous times and need dangerous writing. How many pieces do you read that feel dangerous? The stakes could not be higher. The loss of the possibility of sense is at stake. The content of human connection is at stake. Logos, ethos, and pathos have been stirred into a hot sticky mess. The willingness to blur fact and fiction, in a world of fulminant identity-creation, turns out not to be revelatory at all. It turns out to be stupid—unimaginably stupid, profoundly willfully stupid. The fundamental question for writing today is how to make the world less stupid. That is also the fundamental political question of our time.

And just one more sentence from this fabulous essay: "The post-fact world no longer demands, as the condition of creative fluidity, a rush away from the tyranny of facts, as Shields imagined. Rather the opposite: the moment demands an art of focused observation. The essay is the theater of the brain, but it is also a harvest of vision. We need a new art of information. We need to start building it right now."

Everyone knows that satire, besides being cruel and funny, is also an indictment of whatever social situation the satirist finds himself in. In that, it's different than our current popular artistic forms. My friend Michael Boughn and I were talking about TV on Facebook a few months ago. I had posted this:

> A long time ago, when I lived in Seattle, I became conscious of a game called "Dungeons and Dragons," which a certain type of college student seemed obsessively interested in playing. Now the country seems enchanted by a TV show about dragons, to which they pay more attention than the political chaos currently enveloping us. Coleridge wrote about the difference between fantasy and imagination; in the early years of the 19th century, it must have seemed possible that imagination would find its way in the world. Today, not so much.

So what was I saying in my somewhat snarky way? Something about how I disliked *Game of Thrones* because of its fantasy setting, which bore no possible relation to my life or the life of the republic. But Michael seemed to be a fan:

> Oh, come on, don't moralize a decent entertainment. I can watch *Game of Thrones* and pay attention to His Dumpster at the same time. I can pat my head and rub my tummy at the same time, too. And whistle the Battle Hymn of the Republic. [adding] The dragons are very cool. Best dragons ever, and I have watched quite a few dragons.

Had I been moralizing? Perhaps. But his response seemed too self-satisfied. So I at first allowed that I had been watching the show the last few weeks as well (establishing common ground with one's opponent is a technique frequently taught in argument classes). I added:

> But I do think we disagree about such matters; I'm much less sanguine with the entertainment-industrial complex than you appear to be, and think it's all part of Debord's spectacle run amock. Historicize everything, said Jameson; everything matters, or could.

We were off and running now:

> Yeah, OK, Debord and Baudrillard nail the big picture of historical doom, the Empire's conspiracy to control our minds and yoke us to its wheel. But they seem to miss out on the more human dimension, the need to unwind after another day dealing with shit, the relief that comes with that. Is it all a conspiracy, a control mechanism? I like to think not. People like to tell stories and people like to hear stories. They always have. For many many reasons. I read in a book on Sinatra by Will Friedlander years ago that the American Song Book was the result of a unique set of circumstances that included a confluence of commerce and genius. Sometimes it happens. I think it's happening now with television (not that I think *GoT* is genius—just a damn good story well and lavishly told).

It would take too long to explain this, but I do think it's all a conspiracy and control mechanism. That doesn't prohibit me from enjoying the ride. As noted, I watch TV a lot (the Yankees are winning the Wild Card game on the TV just to the left as I'm writing). In fact, I'm a relative slave of the media, and wouldn't want to get off the grid even if I could. But that doesn't mean we have to give up our historical and critical sensibilities when so indulging ourselves.

Besides, satire can be helpful, useful information. Here's Juvenal's advice to a friend who's contemplating marriage:

> Why stand such bitch-tyranny when there's rope available,
> when those dizzying top-floor windows are all wide open,
> when there's a bridge near by from which you can make your jump?
> Supposing none of those exists catches your fancy,
> don't you think it better to sleep with a pretty boy?
> Boys don't quarrel all night, or nag you for little presents
> while they're on the job, or complain that you don't come
> up to their expectations, or demand more gasping passion. (VI. 30–37, tr. Peter Green)

Not that I'm recommending that; I wouldn't want to get disinvited from Berkeley. I do like the tone, though, and the no-nonsense approach to reality. "Is this not something more than fantasy, my Lord?" We went to see *Hamlet* at the Old Globe a few nights ago, and that's a line I thought might end this piece, as well as the philosophical young lad's take-down of Polonius: "Why sir, this satirical rogue says that old men have gray beards."

That's what I saw—and see—in Nason's *A Modern Dunciad:* satire as a way of bringing back the real. Or we could keep playing the game, the scoreboard of which, I'm afraid, will never change:

	1	2	3	4	5	6	7	8	9	TOTAL
REALISTS	2	0	1	4	2	1	0	6	2	0
IDEALISTS	0	0	0	0	0	0	0	0	0	1

Kent Johnson and the Future of Poetic Satire

Because of Poetry, I Have a Really Big House by Kent Johnson.
Shearsman, United Kingdom: 2020. 90 pages. $18

Don Juan can survive comparison with the poetry of Shelley and Wordsworth, not indeed on their own ground, but because it satisfies deep human needs which their poetry, great and beautiful as it is, can never satisfy. For to Wordsworth and Shelley was unhappily denied the genius of laughter, and the comic spirit has its own beneficent influence upon us;—it dissolves our fanaticisms and dogmatisms, it stimulates the free play of intelligence, it preserves our sanity even where it crosses our convictions. Byron mocked at everything as only the complete skeptic can.
—Louis I. Bredvold, 1935

"Satire," said George S. Kaufman, famously, "is what closes on Saturday night." It certainly seems to have closed in American poetry: by and large, and despite its long history,[1] examples of satire in our poetry since 1900 have been few and far between. There are reasons for that: for one thing, satire traffics in shaming, and it's hard to defend holding anyone up to ridicule; for another, one person's vice is another's kink, and we've become, these days, notoriously shy about inhabiting any sort of moral high ground. And at the moment, there's one more possibility for its unpopularity, namely, that there are some historical periods when real life would seem to make satire totally unnecessary.

---

1. The tombstone of Archilochus, the second poet of the Western world after Homer, says "Hasten on, Wayfarer / lest you stir up the hornets"; he was rumored to have killed people by means of his iambs.

But I think critics of satire ignore one of its prime virtues, namely its humor, or as Louis Bredvold called it in 1935 the "comic spirit." What was it, exactly, that Byron had and Wordsworth and Shelley didn't? Many poets will know these humorous lines from the first canto of *Don Juan*:

> Thou shalt believe in Milton, Dryden, Pope;
>   Thou shalt not set up Wordsworth, Coleridge, Southey;
> Because the first is crazed beyond all hope,
>   The second drunk, the third so quaint and mouthy (I 1633–36)

But they may not be as familiar with some from the third, which takes the quarrel with Wordsworth into darker, more vituperative channels: this is the Wordsworth who was "unexcised, unhired, who then / Season'd his pedlar poems with democracy":

> We learn from Horace, "Homer sometimes sleeps;"
>   We feel without him, Wordsworth sometimes wakes,—
> To show with what complacency he creeps,
>   With his dear "*Waggoners*," around his lakes,
> He wishes for "a boat" to sail the deeps—
>   Of ocean?—No, of air; and then he makes
> Another outcry for "a little boat,"
> And drivels seas to set it well afloat. (III, 873–880)

Ouch. We're here confronted immediately with satire's double edge: sure, it's funny, or can be, but it can also be—to use one of the ex-president's favorite words—nasty. What accounts for such scorn? Byron's case is simple: he was operating under a completely different poetics than the Lake Poets, formed first by a close study of his eighteenth-century predecessors and then by the comic epics of the Italian Renaissance, which gave him his form, and those amazingly versatile eight-line stanzas enabled him, he wrote in a letter to his publisher in 1820, "to be a little quietly facetious upon every thing" … "I *have* no plan—I *had* no plan; but I had or have materials." For Byron, those materials included the moral and political hypocrisies of the ruling castes of all European countries. Still, the *object* of satire can be anything: Juvenal didn't care much for the decadent aristocrats of his imperial society, while Swift hated the entire human race. We don't have to subscribe to a satirist's beliefs to appreciate the poems any more than we have to believe in God to appreciate the *Commedia*. It's just that good satire is always waspish in some manner; it never adopts the party line, no matter what it is at the moment. Satirists live in a kind of poetic permanent revolution: "to mock," a Greek proverb goes, "is to thumb through Archilochus" (Guy Davenport, *7 Greeks*)

Happily, there are still some practitioners who aspire to that particular laurel, the prize for a "contest" that might have started with Archilochus yet includes Hipponax, Horace and Juvenal among the classic poets and Dryden, Pope and Swift in seventeenth-to-eighteenth-century England. Perhaps Edward Dorn was our last great satiric poet, but Kent Johnson, with his new book *Because of Poetry I Have a Really Big House* (Shearsman Books, 2020) has officially joined the list. To explain why involves exploring the changes he's rung on satire in this, his most impressive work, which are at once traditional and completely new.

We might start with an example close to home: in early summer of this year, the *New York Times Book Review* featured two poets on their front and back pages (something it will probably never do again), Claudia Rankine and Jericho Brown. The poems were fine, if not remarkable, but the reason for their display wasn't their merit, exactly, but because these Black poets were seen as authentic spokespeople to address the protests for social and racial justice that will hopefully continue on the streets of American cities. I think most poets who saw that issue were probably happy that their art had been recognized, but there was a troubling subtext: poetry, the *Book Review* seemed to imply, is something we turn to *in extremis*, when social conditions become so intolerable that "normal language"—whether political rant or Facebook post or cable pundit—isn't qualified to address them; similar efforts like the "Shelter-in-Place" poems sponsored by the Academy of American Poets would seem to agree. In other words, poetry is rarified air, the kind of thing John Adams was talking about when he said he had to learn politics and war so his grandchildren could dabble in the humanities: it's high rhetoric, like the recent eulogies for John Lewis or Auden's "September 1939."[2] Johnson, apparently, feels differently:

> I don't read poetry unless I have to, which
> would be when a guard from Penn is pressing
> a knife to my throat in a penitentiary, where I
> am residing for protesting some Poetry Institution.
> He orders me to squeal, again and again, that I, too,
> dislike it, that I wish I were a poet, but I am not.
>   ("With Fred Seidel, near the Matterhorn, in 2020")

Of course, Johnson reads a lot of poetry; his book shows familiarity with every major poetic group and community in the U.S. over the last 60 years. It's just that satiric poets know there's a crack in the edifice ... any edifice. For Johnson, that edifice is the Poetry Foundation and its billion-dollar endowment that isn't being spent to promote and protect poets. In that building, however, also live language poets, "post-avant" poets (Johnson's column in the sadly departed journal *Dispatches from the Poetry Wars* was called "Emily Post-Avant"), conceptual poets, poets too indebted to theory, Gertrude Stein, and any writers who are being paid off by the "virtual Poetry Bank" of the times, including the poet himself: "True enough: I, too, am a literati-stiff" ("To Those Who May Come After"). Things used to be different, he mourns, but now "Bolinas is condo strata. Nanluoguxiang's / a Po-bourgeois tourist-trap" ("Departing Qinzhou"), and in another poem from the masterful "One Hundred Poems from the Chinese" section, he admits that he's "grown old / and surly. My liver is shot. Almost all the friends / of my youth have abandoned me." So he leaves instructions for a friend:

> If you're coming
> down through the narrows of the River Kiang,
> give me a ring, my cell is 815-234-8004. I'll
> come out to meet you, as far as Cho-fu-sa, by the
> mist-shrouded ruins, on deserted Black Mountain. ("Near Black Mountain")

---

2. All these years later I still don't understand why he took out the line "We must love one another or die" and later renounced the entire poem: that we'll all die whether we love one another or not misses the point.

These lines might be funny even to people who don't know the famous Pound translation they mimic, but they're not *only* funny; Johnson is serious about the corruption of the present Institutional Culture of poetry, calling it "a virtual Poetry Bank exist[ing] to buy poets off" and excoriating the "Big Tent, Third Way nature of its canny / putsch (crucially aided by Capital gifts), likely / tweaked by intelligence ops." The Chinese section closes with a haunting verse that may or may not be an actual translation:

> *My dear poets, here and there,*
> *today and long ago,*
> *Paradise is a wandering ghost,*
> *for ten thousand years,*
> *before it will be born.*
>   ("Three Days After")

Some people might wish to abstain from appreciating poems the subject matter of which is primarily other poems (and poets). But to return to Johnson's predecessors for a minute, Dorn wasn't above taking a few shots at the poetry world, from his comparison of poetry criticism to "grades assigned to meat" in Hello La Jolla to the poem in his last book, Chemo Sábe, "The Dull Relief of General Pain":

> millions of people in North Korea
> are succumbing to starvation ...
> Doesn't Michael Jackson like children anymore?
> Or did he never like communist children?
> What's going on? This is poetry calling!
> Poetry is waiting for an answer.

Ariana Reines is a poet I've been paying attention to lately who's making similar moves:

> Poem being extremely careful and giving praise as peculiar as possible
> Try hard little poem
> Where is the reward asks the poem it will come someday
> Says the poem

while on the next page she seemingly mocks herself: "Oh yeah her stuff is so fresh compared to, compared to / Her stuff is really fresh /

Yeah" ("Save the World," *Mercury*). And a few centuries ago, Juvenal suggested there may be other factors to poetic success besides skill:

> How can grim poverty grasp
> Inspiration's enchanted wand, how find that singing grotto
> if you're forced to scrape and pinch to satisfy the body's
> demands for cash? Horace cried "Rejoice!" on a full stomach....
> For if Virgil had not had one slave-boy and a fairly comfortable
> lodging, all those snakes would have dropped from the Fury's hair,
> her grave trumpet would have been voiceless. ("Satire VII")

That passage could also serve as a gloss to much of Byron's *Don Juan*. So one answer to the objection that these poems are too absorbed with poetry is that poets always hear other poets' voices in their minds: why not just cop to it? But let Johnson tell it:

> For we did what we could, switching our homes
> More often than our shoes, all through the small
> Poetry wars and the great war of the classes, despairing
> At the sins in the latter, and no doubt too much
> At the ones in the former. We crossed deserts, rivers,
> And seas, and still we never arrived, for we were nothing.

That's from "To Those Who May Come After," what he calls a "translucination after Bertolt Brecht," in which he confesses "Yeah, I know, it's not 1939, so the language is 'off.'"

So there are two things to keep in mind about good satire: 1) it ridicules people and ideas, and 2) it's funny. Johnson's *Because of Poetry I Have a Really Big House* amply fulfills both of these criteria, but more importantly, it perpetuates a once-noble tradition that's in serious danger today of being choked off by woke and humorless commissars who wouldn't know satire and parody if it bit them. Sadly, that's not only in the poetry world: the best thing about this book is that it creates a world where more of our sensibilities can be employed than in the terrible, straitened year just completed.

Isn't It Romantic?

Poems for the Millennium, Volume III: Romantic and Post-Romantic Poetry
Edited by Jerome Rothenberg & Pierre Joris

The appearance of *Poems for the Millennium, Volume Three: The University of California Book of Romantic & Postromantic Poetry*, edited with commentaries by Jerome Rothenberg and Jeffrey C. Robinson, raises a few questions. Why another anthology of Romantic poems? Does this anthology bear any resemblance to the first two in the series? Who is its intended audience? And last and probably least, what would Harold Bloom think about it?

Let's take those questions in reverse order. Bloom's famous concerns about the "anxiety of influence" and canon-formation were criticized extensively in a 1981 essay by Rothenberg called "The Critic as Exterminating Angel,"[1] and one way to look at this gathering—along with the other anthologies Rothenberg has produced or collaborated on, including the two previous volumes of this series and other hugely influential volumes dating back to 1968's *Technicians of the Sacred*—is as a manifesto antithetical to everything Bloom stood for. Instead, it

---

1. The anthology appears at the same time as a collection of Rothenberg's long and short essays and interviews called *Poetics & Polemics: 1980–2005* (University of Alabama Press). Without slighting the contributions of the Romantic scholar Jeffrey C. Robinson to the anthology in any way — indeed, his recent *Unfettering Poetry: The Fancy in British Romanticism* intriguingly reverses Coleridge's famous dictum about the fancy being subsidiary to the imagination, and is one of this volume's guiding "re-imaginings" — I will be quoting or paraphrasing many of Rothenberg's essays in this review, and will make clear when I'm talking about one of them (*Poetics & Polemics*) as opposed to commentary or poems from the anthology (*Poems*).

represents "a poetics of the open as against the closed, the free against the fettered, the transgressive and forbidden against the settled" (Rothenberg, *Poetics & Polemics* 7). In that context, it advances a radical Romanticism that recalls its associations with revolutionary thought of all kinds, and seeks to re-imagine the familiar dichotomies between reason and imagination or the individual and social reality that have become part and parcel of the cultural mainstream.

But while it's easy to dismiss Bloom's limitations—his conservative Oedipal complex, his anti-liberation theology—it's still daunting to see this "big Romantic book" as "a radical usurpation of the canon" (*Poems* 8), some sort of anti- or counter-canonical enterprise that might change the prevailing views about Romanticism and even give the venerable *Norton Anthology* a run for its money. If anything like that is going to happen, we'll need to unpack some of the assumptions behind this book, which will also allow us to explore the function of anthologies in general.

In the introduction to Volume I of this series, Rothenberg and Pierre Joris wrote that they wanted to accomplish their ends "without turning the selection of authors into the projection of a new canon of famous names" (3). No danger of that here: while it's true that only 37 of the 66 authors who appear in the three main "galleries" of the anthology also appear in one or another version of the *Norton Anthology* (World, English or American), many of the omitted are better known for other genres of writing (Charles Fourier, Kierkegaard, Nietzsche) or are well-known and widely available (Nerval, Laforgue, Apollinaire) or are writers whose choice of dialect(s) make translation difficult (Giuseppe Belli). But considerations of this sort are usually equivocal: for example, the Spanish writers Gustavo Adolfo Bécquer and Rosalía de Castro are in the World *Norton* but not here, while the English Romantic *Norton* opens with Anna Letitia Barbauld and Charlotte Smith, also absent from these pages. There are a few writers I confess I never heard of until finding them here—the Greek experimentalist Dionysios Solomos, Cyprian Norwid of Poland, Victor Segalen, writing in French, Arno Holz (an early adherent of Visual Poetry) in German, the Colombian José Silva—and discovering new and interesting work is always a good reason to pick up a book. But surely its necessity, its *raison d'etre,* lies elsewhere.

Mentioning people like Laforgue and Apollinaire does imply one huge change: rather than seeing the chronological "end" of Romanticism in about 1830 (the English Romantic *Norton* ends with the passage of the first Reform Act in 1832, an important but not earth-shattering event), the editors extend the movement—or that part of it that was "experimental and visionary"—throughout the entire nineteenth century and into the twentieth, thus coining the term "Postromantic" and making it a true "prequel" to the first two volumes of the series. But that, in turn, raises a few more questions: what "experimental and visionary" qualities do these former writers share, exactly, with their successors, and—since very few people are going to pick up a 928-page book at their local bookstores for light summer reading (even though it is available as I type at Amazon for $23.07)—in what undergraduate classes would such a volume be required?

Again, let's go in reverse order. At a recent dinner party, one guest who had seen the book in galleys was enthusiastic, saying that, in comparison, the venerable *Norton Anthology* was pathetic. As I'd been teaching a British Literature survey course for four years, largely using the *Norton,* I filed this piece of information away silently. As it happened, I had also kept a *New York Times* notice from January 2006 on the most recent (8th) incarnation of the English *Norton* and dug it out in preparation for writing this review. The article, an essay by Rachel Donadio called "Keeper of the Canon," mentioned that the English anthology was Norton's top seller, with eight million copies in print since 1962, and that its editor "holds one of the most powerful posts in the world of letters, and is symbolically seen as arbiter of the canon" (27).

In that respect, it's interesting that there's been a changing of the guard: Shakespeare scholar Stephen Greenblatt, who published the entertaining *Will in the World* in 2004 and is one of the leaders of the critical school known as New Historicism, has now taken over main editing duties of the English *Norton* from his predecessor, noted Romantic scholar M. H. Abrams, best known perhaps for his book on Romantic theory, *The Mirror and The Lamp*, in 1953. Abrams lamented some of Greenblatt's changes, which included scaling back on the Romantic poets to make space for more Modernism and Gothic literature. As well, the article noted amusingly that, besides Bloom and Lionel Trilling's *Oxford Anthology of English Literature* in the '70s, Northrop Frye had briefly joined the contest to dethrone the *Norton*, but his proposed Harcourt counter-anthology, which he wanted to call "Burnt Norton," never materialized.[2]

Such scholarly competitions for the attention of thousands of undergraduates might involve many criteria: a better, somehow more representative selection from the major figures, or a re-contextualization of some of their more famous works; a more multicultural gathering, with more women, minorities, post-colonialists and working-class writers; writings organized by theme or subject matter rather than chronologically; the introduction of heretofore "minor" figures, with the connections between majors and minors explained; or a geographically expanded selection, as Romanticism was a worldwide movement. Indeed, all of these tendencies are on view in the volume under consideration here, and some specific details will follow.

On the other hand, any reasonably competent Romantic anthology (and there have been many, over fifteen in the last twenty years) will also offer many of these features … and as Ed Dorn asked in *Hello, La Jolla:* "Sure, there may be some interesting juxtapositions, but so what[?]" (65). We're back to the original questions: why exactly was it necessary for the University of California to extend its imprimatur to this particular version of Romanticism? Why is it important? Why is it necessary?

In beginning to answer those questions, we should remember another crucial audience for this volume is poets, and those deeply involved in the study of poetry, undergraduate or not. And for them especially, we should ask one more: What exactly is the function of an anthology? According to the Greek etymology, it's "a gathering

---

2. Coincidentally enough, Bloom claims Abrams as his intellectual "father" … "a precarious position to be in," said Abrams dryly, considering the "strongly Oedipal" nature of Bloom's theories.

of flowers" (viz., Zukofsky's *80 Flowers*), and in an essay called "The Anthology as a Manifesto and as an Epic," Rothenberg describes the meadows he's gathered his in, quoting Gertrude Stein: "as it is old it is new and as it is new it is old." Also in that essay, he says that there are two main kinds of anthologies:

1. those that *deceive* me/us by a false sense of closure and authority ... the canonical anthologies we all know as the great conservatizing force in our literature(s) ... gatherings of acceptable/ accepted poets ...

2. those I had hoped to do with regard to the *past* and those still more rare and useful ones that opened up and thereby changed the *present.*

The first kind, he goes on, serves to "rein in or exclude those moves that challenge too overtly the boundaries of form and meaning or that call into question the boundaries (genre boundaries) of poetry itself," while the second "use[s] the form as a kind of manifesto-assemblage: to present, to bring to light, or to create works that have been excluded or that collectively present a challenge to the dominant system-makers or the world at large" (*Poetics & Polemics* 14).

Thinking back to the anthologies that have probably influenced many of *Jacket*'s readers—Don Allen's *New American Poetry* in 1960, certainly, or *An Anthology of New York Poets* ten years later, or perhaps *Another Republic,* an international anthology of the 1970s, or any of the others that Rothenberg has worked on, with various collaborators—it seems clear that they fall under category #2. As Rothenberg has it, that means that they're a) manifestos; b) ways of laying out an active poetics, by example and by commentary; and c) grand assemblages, including past work "that had been kept beyond the pale" and present work "that has been kept from comparisons" (*Poetics & Polemics* 15).

They can also be combinations of "avant-garde" work (however defined) and so-called multicultural work. An example of that crucial blend can be seen in Rothenberg's view of Pound's book *Cathay*:

> Rather than a capsule glimpse at an ancient—and from a Western perspective, exotic—poetry, it represented Pound's

sense of what it was to be alive and writing poetry in 1915 (in the midst of the First World War). "Largely a war book," as Hugh Kenner describes it, "its exiled bowmen, deserted women, leveled dynasties, departures for far places, lonely frontier guardsmen, and glories remembered from afar, were selected from the diverse wealth in the Fenollosa notebooks Pound was working from by a sensibility responsive to torn Belgium and disrupted London." (*Poetics & Polemics* 9)

In other words, "something in Chinese language and culture served as both a model and a confirmation" to "the objective of Pound's imagism and that version of it 'in motion' that he called vorticism," namely, "connecting to the concrete particulars of the world around us" (*Poetics & Polemics* 10). The connection between multicultural work and radical poetic techniques is the crucial point here, just as the cluster "Some Orientalisms" in the anthology refers both to the nineteenth-century colonialist drive for control over non-European people and the corresponding opening to unfamiliar poetic horizons and techniques: "the locus, in Emily Dickinson's phrase, of the 'unreportable place,' unknown myths, unknown subjectivities" (*Poems* 806).

Including in other "clusters" such things as excerpts from the Egyptian Book of the Dead and unfamiliar translations from Sanskrit, Serbo-Croatian and Icelandic is again not meant as a collection of exotic antiquities, but as an experimental gathering of modes that might speak to us in our various contemporary situations; like the previous two volumes, the chronological "galleries," which stretch from the late eighteenth century to the early twentieth, are intermixed with the afore-mentioned "clusters" and thematic "books" of "extensions" and "origins," the former featuring visual, performative and conceptual works not usually associated with Romanticism and the latter "tilted toward the ethnopoetic" (*Poems* 17).

These principles create a book with stunning surprises: different readers will have to choose their own favorite discoveries—one of mine was the absolutely insane Pushkin poem, "Tsar Nikita and His Daughters"—but one more point needs to be stressed: the unfamiliar works collected here, some of them, no doubt, falling into what Bloom has sneeringly called "The School of Resentment" (postcolonialist and political literature), are not being offered against a deeper historical grounding of the material. Rather, it's exactly the hidden connections between the literature of the past and present that the editors seek to uncover. In this light, Bloom's insistence that "everyone who now reads and writes in the West, of whatever racial background, sex, or ideological camp, is still a son or daughter of Homer" (qtd. in *Poetics & Polemics* 71), even though "No Coyotes or Taras appear in his mythologies, no Milarepas or Li Pos among his canonized poets" (71) is doubly inadequate: "Western definitions of poetry and art were no longer, indeed had never been, sufficient and ... our continued reliance on them was distorting our view both of the larger human experience and of our own possibilities within it" (*Poetics & Polemics* 12).

Another basic principle of much of Rothenberg's previous anthology work has been to rescue un-canonical traditional material. Writers date themselves by which of his anthologies they consider most important or influential; for me it was *America A Prophecy* (1974), edited with George Quasha, with its gatherings from (on consecutive pages) the Mayan *Popol Vuh*, the Nez Perce Indians and Archibald McLeish, or Pound preceded by Frances Densmore and succeeded by Else von Freytag-Loringhoven, knitted together with small dollops of commentary (smaller than in this volume). There was a "Book of Origins" in that book as well; in the introduction to this one, the editors say that, at the end of the eighteenth century, "Something had happened—Enlightenment or Revolution or, on its more doubtful side, Imperium—that brought other worlds into view & put the inherited past into question" (395). Some lines from Whitman's "Song of Myself" serve as that book's epigraph:

> Through me many long dumb voices,
> Voices of the interminable generations of prisoners and slaves,
> Voices of the diseas'd and despairing and of thieves and dwarfs,
> Voices of cycles of preparation and accretion,
> And of the threads that connect the stars, and of wombs and of
>   the father-stuff,
> And of the rights of them the others are down upon,

> Of the deform'd, trivial, flat, foolish, despised,
> Fog in the air, beetles rolling balls of dung. (qtd. in *Poems* 395)

Indeed, this might serve as yet another of the organizing principles of the book. Finally, one of the more interesting sections for me are the selections from the canonical Romantic authors: for example, I'd seen and admired Browning's gritty "Caliban upon Setebos" before—it's in the English *Norton*—but somehow missed Tennyson's intensely musical "Hesperides" and these lines from "Maud":

> See, there is one of us sobbing,
> No limit to his distress;
> And another, a lord of all things, praying
> To his own great self, I guess;
> And another, a statesman there, betraying
> His party-secret, fool, to the press;
> And yonder a vile physician, blabbing
> The case of his patient—all for what?
> To tickle the maggot born in an empty head,
> And wheedle a world that loves him not,
> For it is but a world of the dead. (*Poems* 516–17)

I wish Lord Alfred had done more of this, myself.

Having said all this, I do have a slight qualm, and it arises from the editors' admission in the introduction that "there has always been a conservative view of Romanticism and a radical one, and, moreover, a conservative later history of the fate of Romanticism and a radical history." The conservative view, they write, sees the visionary, expansive side of Romanticism as having built-in limits, "as if 'common sense,' a sense of the 'tragic' nature of human life, or the knowledge of a 'realist' account of modern life asserts itself as a thankful check upon Romantic visionary excess and experiment" (4–5).

But doesn't everything have its limits? Opening the anthology at random, as I do frequently, I recently came across what at first seemed a parodic stereotype of romanticism in part two of Heinrich Heine's poem "Morphine":

> o lamb lamb I was your shepherd once
> guarded you against the world

> I fed you with my bread
> with water from this well—
> o rage of winter storms
> my breast was warm to you
> I gripped you in tight love—
> the rain had thickened
> wolves & mountain rivers howled from their stone beds (316)

A few pages later, however, reveals the same poet's change of styles into a more hard-bitten realist: in an excerpt from "Germany: A Winter's Tale," he sounds a bit like Byron making fun of Wordsworth and Coleridge in "Don Juan":

> Here's Wille, whose face is a register;
> His academic foes
> Had signed inscriptions in that book
> Too legibly—with blows.
>
> Here was that thorough pagan, Fuchs,
> A personal foe of Jehovah—
> Devoted to Hegel, and also, perhaps,
> To the Venus of Canova. (322)

Later, the speaker meets up with "Hamburg's protecting goddess," Hammonia, who turns out, despite her "wondrous high breasts" and "superhuman rear," to be rather priggish, fond of patriotic lyrics by Klopstock; she urges Heine to

> Stay with us in Germany;
> You'll find things more to your liking;
> You've surely seen with your own eyes
> That progress has been striking.
>
> And the censorship is harsh no more—
> Hoffmann grows milder with age;
> No more will he mutilate your books
> As he did in his youthful rage. (328)

It's probably just a matter of taste, but I enjoyed the urban narrative momentum of these lines after so many rages of winter storms. In the note that follows the Heine selections, the editors note that his work marks

"A turning from Romanticism as previously practiced & a reminder of how much tension existed in such movements"; specifically, he became "a satirist/ironist" whose "oppositional, often courageous practice [was] marked by a strong impulse toward dismissal & invective." And who was he dismissing? "Those 'Goethians' & Jena School Romantics ... who 'allowed themselves to be misled into proclaiming the supremacy of art and turning away from the demands of that original real world which, after all, must take precedence." Raising this issue, write the editors, points "to a conflict that has still to be resolved" (*Poems* 334).

But if we can't resolve it, we might at least explore it a little more. Romanticism is known to be many things, but except for a very few exceptions like Byron, dismissive satire isn't one of them. It's one thing to extend its traditional historical borders to the entire nineteenth century and part of the twentieth, thereby being able to trace the similarities between the familiar and unknown Romantics and those that followed them, like both Brownings, Poe, Baudelaire, Martí, Edward Lear (!) and the Russian Futurists (instead of splitting those latter writers off into other volumes, as the *Norton* does, with critical tags like "Victorian" or "realist"). But what's the real value of "blur[ring] the distinctions of Romantic and Postromantic as much as ... insist[ing] on them"? (*Poems* 7) For example, in an essay that Robert Browning wrote about Shelley, part of which is reprinted here, he writes:

> For it is with this world, as starting point and basis alike, that we shall always have to concern ourselves: the world is not to be learned and thrown aside, but reverted to and relearned.... There may be no end of the poets who communicate to us what they see in an object with reference to their own individuality; what it was before they saw it, in reference to the aggregate human mind, will be as desirable to know as ever. (*Poems* 530)

Not only is this not Romanticism traditionally conceived, it's not Romanticism of any sort. It's more in the spirit of the Enlightenment, and (speaking of connections) is also picked up in Olson's "Projective Verse":

> Objectism is the getting rid of the lyrical interference of the individual as ego, of the "subject" and his soul, that peculiar

presumption by which western man has interposed himself between what he is as a creature of nature (with certain instructions to carry out) and those other creations of nature which we may, with no derogation, call objects. (24)

But isn't Blake's determination to see more in the "guinea" sun than is "really" there one of the guiding lights of Romanticism? And haven't we been taught (since Abrams' book, but also since Wordsworth), to see Romanticism as some sort of glorification of the individual, notwithstanding Keats' criticism of Wordsworth's "egotistical sublime"? It's one thing to blame "conservatives" for the view of Romanticism that enshrines it as "primarily a poetry of the individual subject asserting an inner freedom in the face of growing industrialization" (4), but I'd think that view would be widely shared among people with a casual knowledge of it, and among many of those afore-mentioned undergraduates as well. In fact, it is how Byron saw the "Romantic" poetry written by Wordsworth and Coleridge. As material from the anthology started to appear on Rothenberg's blog, I asked him whether it was just going to champion imaginative transcendence and not mention the political real-world conditions many Romantic writers were trying to transcend … for example, whether it would include Shelley's great political sonnet "England in 1819" as well as the dream visions of "Queen Mab" or the bleeding of "Ode to the West Wind." On that point, I needn't have worried: the introduction mentions several concerns of the early nineteenth century, which, the editors write, have now returned to plague us … nationalism, colonialism and imperialism, ethnic violence, growing extremes of wealth and poverty under hegemonies of industrial capitalism, and reemerging religious fundamentalisms among them. But such concerns seem to disappear in the celebration of the "visionary and experimental Romanticism" collected here; to use the editors' own terms, Romanticism's transgressive side is often superceded by its experimental side. In fact, if avant-garde artists feel they can ignore or "transcend" these unpleasant realities, or indulge their radical sensibilities in one or another reincarnation of "art for art's sake," the very separations that Rothenberg and Robinson are working against might re-emerge.

Rothenberg, at least, is aware of the danger. In his essay "The Poetics of the Sacred," he writes "the transcendent ... implies for me too great a denial of the here and now; and the source of poetry, as I understand it, is deeply rooted in the world around us: doesn't deny it so much as brings it back to life" (*Poetics & Polemics* 5). Or, as Byron has it in an excerpt from "Childe Harold's Pilgrimage" included here, "But this is not my theme; and I return / To that which is immediate" (234). Which is why the existence of this anthology is finally a cause for celebration: its editors have done more than resuscitate Romanticism. They've also made it part of a vital tradition, generative of much of the imaginative work that sustains us today, thus "bringing back a sense of innovation, danger, and revolution ... to work too often taken for granted or robbed of its newness and power through repetition and enshrinement (canonization)" (4). And that, Mr. Bloom, is an achievement that even you might want to note.

Works Cited

Abrams, M. -H. *The Mirror and the Lamp: Romantic Theory and the Critical Tradition*: Oxford University Press, 1953.

Donadio, Rachel. "Keeper of the Canon." *The New York Times Book Review*. 8, 2006: 27.

Dorn, Edward. *Hello, La Jolla*: Wingbow Press, 1978.

Greenblatt, Stephen, ed. *The Norton Anthology of English Literature*. Volume D: The Romantic Period. New York: W. W. Norton & Company, 2006.

Olson, Charles. *Selected Writings of Charles Olson*. Creeley, ed. New York: New Directions, 1966.

Rothenberg, Jerome & Pierre Joris, eds. *Poems for the Millennium: The University of California Book of Modern & Postmodern Poetry*. One. Berkeley: University of California Press, 1995.

Rothenberg, Jerome & Jeffrey C. Robinson, eds. *Poems for the Millennium: The University of California Book of Romantic & Postromantic Poetry*. Three. Berkeley: University of California Press, 2009.

Rothenberg, Jerome, with Steve Clay. *Poetics & Polemics: 1980–2005*. The University of Alabama Press, 2008.

Selected Shorter Reviews

In the House Un-American by Benjamin Hollander

Clockroot Books, 2013

A few years ago my wife and I attended a dinner party at my cousin's house; her husband is a philosophy professor at UC–San Diego, and some of his graduate students had also been invited. At one point, I thought I would be a smart-ass and said I'd been reading an author who thought everything in philosophy had gone downhill after Descartes. "A lot of people say that," said the professor, and looked over at the TAs, his eyes rolling. Still, one of the more powerful vignettes in Benjamin Hollander's *In the House Un-American* is the true story of one Eugen Rosenstock-Huessy, a Harvard lecturer who wrote an essay at the time of the Harvard Tercentenary in 1936 called "Farewell to Descartes." In it, he accused the seventeenth-century philosopher of sanctioning a kind of thinking without physical consequence, adding that "When Nobel Prize winners produced poison-gas, their thinking was no longer identified with existence." Unfortunately for Rosenstock-Huessy, the president of Harvard at the time was James Bryant Conant, who had helped that Nobel prize winner, Fritz Haber, to develop poison gas in World War I; the lecturer, who had claimed to be "an impure thinker" (presumably unlike Descartes), was fired one year later.

But Descartes isn't the only authority Hollander questions in his book: I might also have started this review by remembering a famous 1990 essay by Amy Tan called "Mother Tongue," which deals with how her mother's broken English has informed her own writing. The first page of Hollander's book presents us with a young man taking his mother sightseeing in San Francisco. At one point, she says "Those nets up in the air, there, what are they?" but the footnote corrects us: "'Zoze nets up in ze air, zair, vat are zey' was what was really asked, in the original language, accented, pointing to the cable car wires" (3). Tan herself is mentioned a few pages later, but the book's narrator would prefer not to be compared to someone who writes stories of "inspirational difference," positing that the real "second language" in America is poetry, "the sounding of a second language within an American culture that does not count it among its facts" (28).

Or I could have started by quoting Jay Leno, who, after his interview with Barack Obama, said to Lawrence O'Donnell that "Everybody eventually becomes American once they stay here long enough." In fact, I could spin these various openings out a little longer, but I hope they begin to describe what kind of animal *In the House Un-American* is: a kind of trickster book, notably impure, part history, part family chronicle and part tall tale. It's made up of short vignettes, dialogues (real and imagined), flash fictions and lots of citations … most notably from Hannah Arendt, referred to only by her first name as if she were a family relation, and some of Bertolt Brecht's testimony before the House Un-American Activities Committee in 1947. These hybrid forms combine to interrogate the sameness, shallowness and supposed universality of America (often spelled, à la Kafka, with a "k"), the mothership for a host of different aliens. Hollander's prose is sometimes tangled and dense, at times even recalling James Joyce's multi-lingual puns. Early on, the narrator and his immigrant friends admit they've never come to grips with the American language, "its rootedness, its by rote-ness" (6); their conversation takes place in a house that's not a home, "a House on loan." Indeed, part of what's under consideration in this book is language itself, which Hollander twists in order to braid these parallel facts and fables.

Let's return to that footnote on the first page: it announces immediately that this will be a fanciful tale, that the author will take liberties, mess with us, that we'll have to watch our backs (an idiom that itself comes under examination at the end of the book). The notes aren't like the ones that another famous immigrant, Vladimir Nabokov, used in *Pale Fire*, but they do introduce multiple points of view and depths of consciousness—here, the educated, assimilated Jew vs. the old country mom—and the tangled idioms and notions of "shame" that are generated as a result. "It's the matter and the mother of hearing all this I am after," says the narrator, Carlos ben [בן] Carlos Rossman (the Hebrew for the word "son" continually re-printed throughout the text). The mother's question is re-visited later, when Carlos "thinks hard" that if immigrants "sound fluent, and we write poetry which appears to articulate that condition ... a reader will not acknowledge wires as nets in a poem as anything but metaphor for the mill" (12).

This, in turn, sets the table for a dialogue about the nature of language among the narrator and two friends in Chapter 3, "Our Mediterranean." There, Mordico (the Turkish poet and translator Murat Nemet-Nejat), says that "The true power of language, its well of inspiration, for me, lies in its conscious or unconscious errors, cracks, imperfections. I am a poet, an American poet, because I have a defective ear" (44). Which raises the questions: Should language sound "fluent" or expose its imperfect roots? Can it do both? More to the point, what exactly is "lineage"? Is it still with us? Are Nazis still with us (wonders Carlos a little later) if we never lived among them? And if they're not ... have we "assimilated" a bit too much?

Emphasizing linguistic conundrums, however, doesn't give an accurate picture of the genial *talkiness* of Hollander's assemblage; some of its mundane concerns include left-handed third basemen, Viagra, corner bar owners without alcohol permits, and the decline of the word "fascist" among ever-smiling hyphenated-Americans. But even though being "un-American" is "a condition that transcended politics," (8) political comment is never far away: Carlos' father, we learn early on, looked a little "like the future Henry Kissinger ... who sounded when he spoke much more content, as if he had always just finished eating: bloated, self-satisfied, sovereign, like a perched frog" (5). Such speculations are woven throughout, so that readers are always forced to compare their lives to the situations of immigrants, aliens and others, "living between false options" (or as Bob Dylan had it in "Joey," "always on the outside / of whatever side there was"). Hollander never lets us forget that "politically, one can determine who belongs to the un-American camp at any time ... and on that opinion the accused lose jobs and reputations for life" (31). It's a tough thing to assimilate, he writes: mouthing the lies of pop tunes while swaying with a girlfriend in the dark won't always cut it.

At one point Hollander invokes the famous opening of Charles Olson's *Call Me Ishmael*, "I take SPACE to be the central fact to man born in America, ... Some men ride on such space, others have to fasten themselves like a tent stake to survive." Because the traces of his lineage, and others', have mostly disappeared from American life, it sometimes feels as if the narrator has fastened himself to a tent pole that isn't really there, which makes for a few metaphysical problems. However, in the seventh and final chapter, "Just Call Me Al," Carlos orchestrates a conversation between Herman Melville (characteristically referred to as "Uncle Hermann") and Muhammad Asad ("Uncle Leopold"), who debate the extent to which "the Heart of Islam is American." It turns out that there are some similarities—though they have nothing to do with universalism—but it takes Arendt to fully yoke them together:

> It was what Hannah in her letters called the problem of beginning, the coming out of nowhere in a specific time at the same time as one was being *bound* back to one's beginnings, *religare*, religion, as in the foundation of the Republic, "an unconnected new event breaking into the continuous sequence of historical time," and Carlos wondered, where *the Heart of Islam is American*, could this be where "the unconnected new event" might begin a principle entirely new but present at the Republic's beginning? (145)

Call me Al or call me Allah. "It was not just reason," wrote Arendt, but "divinely informed reason" that can intuit such a connection and take up the "unfinished work" of the Republic. Despite the many examples given here about the awful passivity and sameness that the "mundane fact" of equality has brought onto these shores, and despite Carlos being trapped between the two slates of Melville's *The Confidence Man*—one saying "Charity thinketh no evil" and the other "No Trust"—the feeling one takes away from *The House Un-American*, finally, is hopefulness.

Some years ago, I stumbled upon the (for me) astonishing discovery that the great American poet William Carlos Williams had Sephardic Jewish roots, through his Puerto Rican maternal grandfather. I excitedly sent an e-mail to Ammiel Alcalay, the only other writer I knew with a Sephardic background (who, coincidentally, also appears in *In the House Un-American*, as the narrator's friend Gingi). So another question raised in the book is why Williams—a central "character" here, with three names like the narrator—didn't sound like his mom. In that context, one of the sub-themes of the book is Hollander's own journey away from the clear and "polemically American" language into a more diverse, clashing and cosmopolitan vision. "It is only the blind groping weirdness I want to relate," says Carlos in an early part of the book, and he later explains why "we needed to create another real world from the facts on the ground as we could know them." With its impure thinking wedded to physical existence (so unlike Descartes'), *In the House Un-American* creates that other "real world," one that residents of this one might do well to explore.

Like A Dark Rabbi: Modern Poetry and the Jewish Literary Imagination by Norman Finkelstein

Hebrew Union College Press, 2019

My wife and I were walking out of a restaurant last month when she saw a Jewish Federation shop next door and asked me to wait a minute before we got on the road: she wanted to buy a Jewish calendar. I accompanied her to the door, which was locked, with a small sign next to it: "Recent security updates ask visitors to explain their purpose before coming in." So it goes, even (or especially) in liberal Portland, where we have our fair share of Nazis, not all of them bussed in from Vancouver.

Never fear, reader: I'm not about to dip into sociology. In fact, in some ways, I'm the least likely person to review *Like A Dark Rabbi*, a collection of essays on the Jewish literary imagination in modern poetry by Norman Finkelstein, because although I was born Jewish, and will thus always *be* a Jew (or so Bret Stephens and a recent Trump executive order affirm), I'm not an observer or even a believer. As it turns out, though, that's not unusual: if there's a word that recurs throughout these different essays in different ways—remembering that it's a collection written and reworked over years, without a comprehensive argument—that word would be "secular," and a major task of the essays is to trace how a secular culture and attitude can still be steeped in Jewish tradition, history and texts.

What constitutes this "secular religion"? Finkelstein gives several examples in the introduction: Daniel Morris calls it "the public life of imaginative and interpretive, as opposed to fundamentalist, forms of religious life," adding (with Stephen Paul Miller) that the secular should be seen "as a paradoxically religious and in some ways characteristic Jewish concern that is germane to radical poetic processes." "I am no more Jewish than when I set my Jewishness adrift from fundamentalist religious practice," writes Charles Bernstein; "I am no more Jewish than when I refuse imposed definitions of what Jewishness means."[1]

This idea is given context in the introduction, which deals with two Shapiros, Karl and Harvey. Here's part of Finkelstein's analysis of Harvey Shapiro's poem "The Generations":

> The prayer is "still being said," though presumably the son does not know the prayer at all. How can this be? My answer is that the prayer, embodied in the son's gesture, is *in* the poem and maintains its living presence *through* the poem. The poem with its image of the son and the baby, as a secular utterance, literary rather than liturgical, takes the place of the prayer for presumably secular readers. (12)

Following this train of thought, few of the poets analyzed here show any longings for liturgy, and certainly not at the expense of literature: "as another / unbelieving believer / at prayer," writes Rachel Tzvia Back, she "puts one more poem / on the page" ("Like the Believer"). Henry Weinfeld goes further than that, removing the entire scaffolding on which Judaism is based: "The Chosen People are the ones who knew / That no one's ever chosen" ("Praise and Lamentation") and adds, in "My Father Was a Wandering Aramean," "No one is chosen— Hebrew, Greek or pagan— / The self-same cloud encompasses us round." Meanwhile, Chana Bloch thinks "the quarrel with tradition is one of the most distinctive features of Judaism, and one of the most compelling," while for Allen Grossman, poetry is "a mode of sacred utterance that paradoxically maintains its religious status even when

---

[1]. Finkelstein disagrees with Bernstein's use of the word "fundamentalist" (preferring the less inflammatory "observant") and also with his fetishization of the words "radical" and "experimental," believing, with Wallace Stevens, that all poems are experimental. In his essay on Chana Bloch, he writes that the success of Jewish-American poets doesn't depend on whether they're called "mainstream" or not.

the notion of divinity is called into question or perceived as infinitely withdrawn" (77).² Finkelstein's allegiance to the poetic over the liturgic here even goes as far as arguing that Jewish poems can be written by non-Jews—an idea he traces to Jerry Rothenberg's poem "The Connoisseur of Jews"—and analyzes the "Jewish" poems of Wallace Stevens, Robert Duncan and Joseph Donahue as proof (the title of this volume comes from Stevens' poem "Le Monocle de Mon Oncle"). And there is precedent to this questioning of religion: after all, even Adam was a heretic.

In Finkelstein's essay on Charles Reznikoff, one of his finest, Yosef Hayim Yerushalmi characterizes the situation in different terms, witnessing a sharp break in the continuity of Jewish living and hence also an ever-growing decay of Jewish group memory. In this sense, if for no other, history becomes what it had never been before: the faith of fallen Jews. For the first time history, not a sacred text, becomes the arbiter of Judaism (39).

And history, as Finkelstein reminds us, isn't an article of faith. Walter Benjamin, a frequent visitor to these essays, writes that "nothing historical can relate itself on its own account to anything Messianic" ("Theologico-Political Fragment"). The situation more closely resembles Paul Klee's famous painting, in which we're all being propelled backwards by the vast heap of ruins of history, "one single catastrophe" ("Theses on the Philosophy of History"). This accounts for the heartbreaking ending of Reznikoff's poem "Early History of a Writer":

> Perhaps my grandfather was in tears for other reasons:
> perhaps, because, in spite of all the learning I had acquired in high school,
> I knew not a word of the sacred text of the Torah
> and was going out into the world
>
> with none of the accumulated wisdom of my people to guide me,
> with no prayers with which to talk to the God of my people,

---

2. Once I became aware of this theme (as many writers will appreciate), I started finding it everywhere, even in A.O. Scott's review of *The Two Popes* in the *New York Times*: "My own view on the matter is: I'm Jewish, and also temperamentally more inclined to ponder secular details than sacred mysteries."

>   a soul—
>   for it is not easy to be a Jew or, perhaps, a man—
>   doomed by his ignorance to stumble and blunder.

In such a situation, then, traditional religious practice can be remembered, even revered, but not necessarily observed. Finkelstein writes about "the ways in which poems written from 'inside' a particular religious tradition simultaneously occupy a space 'outside' of that tradition by imaginatively, if not transgressively, transforming religious gestures, texts and rituals into poetic utterance" (xvii). But are Jewish themes or subject matter—a few quotes from the Old Testament, for example—enough to constitute a "Jewish poem"? Can someone who's not Jewish, but who may have "a pervasive fascination and strong affinity with Jewish spirituality and Jewish texts" (as Finkelstein says about Robert Duncan and Joseph Donahue) actually help transmit the "Jewish Literary Imagination"?

Anyone familiar with Jewish culture and traditions knows that there's no end to questions, especially in this situation, when "paradox and contradiction prevail," and lines between the sacred and the profane are never easy to draw. But there is some learned testimony about what makes a Jewish story, or in this case, poem. The renowned Jewish folklorist Dov Noy writes that there are three usual but not mandatory elements to such work: some sense of Jewish time (e.g., Shabbat, the fact that holidays start the night before), Jewish space (the chuppah, the synagogue) and representative Jewish characters (King Solomon, Elijah, or the Fool from Chelm). The one essential element, though, is the message or theme: some moral or religious purpose that's future-oriented, an ideal or goal not yet realized. In other words, whereas universal tales might have as their purpose the entertainment or relief of the listener, often with some sort of pat resolution, Jewish stories are always asking about what comes next.[3]

This has to do with what Finkelstein elsewhere calls "Total Midrash," the capacity (or not) of contemporary writers to comment on and thus to change or enhance traditional texts. Some conservative scholars would limit such commentary to gaps in the Torah itself, to

---

[3]. I thank the great story teller Peninnah Schram for guiding me to this material.

what's already been written, but others "commonly rejoice in the gaps, foreground the contradictions, and explore issues ... in a broad sense" (Alicia Ostriker, qtd. by Finkelstein). For them, "Jewish secularism may be seen as the attempt to fashion a counter-tradition, an alternative to Judaism as a religion that has its own intellectual lineage" (David Biale, qtd. by Finkelstein): the etymology of secular, after all, is "age," and we're clearly living in one.

The great kabbalistic scholar Gershom Scholem appears often in these essays, and in their context, it's important to understand him as a secular thinker as well, creating a counter-narrative or counter-tradition. "Perhaps a double way is possible, secular and holy ... Perhaps this holiness will be revealed at the heart of the secular," he writes in his *On Jews and Judaism in Crisis*, which Michael Heller quotes in Finkelstein's essay about him. One might also note Miriam Nichols' idea, in her book *Radical Affections*, that "poetry may catch and hold our experience of the world as larger than ourselves ... a territory traditionally held by religion."

I'll return to these ideas before this review is over, but here it might be wise to remember Heller's idea that a lyric can provide relief from what Finkelstein calls "the relentlessness of philosophical investigation" (105). Here's a nice poem from Chana Block called "The Converts," which I discovered while reading Finkelstein's essay about her work:

> On the holiest day we fast till sundown.
> I watch the sun stand still
> as the horizon edges toward it. Four hours to go.
> The rabbi's mouth opens and closes and opens.
> I think *fish*
> and little steaming potatoes,
> parsley clinging to them like an ancient script.
> Only the converts, six of them in the corner,
> in their prayer shawls and feathery beards,
> sing every syllable.
> What word
> are they savoring now?
> If they go on loving that way, we'll be here all night.
> Why did they follow us here, did they think

> we were happier?
> Did someone tell them we knew
> the lost words
> to open God's mouth?
> The converts sway in white silk,
> their necks bent forward in yearning
> like swans,
> and I covet
> what they think we've got.

I think that's a pretty great poem, and hope it can be appreciated by people who haven't experienced the peculiar requirements of that day. Whether or not the congregants get their names inscribed in the Book of Life, the diaspora will always be with us.

Which is a perfect segue to Heller's term "diasporic poetics," referring to a kind of poetry that can't be traced to one overriding cultural idea, like Judaism or communism, but forms through a constellation of different influences. "Constellation" is an important idea to both Heller and Benjamin: it's what differentiates and protects ideas—at least potentially fresh and new—from their decay in organized systems of knowledge.

This is an important theme in a few of the essays, so it might be worth exploring. A theme from Benjamin's messianic period went something like this: the world is God's creation, all good. The "knowledge" of good and evil that originated after the fall actually meant the inception of a language that differentiated between them; before the fall, when the Tree of Life governed the world, it represented

> the pure, unbroken power of the holy, the diffusion of the divine life through all worlds and the communication of all living things with their divine source. There is no admixture of evil in it, no "shells" which dam up and choke life, no death, and no restriction.... the heart of life beats unconcealed and the isolation in which everything now finds itself is overcome. (Scholem, *The Messianic Idea of Judaism*)

Sounds pretty good, no? Of course, such a state of mind would be scorned by most post-modernists, tangled in their signifiers and insisting that there are no pure states, that everything is mediated. But unlike Benjamin, poets like Heller and some others written about here aren't trying to get back to that state of redeemed life; rather, they're working the spaces between. Between good and evil, holy and unholy, pure and impure, "between the law of religious observance and secular life" (Heller, "Remains of the Diaspora") is a gap—there's that word again—that can be generative. Heller's poem "Diasporic Conundrums," like the Reznikoff poem quoted earlier, both remembers and forgets Jewish tradition; it begins "And now this man is fatherless / because he had a father, / and Israel is no more," and concludes

> The dead are dead.
> This is certain.
> This is what was written, why it was written.
> This need not be said.

But of course, it has been: poets are in the business of saying what mustn't, and often can't, be said. And that has very little to do with knowledge:

> Benjamin identifies "knowledge" with the misplaced philosophical preoccupation with method, which dates from the time of Descartes. The goal of knowledge is the possession of objects and not their emancipation. Knowledge, in this sense identical with the Nietzschean "will to power," will stop at nothing to reach this end, and its preferred technique, from the Cartesian cogito to the transcendental ego of Kant and Husserl, has been the imperious assertion of the primacy of the knowing subject over the object to be known. (Richard Wolin, *Benjamin: An Aesthetics of Redemption*, 93)

I think, in this context, of negative capability, a recognition and acceptance of uncertainty in all acts of imagination, to which several poets in these essays testify. In contrast, knowledge is a paltry thing, handmaiden to power.

I DO have a few mild problems with the book that I'd like to register: one of them is the total absence of my people, the Sephardim, which might cause an uninformed reader to think that Yiddish is an archetypal language for all Jews. The second, though, probably says more about my cynicism than Finkelstein's graceful and lucid criticism: that is, I'm all for syncretism when it's a choice between that and ethnicity as a marker of identity, but at times that practice seems to cover too much ground, and the "constellation" formed as a result skirts perilously close to the abstract and non-existent. This, in turn, forces the dialectical scales of sacred and profane to bend towards the former. For example, Finkelstein writes, in the Duncan section, "the wand of Hermes is the rod of Moses." This recalled for me Charles Boer's entertaining words about Hermes:

> But "pompos" is more than *guide,* and even more than *guide to the underworld.* It means to lead, but Hermes as leader is not quite right either. It means something more like to lead on. Hermes is the god who "leads you on" ... deceiving you, taking advantage of your gullibility, "taking you for a ride." (Introduction to *Hermes, Guide of Souls,* by Karl Kerényi)

Finkelstein is certainly aware of the (potential) problem, saying that Heller "always leads us back down out of the transcendental heights" (123), and in a recent review of Joseph Donahue's *Wind Maps I-VII* published in *Hyperallergic,* he says that the spiritual quest that Donahue and other poets are exploring needs to be accomplished "without falling prey to obscurity or bombast." But in another essay collected in the volume *Radical Poetics and Secular Jewish Culture,* "Secular Jewish Culture and Its Radical Poetic Discontents," he says he has an "allergic reaction to the reference ... of *secular* Jewish culture," and adds that "Jewish poetry ... can never be fully secular." I'd argue, following the logic of many of these important essays, that only the fully secular can be religious, not in the sociological or political sense of it being adopted by evangelicals or supremacist groups, but in the connection it has with mortal life: as Miriam Nichols, again, had it, in talking about Creeley, "what takes place / has no particular time." Or as Benjamin had it:

> Just as a force can, through acting, increase another that is acting in the opposite direction, so the order of the profane assists, through being profane, the coming of the Messianic Kingdom. The profane,

therefore, although not in itself a category of this Kingdom, is a decisive category of its quietest approach. ("Fragment")

As I finished this essay, an online news site on another tab screamed "Sanders after Corbyn: The Jewish Question," while, as noted in my first paragraph, the paper of record recently offered a column by Bret Stephens called "The Secrets of Jewish Genius" that had as its source material an advocate of eugenics. I just got a text from George Soros, so before I return to my secret world-dominating cabal, I'll close by saying that with all the alarming simplifications of religion in the public square, the best thing about Finkelstein's book is that it teases out its deeper meanings, especially, here, in its entanglements with poetry. I enjoyed and learned from this book of essays, and better still, discovered a few poets I'll be following from now on.

DREAMLAND COURT BY DALE HERD

City Point Press, 2022

Earlier this year, a fugitive convict and prison guard in Alabama, Casey White and Vicky White (no relation), were arrested; Vicky, the guard, died in the hospital the next day from a self-inflicted bullet wound, while Casey was returned to prison and his 75-year sentence. They reminded me a little of the characters in Dale Herd's great new novel *Dreamland Court*, one of them constantly in and out of jail and all of whom mistakenly think they know what they're doing.

Herd has been heralded before now for his short prose, poetic in its diamond-like hardness, and here gives us a novel that features language as the main character. This makes *Dreamland Court*—a chorus of different monologues curved around each other, each preceded only by the character's name in bold—difficult to follow at first: it takes a while to sort out who's talking and where they are. But the speeches are similar in that they're all master portraits of futility: all the characters' plans come to nothing, and all their hopes prove fruitless. In this regard, the novel's nearest relatives might be plays like *Waiting for Godot* and *Endgame*, which is apparent as well in Herd's frequent use of biting humor. Here's Johnny, the main character, relating a recent experience in jail:

> The dumb son of a bitch just stood there looking at me, blood pouring down his face. "Dude," I said, "you don't know it, but you better get your ass over to the infirmary muy pronto 'cause you're dying." He was just standing there all steamed-up, looking to kill someone, you know. Now that's a guy to stay away from. Too damn stupid for his own good.

Similarly, Jackie—Johnny's wife but also the object of desire for many men in the novel—often thinks she's figured it out: "I felt no guilt but was sorry over the things I was unable to provide for her [her daughter], but felt I was smarter than other women in similar situations." On the next page, she says to one of her suitors, "that's why I'm here, man. I'm not gonna bullshit you about it. Those are the *facts*, man. I wouldn't be here if they weren't. If I didn't have my *facts* straight. The *facts of life*, man. That's *what facts*." As Bob Dylan once sang, nothing is revealed.

Just when the reader might be feeling superior to these unfortunate characters, it becomes clear that Herd is actually re-running a history of Western philosophy—especially the part about how we know what we know, epistemology. Johnny, who communicates with Jackie mostly through letters, here explains a recent prison psychologist diagnosis:

> Well, you could call it acting out, 'n stuff like that, if you wanna, but most people think I'm totally behind it. They think, here's what they think, they think I don't know that's not really me. See what I'm saying? That even if it looks like I've crossed over, hey, what I'm doing is having a big laugh behind it. Now that's what burns the shit outa me. No one sees that. None of you people do.

This could be Herd talking to his readers, and it raises questions about the ethics of play-acting, and of writing fiction as well. Where is the author, really? Here, he's mostly paring his fingernails, exhibiting uncanny skill in telling the same hard luck story in different voices; Herd's ear for American speech is impeccable. But there's no need to get all high-minded about it—the stories these people tell are like all stories, yours and mine too: "You and her hurt Harold, and God will hurt you and her. You hurt Irene, and God will hurt you. You hurt your friend Eddie, and you will get hurt. You think I'm some crazy old woman, but I'm not."

In a way, each character who speaks in this assemblage is writing his or her own story, but the official language of the authorities in *Dreamland Court* implies a world barren of storytelling's lessons: "You are not eligible for Aid To Families With Dependent Children for Aug. because: Refusal to comply with requirements." According to *E News*, the sheriff who arrested the unfortunate Whites in Alabama—just 270 miles north of where they started from—said he wanted to know more about what really was going on between Casey and Vicky, but "I don't know if Casey White is going to be cooperative in that regard or not. It would be nice to know what they had in mind." Similarly, in one of his letters to Jackie, Johnny writes "It would take a pretty damn good doctor to figure all this shit out, so maybe that's what I'm gonna do."

Damage by Mark Scroggins

Dos Madres Press, 2022

What is the "damage" incurred in Mark Scroggins's new book of the same name, and to whom or what is it applied? In "Damage Poem," it appears to be poetry itself:

> the poem as vicious animal; the poem as
> tumor, bulbous and unclipped umbilicus. No more poems
> as consolation. I want the poem as damage. (160)

Throughout this volume of selected poems, damage is done as well to any "Nostalgia for a mythic unfallen, garden / of single speech" ("World Culture" 89): Scroggins is charting a world of eternal recurrence, but of the less evolved parts of human nature, where, as the poem "Lazarus" puts it, "the vocables of emulation and praise / no longer sound" (126).

We also might consider the poems in "Torture Garden," forty-two dense seven-line poems of five words each he calls "Naked City Pastorelles." Here's the first one, titled "Blood is Thin":

> Shine the starry message-bearing host
> bow down shepherds *insofar* as
> happiness a part of destiny
> *absolute dependence* then the dog's
> the best Christian like sheep
> without a shepherd *stars* a
> gleaming leprosy in the sky. (163)

At the very least, this presents a complicated view of the Christian origin story: the shepherds are bowing before the host like their sheep wandering without direction, a condition of passivity like the dependence of a dog, while the stars, rather than communicating beauty or awe, resemble a dreaded disease. The poem that follows, "Demon Sanctuary," further stipulates that history has nullified "the soil of happiness" and recalls Virgil's famous line about death being present even in pastoral paradises. Or as Scroggins writes in "Goldfinches," "My tongue in your ear is politics.... My tongue in your rear is poetry." (98)

Reviewing a book of selected poems presents opportunities and problems not relevant for individual books. For example, how have the poems changed from early to late (if they have), and which seem more powerful (if either does) and why? In fact, the systematic disentangling of any notion of poetic, sexual, or broadly human autonomy charted above is a far cry from some earlier poems in *Damage*. In the first of the "Early and Uncollected Poems," dated to 1988, we encounter "a woman / singing at the / piano" (279), a romantic image recalling an early D. H. Lawrence poem, while "the black of / night is bed to / the fixed stars," presumably with no trace of leprosy. The next poem blithely assumes "there's nothing / to fret us here" (280). Since pretty much everything "frets us" in the other poems in this volume, the "damage" of the title might apply to any traditional romantic sensibility or perception, any notion that an occasional correspondence (*pace* Baudelaire) will make things turn out okay.

Even those early poems, however, are always precise and concrete—objectivist, to cite the school Scroggins is close to and has written well about—but when those images become incorporated into a larger context, we see the poet's more satiric and learned voices take over, working to dismantle naïve beliefs and unquestioned assumptions, as in the hilarious "Florida Poem (with footnotes)." There, Gertrude Stein is dismissed as a "theorist of narrative and / hairstyle model for generations of lesbians," while Thoreau suffers a worse fate: Guy Davenport suspects that he "'would have married a woodchuck or a / raccoon, if the biology of the union / could have been arranged'" (320–21).

If "learned voice" sounds a bit scholarly, it's important to know that Scroggins uses poems such as "Oliver Cromwell" and two called "John

Milton's Blues" not to commemorate anything those worthy gentlemen might have thought or written, but to act as analogues to our vacuous and witless present. The portrait of Cromwell, for instance, grows more and more fabulous (as in "fable"), from its imagination of "cannons with 'God of Love' scribed round / their barrels" to similar visions granted to the "great men" of our own time, like the shop clerk "whose weekend sends / him — in militiamen's uniform — / to take stock — with a bayonet — of a / tentful of refugees" (133). As far as Milton goes, the author of "When I Consider How My Light is Spent" (not to mention *Paradise Regained*) might have appreciated this stanza:

> Finding it hard to take *obedience*
> as virtue, *nicht wahr?* Clever
> classless and free, but nicer
> in the end to be Napster's microserfs.
> Twenty-first-century forecasts bullish
> on air conditioning concerns, seawalls,
> Kabbalah Energy Drink (*En soph*
> perpetual source of profit and
> enlightenment). Insurance payouts
> on the rise. Best investment New Laputa. (135)

Here, even with (or perhaps because of) the somewhat anachronistic reference to Napster, we might envision thousands of disaffected and recently laid-off tech engineers, not to mention the recent protests in Iran and China. Devotees of the pastoral paradise should definitely look elsewhere.

All these poems demand close readings and re-readings. In a bravura tribute to the photographer and filmmaker Richard Kern, puns, allusions, and scattered memories combine in a collision of discourses that make any linear communication suspect; as a result, what was mere cleverness becomes something more sordid and dangerous:

> that jury built monument to the ten
>   words break two tablets call me
> deep in mourning a barbeque of aureate
>   veal lechon asado chimichurri
> vindaloo nouveau Beaujolais rising

> up like the sun which is we are
> told new each day they leaven the end-
>   less parade of bleached teeth
> and boob jobs with photos of a girl
>   got her face burned off in a wild-
> fire *true life human interest* florida
>   scum on the white house train (130–31)

Kern is known primarily for his photos and videos of young girls in various states of undress, reminders of which show up periodically in this complex yet rigorously formal pastiche ("highlights photoshopped onto that model's / canines and bicuspids"). These recurring images combine with references to Greek mythology, the Old Testament, George Bush's administration, and unbearably banal pop culture ("the evil dead maunder / through an outlet mall of children's / fancies outsourcing nail set / past a laboring proletariat switching / channels swiftly as their thumbs / can twitch"), culminating in a bleak portrait of contemporary life, "just another weeping carnal gash" (132).

In a recent discussion about the work of British poet Keston Sutherland, it was said that "poetry might never have been less able to interfere in the conciliation of collective and individual interests under capital than it is now." This seems plausible, and among the various ways practitioners of the art might react, Scroggins's masterful blend of irony and cynicism directed at the horrors of contemporary society can be counted among the most valuable. Indeed, *Damage* announces him as one of our finest poet-critics.

JUS' SAYN' BY HELLER LEVINSON

Black Widow Press, 2022, $10.00

Heller Levinson's last few books—*Seep, Lurk* and *Lure* among them—seek (as he said in a recent email) "to free the word/term from lexiconic stasticity & enflower it with vivacity." They're further extensions of Hinge Theory, which he started elaborating in the books *Smelling Mary* and *From Stone This Running*, now over a decade old; in them, he created a new poetics of sorts, based on the interplay of language, sound, mathematics and philosophy to regain for poetry more possibilities of meaning than can be found in current mainstream practice. Upon being introduced to it some months ago, I was sympathetic to the intention but hadn't been able to fully appreciate its manifestation.

Until now. The book under review here, *jus' sayn'*, is a re-creation of John Coltrane's legendary performance of "One Up One Down" at the Half Note Club in New York in 1965. First released a few years ago, the tune is his longest solo on record—the entire cut lasts 27 minutes, a time period noted by Levinson in the text—and the book-length poem seeks to do it justice in a complicated and polyphonic call-and-response. Much more ambitious than liner notes, *jus' sayn'* employs philosophy, cultural history, science, jazz history and Hinge Theory as Levinson attempts to communicate the enormity of what this music means to him. It's an astonishing accomplishment.

Jazz poetry and poems about jazz have a long history in North America, and poems about John Coltrane make up a large part of that history; Amiri Baraka, George Economou, Michael S. Harper, Nate Mackey, Garret Hongo, and Sonia Sanchez are only some of the poets who have written poems to him, mostly of praise and tribute. I admire many of these poems, but *jus' sayn'* is something different: not quite praise, although there's plenty of it, and not quite tribute, though there's plenty of that too. Rather, it's an attempt "to give speech to the unspeakable, to the void that swells" (38), or, as the first line of the book has it

a manner a bid to spell out make sound swell forth (7)

Part of the method lays in asking questions and not taking any previous statement at face value. For example, one recurring theme of the book involves philosophical speculations about "the void" just quoted, and more precisely, the ever-changing relationship between sound and silence:

> Something, then, is that nothing which achieves its status by virtue of negating. Nothing spurls through the ether by scraping away *nots,* breath replaces breath, note..., note. cancellation hopping the oscillate transpires, the vacuum of abyss surges. *undulation hatch deep respiration   rural life   rum & border collies* (21)

This is followed soon after by the questions

> where in the upsurge
> is
> void
>
> how much of
> void
> is
> hearable (22)

Coltrane, he says in a later section, "Cover[s] the Unsaid with sound" (38) in an effort "To Robe the Cosmos in Revelation" (45). But lest I give the impression that the book is some sort of philosophical (or religious!) treatise, it's also a portrait of what else people were listening to in 1965 ("Stop! in the Name of Love" by the Supremes, and "Wooly Bully" by Sam the Sham and the Pharoahs, the lyrics of which, in a gift to humanity, are quoted in full), who won the World Series (the Dodgers over the Twins in seven), and the conditions at the club itself:

WABC hosting live for their Friday nights "portraits in Jazz," Mike Canterino (Half Note founder) goes into kitchen asks his pop (the cook) where the veal parmesan sandwiches are he's got a table of five hungry, pop says "*Ma fammi il favore!*" four suits white shirts & ties stroll through door eyes magnify mouths petrify to check out these musical gangsters these watershed angel Giant Steppers McCoy stands over the piano plinks an F# Elvin mounts his cymbals Jimmy picks up his bass & Trane stares at his Selmer Mark VI sax (7-8)

If this book were mostly another exemplification of Hinge Theory, where, to quote Levinson in "Hinge by the Slice," the hinge is "the pivot ... whose function is to spring (to unleash, to unmoor) the particle into a climate of free fall and unpredictability," there would be more passages like this:

Trane brings the sax to his mouth, limbers his fingers, his eyes don't leave the painting, he plays: *golden bicycle wind river rend beaver hustle quartet colloquy proud pastures green animals dandelion grasshopper   glide   slide   sideslip   rock gardens   emerald*

*molten
moccasin
moss*

starlight   fugues   Ravel

butterscotch (40–41)

And there are plenty: in the age of AI and ChatGPT, Heller is serious about re-vivifying language, capturing its liminality, holding its flow, taking Heraclitus seriously. "[H]inge," he said in an interview, "functions more as a type of counter-language than a vehicle for ideas, it is the freshly laid highway, the sound of a hidden river, bringing hope and ideas of infrastructure to tired settlers—it is the wormhole." But what makes this an altogether uncategorizable book, appealing as much to curiosity as to the imagination, is that there's so much more: the history of the cymbal going back to the Janissaries, a description of the Var region of France, where most of the cane for saxophone reeds is grown, quotes from the Duino Elegies ("Are we, perhaps, here *just for saying*") (44), and even a nod to those who might feel uncomfortable with such linguistic and musical virtuosity, like the critic Kenneth Tynan, who described Coltrane's playing in 1957 as "superficially stimulating, lonely, & rather pathetic self-seeking" (30). His opinion hadn't warmed much more in 1969, where he called Trane's solos "overtones of neurotic compulsion & contempt for the audience" (30). But while it might be easy to dismiss these opinions as unenlightened, Levinson also offers a conversation between Miles and Trane:

> "It takes me that long to say what I got to say," Trane responded when Miles asked him "Why you got to play that long?"
>
> And when Trane said, "I just don't know how to stop," Miles replied: "Try taking the horn out of your mouth" (38).

"One of the reasons Trane kept playing chorus after chorus," says Jimmy Heath near the end of the book, "was that, as he himself said, he 'could not find anything good to stop on'" (55). "Could Beckett have written *Endgame* if he had been exposed to 27 minutes & 39 seconds of Trane?" (12) asks Levinson, rhetorically, at its beginning. But the real question, posed and re-posed in many different ways in this marvel of a book, is "how does the sayin' get said?" (47) For poets, the year 1965 offered a few answers: in June Jack Spicer delivered his now legendary Vancouver Lectures, and a month later Charles Olson gave a four-hour reading/lecture/manifesto at the Berkeley Poetry Conference. *jus' sayn'* is a record of where we've arrived a half century later,

> when all is said & done there's say. we're back to that. or start
> to that. say said sing song sayn' song sayn' wind breeze
> lunglungelonging,.... hug
> nocturnes   pathos ponds   syzygal gusts   dive bars (66)

You could, of course, just listen, which I did several times in the composition of this review. But listening to what this book has to say will help.

Image & Nation

Musing about The Muses

A talk commissioned by the Centre for Myth, Cosmology & The Sacred
Delivered on Zoom October 13, 2021
for Billie Chernicoff, and others

Could you completely forget yourself even for an instant, you would be given everything
—13th-century German mystic Meister Eckhart

Thank you, Mary [Attwood], and thanks to the Centre itself for being one of my muses since I discovered it last year ... and in very specific ways, in that the last several presentations I've seen on the Centre website, including yours just last week on the art of memory, all seem to have said what I want to say today much more cogently. So in that sense, thanks especially to William Rowlandson on the wild, Mark Vernon on Dante and Patrick Curry on Enchantment in the past months: all of these should be available on the Centre website, or soon will be. And, of course, thanks to all of you here on Zoom; there should be plenty of time at the end for questions and comments, but don't be shy about using the chat box as we go either.

So if I had monitored the publicity for this talk tonight a little more closely, I might have de-emphasized the concept of inspiration and instead called it something else, like "Embedded Cognition, Metaphor and the Muses," because what I'm *not* going to do is offer a self-help session in learning how to be more creative in your daily life or pretend I know anything about "invoking your personal muse." I actually downloaded an article last month with exactly that title, because I thought it might have something I could use tonight, but it wasn't to be. In fact, the Muses aren't very good role models for developing self-esteem: when they first greet Hesiod in his *Theogony*, they call him "a poor fool" and "nothing but a belly," and proceed to tell him that they lie all the time ... but can tell the truth when they want to. If that sounds a little capricious, remember that many of the gods and mortals of Greek mythology act in exactly the same way.

Still, some very great poets, as we'll see, seemed to need what the Muses were selling. So what was that? For one thing, it was as much information as inspiration, and it had a lot to do with memory, and metaphor, and both together. Their genealogy was important: genuine goddesses, their father was Zeus, but their mother was Memory—Mnemosyne in Greek—so metaphorically (and it's hard to speak about the Muses without metaphor), the Muses are memories charged through with thunderbolts. And those kinds of memories don't only concern the past; when we're reminded of someone, or something, we're exactly that: re-minded, minded again in the present, with the opportunity to make things new. It's in that sense that the Muses "tell of what is, and what is to be / and what was before": they're bridging the past and present, metaphors for metaphorical thinking itself. When poets invoke them—re-call them—they're asking for the chance to amplify those past stories in the voices of the present. "Make my poem bigger," they ask; "let it encompass more of the world than I'm able to alone."

Eric Havelock, whose book *The Muse Learns to Write* is one of the main resources for this talk, wrote in it "Not creativity, whatever that may mean, but recall and recollection pose the key to our civilized existence." And my old teacher Ed Dorn, in an early statement for the Paterson Society, wrote "Culture is based on what men remember, not what they do ... Even a civilized man who can read and write will occasionally exhibit this memory, at which times it is said of a man he acted with loveliness." The classics scholar E.R. Dodds, in a great book called *The Greeks and the Irrational*, had this to say about the action of the Muses:

> Just as the truth about the future would be attained only if man were in touch with a knowledge wider than his own, so the truth

about the past could be preserved only on a like condition. Its human repositories, the poets, had (like the seers) their technical resources, their professional training; but *vision of the past, like insight into the future, remained a mysterious faculty, only partially under its owner's control, and dependent in the last resort on divine grace* (81) (my italics).

Finally in this introduction, the American poet Jack Spicer is the poet most beholden to the practice of dictation from the outside that I know of—although he called those voices "Martians" and not Muses—and I'll come back to an important lecture he gave in Vancouver in 1965 a little later on, but here's just one snippet that rhymes with the ideas I've mentioned so far:

> In the long run, the past and the present and the future are pretty much the same kind of furniture in the room. Just because a thing happens tomorrow that is in the poem today doesn't really mean that there's anything more mysterious than something that happened yesterday being in the poem today. I mean, the future, the past and the present are in some ways entangled. I don't know how, but they are....

So with that entanglement in mind, here are the topics I want to touch on today before we open things up for your comments and questions. I'm halfway through my introduction:

I   Introduction to the Muses
II Invoking the Muse: The Roll Call of Poets
III Embedded Cognition and Hesiod
IV Conclusion: The Muses and the Wild

That is, after a quick dive into the poetic history of the muses, we'll come back to Hesiod's *Theogony*—the most extended description of the Muses and their work that we have—and also, less traditionally, his *Works and Days*. That latter poem features what we might call "embedded cognition," a neuro-scientific term that basically means letting the world and immediate environment in as part of one's thought, which, as Iain McGilchrist has shown us, activates the right hemisphere of the brain:

gods were seen at the implicit level as aligned in some sense with the self, however distinct they may have been at the explicit level ... sudden thoughts and emotions are seen both as the intervention of personal deities and at the same time as an aspect of independent human psychology. (*The Master and His Emissary*, 265)

McGilchrist adds "The crux is that the two planes exist in harmony, and the god's intervention need not imply that the mortal man is less fully responsible for his actions. Similarly poetic skills come from oneself *and* from the gods; and, in general, thought comes from oneself *and* from divine prompting." Or as my friend the poet Charles Stein wrote on Facebook in August, "Hesiod's evocation of the muses is neither in the active voice indicating masterful agency nor complete passive voice receptivity, but middle. Hesiod says the muses 'blew a singer's voice into (his) own.'"

Speaking of singing, it's a shame that I don't have a soundtrack for you, because for the Greeks, the Muses *were* music, all aspects of it, including singing, dancing, festivals, celebrations ... and poetry; in fact, all of the ancient Greek poetry we read and study today was set to music, and the Greek word *Musa*, with a capital "M," is the same as the small "m" *musa*, music. Music, after all, came before words: it was "the oral tradition," and the Muses had been alive for centuries on the lips of oral bards and singers and storytellers before appearing in the first written poems of Homer and Hesiod. But I lied; I do have a snippet of what that music sounded like, and by great good luck, it's a song-poem that starts off with an invocation to the Muses: https://www.youtube.com/watch?v=SgpWXDSSHE0. You can see the lyrics translated into English at the bottom.

You might also be interested in how various Greek sculptors and urn painters imagined the Muses:

The Muses Dancing on Mt. Helicon

https://hadrian6.tumblr.com/post/66610419299/dance-of-the-muses-on-mount-helicon-1807-berthel

The Muses Dancing around Apollo

https://en.wikipedia.org/wiki/File:Baldassare_Peruzzi_-_Dance_of_Apollo_and_the_Muses.jpg

The Muses' Contest with the Sirens
https://www.metmuseum.org/learn/educators/lesson-plans/muses-vs-sirens

There are quite a few stories in Greek mythology about the Muses having contests with other singers, all of which they won, and they weren't exactly grateful winners: I'll mention a famous one in a few minutes. But it's important to remember the time of the poems; in a sense, the Muses were the guests of honor at a party at the beginning of written language, the Homeric and Hesiodic poems, and that wasn't really very far away, not before 700 BCE. The oral memory, aided as it was by rhythm, harmonies, and gestures, was very different than the literate souls we've all become. As Walter J Ong wrote in *Orality and Literacy*:

> Persons whose world view has been formed by high literacy need to remind themselves that in functionally oral cultures, the past is not felt as an itemized terrain, peppered with verifiable and disputed "facts" or bits of information. It is the domain of the ancestors, a resonant source for renewing awareness of present existence, which itself is not an itemized terrain either. Orality knows no lists or charts or figures.

And, of course, neither did the Muses. But again, I want to disabuse us of the notion that the Muses are some kind of mystical, otherworldly personages: metaphor is actually very concrete, very here-and-now. Here's Havelock again, in his earlier *Preface to Plato*:

> The evocative effects described by Hesiod and prefigured as the gift conferred by the Muse were not a spiritual transfiguration, but a set of psychosomatic mechanisms exploited for a very definite purpose. Their effective employment required a degree of virtuosity in the manipulation of verbal, musical and bodily rhythms which was extreme.

And rhythm, he writes elsewhere, is "the foundation of all biological pleasures—all the natural ones, sex included—and possibly of the so-called intellectual pleasures as well." Be that as it may, it's the opposite of the more well-known theory of poetic inspiration brought to us mainly by Plato: as he saw it, the functional purpose of poetry as tribal education was being transferred to prose, so the people who thought in prose—that is, philosophers—needed to relegate the poetic experience to something non-conceptual, non-rational and non-reflective. It was a kind of ecstatic possession, wrote Plato, and that's why he kicked poets out of his ideal republic … and when they left, they took the Muses with them.

Invoking the Muse

Most of us know the Muses as forces to be invoked, or called (or re-called), at the beginnings of epic poems. An invocation is often a prologue to the events to come, a prayer of sorts, usually made to one of the nine muses of Greco-Roman mythology; I'll show you their names in a minute. The poet asks for the inspiration, skill, knowledge, or the right emotion to continue with the poem. So, in the *Odyssey*, Homer asks for inspiration and a blessing for the retelling of the epic: "Speak, Memory—of the cunning hero the wanderer, / blown off course time and again / after he plundered Troy's sacred heights."

So in that translation at least, the muse *was* memory. But it's important to remember that other Homeric invocations of the Muses came before detailing a complex catalog of ships, or, in the *Iliad*, in the midst of ferocious battles, with mangled limbs strewn around the battlefield, and suddenly the poet says "Speak, Muse, of the first Achaean to seek revenge," an example of asking for one's memory to be refreshed, so the poet can go on with his or her tale. I don't have time today to go into the intricacies of what's been called "the Homeric question," but the work of Millman Parry and people who came after him have pretty much established that Homer's poems were full of stock formulas and phrases, dependent on the meter of the particular line they occur in, rather than inventions: calls to the Muses were no different.

We'll come back to ancient Greece and Hesiod, but the Muses also figure in a famous contest with some rival singers that they turn into magpies in Ovid's *Metamorphoses*. And that story, in turn, is recalled in Dante's *Divine Comedy*, at the beginning of the *Purgatorio*:

> But here let my dead poem rise again,
> O sacred Muses! for it's you I serve,
> and here too let Calliope rise a little
>   so that she may accompany my song
> with that same sound that hit the wretched magpies
> so hard they lost all hope of future pardon. (I, 7–12)

That's a new translation that I can recommend by D.M. Black, and I wanted to quote it here for two reasons: 1) it remembers the dual function of the Muses, not only to serve as inspiration for the rest of the poem, but as a reminder that they're not particularly nice, and have no compunctions about being violent with anyone who might claim poetic skills without their guidance; and 2) at the beginning of this second book, Dante and Virgil are walking against the stream of Lethe, or forgetfulness, the river that works against what the Muses do. One final connection with Dante's poem that might be relevant is the difference between the *Inferno* and the *Purgatorio*, in that the characters in the first work are fixed in their sins forever—literal vision, or what Blake called "single vision and Newton's sleep"—while the *Purgatorio* reviews those exact same sins as opportunities to repent, or move on, as in allegory. So again, the Muses are acting as metaphors for metaphor itself.

Shakespeare's most famous mention of the Muses might be in *Henry V*, "O for a Muse of Fire that would ascend the highest heaven of invention" but he also performed an on-again/off-again dance with them in Sonnet 38:

> How can my muse want subject to invent
> While thou dost breathe that pour'st into my verse
> Thine own sweet argument, too excellent
> For every vulgar paper to rehearse? ...
> Be thou the tenth muse, ten times more in worth
> Than those old nine which rhymers invocate;
> And he that calls on thee, let him bring forth
> Eternal numbers to outlive long date.
> If my slight muse do please these curious days,
> The pain be mine, but thine shall be the praise.

Here Shakespeare prefers his human lovers, male here and female in the later "Dark Lady" sonnets, to the somewhat dubious realities of the classic muses. Likewise, in *Othello*, the villainous Iago complains of his own lack of "invention" and says, "My muse labors, and thus she is delivered," thus drawing a parallel between literary creation and childbirth.

Things changed again with John Milton's *Paradise Lost*:

> OF Mans First Disobedience, and the Fruit
> Of that Forbidden Tree, whose mortal taste
> Brought Death into the World, and all our woe,
> With loss of *Eden*, till one greater Man
> Restore us, and regain the blissful Seat,
> Sing Heav'nly Muse....

Milton is still invoking the muse, or muses, to inspire him to write his epic poem, but *Paradise Lost* is a re-telling of the first book of Genesis in the Old Testament, so the muse now switches identities and becomes the Holy Spirit who inspired the Christian Bible, not one of the nine classical muses in Hesiod. Milton wanted his muse to fly above those muses because he was writing about the creation of the Bible and the universe; in that, *Paradise Lost* is a direct descendant of Dante's *Commedia* (although Hesiod was writing about the creation of the universe as well). But like those previous poets, Milton had a prodigious memory: one of the most amazing things to remember about him is that he didn't write *Paradise Lost*, he dictated it from memory, like the blind Homer taking dictation from oral singers.

Moving through the pantheon of great poets, here's William Blake, in a 1799 letter: "[I] cannot previously describe in words what I mean to design, for fear I should evaporate the spirit of my invention ... And tho' I call them mine, I know that they are not mine, being of the same opinion with Milton when he says that the Muse visits his slumbers and awakes and governs his song when morn purples the East, and being also in the predicament of that prophet who says: 'I cannot go beyond the command of the Lord, to speak good or bad.'" And even though the Romantic poets as a whole aren't the best place to look for evidence of the Muses because of their idealization of the poet, we shouldn't forget Keats' notion of negative capability—"when one is capable of being in uncertainties, Mysteries, and doubts, without any irritable reaching for fact and reason"—nor this lovely quote by Shelley in his *Defense of Poetry*: "The mind in creation is as a fading coal, which some invisible influence, like an inconstant wind, awakens to transitory brightness."

And the Muses haven't disappeared with contemporary poets either: here are two.

> Norman Finkelstein: The muse—and the Outside, and hearing voices—is a metaphor for the important listening that a poet has to do. If it's not from the outside, it's from the inside, from the unconscious ... but that's unreachable: stuff wells up, and then you work it.

> Ed Dorn: There are certain Obligations of the Divine, whether those can be met or not. Part of the function is to be alert to Spirit, and not so much write poetry as to compose the poetry that's constantly written on air. What I've read and what I hear merge to make the field in which I compose.

All of this is a way, writes another poet, Don Byrd, to experience "the richness of the world apprehended without the habits of recognition." Finally, I mentioned Jack Spicer a few minutes ago as the poet most beholden to outside dictation. He started a lecture in Vancouver, Canada, on June 13, 1965—the 100th anniversary of William Butler Yeats' birth—by talking about Yeats' wife channeling what Spicer calls "spooks." But these voices weren't there to offer any self-help advice; rather, they came, they said, in a response to Yeats' question, to give him metaphors for his poetry. Spicer has a number of juicy quotes relevant to this talk but, for reasons of time, I can only offer a few of them: "But occasionally, after an hour or so of me trying to write the poem ... a poem nudges me on the back and starts coming through"; or this—"you have the alphabet blocks in your room: your memories, your language, all of these other things which are yours which they rearrange to try to say something they want to say. They are using my memories"; or this—"You have to keep a kind of lookout for them. You can't catch them like canaries by putting salt on their tails, but you sort of give them an even chance. I mean, show them there's a good dinner of blood like in The Odyssey where they dug the trench and slit the throats of the sacrificed animals." Ultimately, he says, what's important is "just cleaning things up so that the invaders, the things which are parasitical on you and create poems, can come in." Anything which takes us out of the trap of the personal, he says, is a good thing.

You might think that as the centuries roll on, we would see shifts from dependence on deified inspiration to the development of personal insight, and we do in fact see glimpses of that, culminating, somewhat hilariously, with Byron's introduction to a canto of *Don Juan:* "Hail muse, etc." But Byron was preceded by a gentleman named Persius in the first century CE:

> The maidens of Mount Helicon
> and the blanching waters of Pirene
> I give up to the gentlemen round whose busts
> the clinging ivy twines; it is only
> as a half-member of the community
> that I bring my lay to the holy feast of the bards.

So from the very beginning, there were people who thought they heard the voices of the Muses, and others, like Aristophanes, who were sure those people were deluded. But I want to end this little survey by quoting some lines from someone who did believe in the muses, Sappho. These recovered lines seem like a curse:

> you have no share
> in the roses from Pieria
> but in the House of Death also
> you shall walk unseen
> with the unsubstantial dead

The Specialties of the Muses

Calliope—"she of the beautiful voice"—was widely revered as the goddess who inspired epic poems and songs. The mother of Orpheus, she was often considered the most powerful of the Muses: Milton criticized her for not being able to save Orpheus from the maenads. But

Calliope's eight sisters each had spheres of influence and were important in their own ways. The other Muses, as named by Hesiod, were:

- Kleio—"the giver of fame," "Celebrator"; the Muse of history, she inherited the memory of past events from her mother, Mnemosyne.
- Euterpe—"the giver of joy," "Delighter"; like Calliope, associated with music and poetry. Her specialty, though, was lyric poetry that told personal stories instead of epic tales of the past; mistress of the flute.
- Erato—"the awakener of desire,""Enrapturer"; her name meant "desired" or "lovely" and was related to that of Eros; the goddess of love poetry and the dance.
- Melpomene—"the singer,""Song Player"; one of the two Muses of theatre, she inspired the playwrights and actors of elegies and tragedy; also associated with lyre playing.
- Thaleia—"the festive," "Luxuriator"; the counterpart of Melpomene, she inspired theatrical comedies.
- Urania—"the heavenly,""Heaven Dweller"; she gave inspiration to astronomers. In the later years of the Roman Empire she was said to inspire Christian poetry.
- Polymnia—"she of many hymns"; hymns, or poems of praise, were her specialty. She was also a mathematical muse who inspired work in geometry; a storyteller.
- Terpsichore—"she who enjoys dancing," "Dance-Delighter"; the Muse of dance. She also gave inspiration to the chorus in Greek theatre; associated with the lyre.

While I was writing this talk, my wife asked me a question I couldn't answer: why were the Muses all women? If any of you have ideas, please say so at the end; I think it's probably too easy to say that ancient Greece was a culture where women were subservient. Anyway, according to Karl Kerenyi, "Whenever they went in procession to Olympus, they were wrapped in clouds. One could only hear their wondrously beautiful voices in the night." And with all this focus on being hidden, it might not be surprising to hear another famous story regarding the Muses: they gave the Sphinx its riddle.

Embedded Cognition and Hesiod

As I mentioned, the *Theogony* wasn't the only poem of Hesiod's we read today; there's also *Works and Days*, at first glance far away from "creative inspiration," in that it's the record of a farmer and the different things good farmers have to do throughout the year, one of which was to keep track of the weather and observe the skies. It demonstrates "how the rising and setting of constellations were used as a calendrical guide to agricultural events, from which were drawn mundane astrological predictions, for example:

> Fifty days after the solstice, when the season of wearisome heat is come to an end, is the right time to go sailing. Then you will not wreck your ship, nor will the sea destroy the sailors, unless Poseidon the Earth-Shaker be set upon it, or Zeus, the king of the deathless gods (II. 663–677).

And this was already ancient knowledge by Hesiod's time: lunar cycles were being charted as early as 25,000 years ago, the first step towards recording the Moon's influence upon tides and rivers, and towards organizing a communal calendar. The agricultural revolution brought increasing knowledge of constellations, whose appearances in the night-time sky change with the seasons, allowed the rising of particular star-groups to herald annual floods or seasonal activities. And this preview of astrology, along with a certain crabbiness, is a good summary of *Works and Days*. "As above, so below" wasn't just Hermetic esoteric doctrine: what was happening in the environment had direct influence on what was happening in their psyches. And that's basically what the concept of "embedded cognition" means: that the brain, and rationality, aren't the only cognitive resources at our disposal.

Again, it's beyond the scope of this talk to rehearse the battle between the folks who believe this and their academic opponents, the cognitive psychologists, who believe that it's all in the mind, but that latter viewpoint is a holdover from Descartes doubting everything he could perceive with his senses, thus bringing about the mind-body split, which was no good for anyone. Embedded cognition believes that we actually have extremely high quality, direct perceptual access to the world, and emphasizes the role perception, action and the environment can play in our actions. I can tell one story about this; it concerns the Inuit tribe in the Canadian north, and comes from Nicholas Carr, one of our most famous skeptics of technology, in his book *The Glass Cage*.

He started this particular chapter by describing their environment: "The average temperature hovers around twenty degrees below zero. Thick sheets of sea ice cover the surrounding waters. The sun is absent.... landmarks are few, snow formations are in constant flux, and trails disappear overnight" (125). Because it was pretty much winter 365 days a year, the Inuit tribespeople had to develop "wayfinding" skills, to be able to know where they were going based on their knowledge of "winds, snowdrift patterns, animal behavior, stars, tides, and currents." This was an inherited knowledge and skill that was continuously taught and developed over thousands of years. But then, in the year 2000 or so, came the use of the global positioning system. And once GPS became popular, those trustworthy Inuit guides started having accidents: they relied too much on satellites; their feeling for the land weakened; they lost sight of their surroundings. And wayfinding, this singular talent of their tribe for thousands of years, wrote Carr, might evaporate over the course of one generation.

So what I would say to you is that this seems very much like the transition from orality to literacy, and very much like what's happening to all our memories from our overuse—or misuse—of technology. And it might be one reason why the Muses are so elusive these days.

Conclusion: The Muses and the Wild

I mentioned at the beginning the publicity for this talk on the Centre website, part of which raised the question, "Are the Muses Still Around?"

> Some people say the muses are imaginary, and that's true: more true than when an inspired artist labels this or that person a muse. But the muses are invisible; they're never more than sojourners in our realm, and we in theirs. But we can sense them, every so often,

even though we don't speak their language (that's actually why we need them). As Wordsworth wrote (not about them), "They're an amplitude of mind." Or as Dante had it, in the *Inferno*, "poet   by the God you did not know   lead on."

The great Islamist scholar Henry Corbin, in a lecture from 1974, spoke about this as well:

> Saving the appearances: what does this mean? The phenomenon is that which shows itself, that which is apparent and which in its appearance shows forth something which can reveal itself ... only by remaining concealed beneath the appearance. Something shows itself in the phenomenon and can show itself there only by remaining hidden.

I can't think of a better description of how the Muses work. And of course, when things are hidden, there's mystery, or bewilderment, here recalling a previous Centre session on the wild by William Rowlandson. The definition of "bewilder" is to "confuse as to direction or situation"; my faithful 1961 Websters dictionary suggests "to cause to lose one's bearings" ... which is, I think, a necessary prelude to any sort of creativity: to get lost, not seeing anything familiar, is potentially to see the new. Likewise, "wild" ... living in a state of nature, not domesticated; growing, produced, or prepared without the aid and care of man, not cultivated; not inhabited; uncivilized. Because in these matters, there's no guarantee: what's unknown is best. As the Greeks knew, the truth is always a mystery.

So a start to summoning the muses might be to get out of our own way, to de-emphasize ourselves and pay more attention to what's going on around us. "'When humans aren't center stage,' writes environmental geographer Jamie Lorimer, 'the expertise of animals is valued, and organisms and landscapes are given more scope to determine their own futures.' A knotty, weedy wild is produced, in which ecology is allowed a kind of agency, and biodiversity is restored."

This chimes with the fact that while the muses are personifications, they're not exactly human. They may be invisible, but the works they support become visible; they "bubble up," as in the birth of the soul.

It's also smart to figure out what's blocking them (usually, thinking too much, or depending too much on rationality).

I'll close with a few questions, after calming the mind, and letting the imagination breathe—remembering that the word "soothe" has close relations to "sooth"—what is it that the Muses need? What in us is necessary for them? The answers we come up with will determine whether we can still hear their singing.

IMAGE & NATION: WRITING VISUAL CULTURE

Preface

It's highly ironic that I've written a book about seeing, as I've suffered from myopia for as long as I can remember. My difficulty with seeing things that weren't directly in front of me started, so it's said, because I got too close to the TV, entranced by the black-and-white images flickering from the magic box (I was born in 1953 when, some sources say, TV itself was born). So I've lived with glasses all my life, and when contact lenses—first hard, then soft—came along, was an early convert, because everyone knows that glasses make people look dorky, even now, when nerds have developed some cultural cachet. Besides, I still had hopes at the time of being a successful student athlete and making it to the NBA, even when I had to wear that silly elastic strap to keep my glasses in place, like the goggles NBA players wear after they've been poked in the eye. Sadly, my hands never grew wide enough for me to be able to palm a basketball, and I even used two hands to shoot my jump shots ... which, though often successful, never earned any style points.

I start with these details because the writing being encouraged here has certain qualities, one of which is that "objective" appraisals of the images and texts contained herein are best blended with "subjective" stories and biases: indeed, for the purposes of this book, it might be best for those adjectives to be retired, at least temporarily. Rather, readers (and viewers) should feel free to connect the texts and images to personal experiences, whether pleasant or disturbing, and/or describe other emotional, intellectual and philosophical responses, perhaps as a stage to more formal writing and perhaps not: the idea is to discover how this material—both texts and images—might affect our future perceptions, and along the way, our beliefs and values as well.

In other words, this isn't a guidebook for writing standard five-paragraph essays, and the suggested informal exercises and open-form academic writing assignments are as important as the formal essay prompts. In that sense, I hope it will be valuable for any class that includes writing assignments, whether academic or creative in nature.

Nor is it a textbook about "visual literacy," which has many definitions and a surprisingly long critical history. In my research I came across some interesting scholarly disputes, but they mainly focused on things that weren't strictly relevant to a process for effective writing. Some argued that visual literacy should be a subject taught across the curriculum, while others thought it should be a major onto itself; some wanted it to spring from the methods and techniques of art history, while others preferred it to focus on everyday images; there were arguments about whether we should concentrate on the seeing subject rather than the perceived object, and whether we had really entered a period that could be labeled a "pictorial turn" or whether there were other such periods in history; the difference between objects, pictures and images were the occasion of long monographs, as were the political necessities for developing this skill.

I learned a lot from these scholars—who included Eva Brann, Colin McGinn, James Elkins, W.J.T. Mitchell, Barbara Stafford, Peter Dallow, Susan Shifrin, William Washabaugh, Lester Faigley, Diana George, Anna Palchik and Cynthia Selfe—and I appreciate their work more than I can say. Still, my purpose in writing this book was to create something that would help generate good writing. I hope other teachers feel that this book does that, and that students who use it will feel helped as well.

I owe a special debt of gratitude to Donald and Christine McQuade, editors of the textbook *Seeing & Writing*, which I used faithfully in my freshman composition classes for 14 years through four iterations, and from which I learned a lot about valuable techniques to use in those classrooms, both online and face-to-face; and to John C. Bean, whose book *Engaging Ideas* is a gold mine of techniques and suggestions for any teachers who want to incorporate critical thinking opportunities into their classes. But my main debt is to some extraordinary scholars and writers who eventually prodded me to chisel the shape this book has assumed, and whose skill, intelligence and humanity leave me speechless. I'm talking about Diane Ackerman, John Berger, Angus Fletcher, Northrop Frye, and Ludmilla Jordanova, whom I quote frequently; their works are listed more fully in the index, and if you haven't already made their acquaintance, you should.

Finally, this book is for my wife Sara, who makes all things possible.

Introduction: To the Teachers and Students Who use This Book

The vast majority of what we see every day is seen on some kind of screen. That shouldn't be surprising: the great majority of people at any college in America look down at their phones as they walk across the campus, paying attention to texts or to the images of the latest app they've downloaded. Still, the statistics might give us pause: "in the last quarter of 2011, the birth of iPhones alone (at a rate of 4.37 per second) exceeded the birth of human babies on this planet (which came in at a rate of 4.2 births per second)" (Apkon 9).

And it's not only our cell phones: if we commute to work or school, most of what we see will be through windows—windshields or the GPS navigation screen—and when we get to work or school, another large percentage will be on computer screens. We'll see our co-workers or other students, of course, say hello, sometimes make eye contact, but a relatively small part of our conscious existence these days is spent looking at actual things and people, much less noticing something distinctive about them. In fact, we're "awash in a world of screens and moving images," as Stephen Apkon says in his book *The Age of the Image: Redefining Literacy in a World of Screens*. Besides the examples I've given, he adds "grocery checkout lines, retail stores, gas stations, airports, airplane seats, and taxicabs" (9). And we haven't even mentioned TV, whether used for streaming, gaming, or watching traditional network and cable shows.

Some cultural critics don't think this is anything to worry about, but others have bemoaned our dependence on technology and the mediation of perception it's brought about. Nicholas Carr's *The Shallows* (W. W. Norton, 2011) is an indictment of the scattered state of mind he's observed—in himself as well as others—that's come about (he thinks) as a result of virtual electronics, while Sherry Turkle has focused, most recently, on the damage the Net has done to conversation.[1] This book leaves the question open, but it does try to leverage our fascination with images and "visual culture"; like any writing textbook, it wants to help you write better—more clearly, more effectively, in a shape and form that's appealing to readers—but here, that starts with learning to see better.

"See better, Lear," says Kent at the beginning of Shakespeare's *King Lear*, and a few hundred years later, William Blake offered a lesson in that enterprise: "We are led to believe a lie / When we see not through, but with the eye." Blake is saying that it's not just the eyes that see—in a scientific process involving light and the retina's rods and cones—but the brain through the eyes: we're not passive recipients when we receive impressions, nor, for that matter, completely in control of what we choose to notice. Although metaphors from technology are more and more frequently used to describe human behavior, the cell phone videos and surveillance camera footage that have become so important in this cultural moment don't really represent that reality; we might record much of what we see these days, but that doesn't mean we see only what we record.[2]

So one problem with what we might call "screen culture" is that the context for the images on those screens, the overall environment and social interchanges that helped create them in the first place, is often lacking: that's one thing a heightened attention to visual culture might be able to provide. Indeed, in these days when "image is everything," it's

---

1. *Reclaiming Conversation: The Power of Talk in a Digital Age*. Penguin, 2015.
2. Iain McGilchrist develops this point with some eloquence in the selections excerpted here in the appendix from his book *The Master and His Emissary*.

important to understand not only what images we're paying attention to, but why, and why they might exist in the first place: it's also important to try to notice more. If we look mostly at our cell phones or other screens all day, we might not be exercising the visual cortex of the brain as well as we might; still, nothing is preventing us from doing those exercises. So this book, among other things, can be seen as a visual fitness manual.

In fact, the basic ideas of *Image & Nation* can be stated rather simply:
1. **how** we see and **why** we see has a big influence on **what** we see
2. what we attend to (and how we attend to it) changes it and changes us;
3. what we see always has a context, or depth, which we ignore at our peril;
4. what we see, or don't see, has a big influence on what and how we write.

Several texts over the last decades have operated under the assumption that developing a sense of "visual literacy" will also help improve our writing skills.[3] I hope that's true, but I'm not a scholar in the field; again, I'd rather leave the question open. However, there are two premises to keep in mind at the beginning. One is that developing our powers of perception and observation takes time, and devoting that time is essential; without it, what we see can't be transformed into what we say, nor can sight become insight. And the second principle is that you—the students and teachers reading these words—need to use this book actively: take it out for a test drive, put it through its paces, and judge for yourself if the images it asks you to look at (and see, and describe, and analyze), along with the accompanying texts, change your writing and critical thinking for the better.

Here's a process for a way that might happen, tweaked from Brian Richards of the Toledo Museum of Art: (https://www.toledomuseum.org/education/visual-literacy/why-visual-literacy)

---

3. I mentioned *Seeing & Writing* from Bedford/St. Martins in the preface, now out of print; another is *picturing texts* by Lester Faigley, Diana George, Anna Palchik and Cynthia Selfe, published by W. W. Norton.

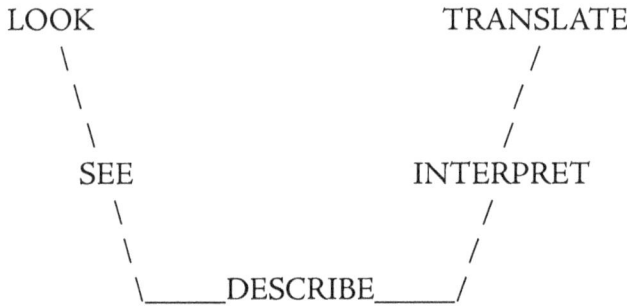

Ideally, these steps would be arranged in a circle, not a rigid sequence; I could have also outlined a three-part process, "seeing" leading to description—a reflection or accounting of what was seen—leading to interpretation. For that matter, I could probably have written a whole book about the difference between looking and seeing! These stages are tools, not rules: the purpose is to broaden our perception and enhance our understanding. As Elliot Eisner has it in *The Enlightened Eye*, "the world we experience is a mix that we often try to sort out later, but the mix once sorted is no longer the mix, even if the sorting itself sheds some light upon it." What's important is that any final evaluation or "translation" cycle back into that mix, into the chaos of initial discovery: there's never an end to seeing, and its purpose is to arrive at an appropriate cognitive response, or action.

However represented, the foundation for the kind of writing this book is trying to generate does depend heavily on description, and since descriptive writing has gotten a bad rap in some quarters, part of this introduction will try to defend it. But in each of the four chapters, this exploration and investigation of images can also correlate with a variety of writing projects, both formal and informal in nature:

- **Looking:** initial pre-writes, tweets, and/or free-writing about the images (which might be shared with partners or in groups)
- **Seeing:** journal entries or micro-themes involving closer attention to the image (which might include personal narrative and/or inquiry)
- **Describing:** an enhanced sense of description in expository essays (see below)

- **Interpreting:** research questions and thesis statements (which might include more contextualization through research and also feature expository writing)
- **Translating:** a trans-mediation or final evaluation of the image and its value (argumentative writing, formal essays)

At the end of this introduction, I've broken down the way I use this process in my classes, giving a suggested list of assignments over the course of a semester and how much they might be valued. Having said that, the chapters can be assigned in any order, and anyone is free to use the book as he or she likes.

Descriptive Writing

I've said that this book will focus on descriptive writing, and that description can be the foundation for all kinds of writing. How is that possible? For one thing, it's in the etymology: the word "describe" is from the Latin *de* + *scriber*, "to write." Some synonyms are "relate, account, narrate," and the prefix *de-* can also mean an intensification, so to describe might also mean "realizing something more completely through script."

But we should start more modestly. "Lift your eyes from the screen," begins a long-standing exercise I use in online writing classes, "and look around your house or apartment. Focus on an object you haven't noticed for some time; maybe you see this thing every day, but haven't really observed it closely. Now, describe this thing, using as many concrete and sensory details as you can. There's only one catch: *don't tell us what it is!* If your description is accurate enough, we should be able to guess."

This is an informal writing exercise that usually engages students (especially the guessing part!) and provides a scaffold for more complex tasks. But it also suggests, in its modest way, the central importance of description, as a mid-stage between seeing (perceiving, observing, noticing) and writing, the image still fresh in mind. It also implies that there has to be a purpose for description, and that description should lead to discovery; some students, as they compare each other's descriptions, might even realize that there isn't just one acceptable mode for representing reality. Indeed, this "ancient art of rendering scenes and persons," as Angus Fletcher calls it, has employed different rules and forms throughout history, from medieval times through the Renaissance, from the relative purity and clipped nature of scientific explanation to the conversely lush and sensuous Romantic variety, which incorporates mood and flux into the described object.

Another approach to descriptive writing can be found in most genre-based textbooks. "Whenever you use words to depict or re-create a scene, an object, a person, a feeling, you use *description*," say the authors of a new thematic composition reader.[4] Of course, "depicting or re-creating a scene" could also apply to ideas; images can be both mental and physical. But let's stay with this book a little longer:

> A mainstay of conversation between people, description is likely to figure in almost any writing situation: a Facebook post may praise a friend's new spiky purple hair; a laboratory report may examine the colors and odors of chemicals; a business memo may distinguish the tastes of two competitors' gluten-free pizzas; an insurance claim may explain the condition of an apartment after a kitchen fire. Because the method builds detail and brings immediacy to a subject, description is an important part of most essay writing as well. (Aaron and Repetto 91)

So far, so good. I think these are fine examples, and there's even more to appreciate: "Description draws on perceptions of the five senses—sight, sound, smell, taste, and touch—to understand and communicate a particular experience of the world." (Some of the "Vision Writing" quotes sprinkled throughout this book show this abstract principle in operation.) Standard cautions about confusing subjective and objective perceptions—and how good description can blend the two—follow, and then a concept I've seen in other texts as well: "Effective description requires a *dominant impression*—a central theme or idea about the subject to which readers can relate all the details.... The dominant impression serves as a unifying principle that guides both the writer's selection of details and the reader's understanding of the subject" (92).

And here's where we part ways; I've taught composition for a number

---

4. *The Compact Reader*, ed. by Jane E. Aaron and Ellen Kuhl Repetto. Boston: Bedford/St. Martin's, 2016.

of years, and over that time have become more than a little nervous about the concept of a "unifying principle," for the simple reason that it runs the risk of ignoring the subject matter being described in the first place. I feel the same way about privileging thesis statements; too often, they're premature. Coherence is a valuable quality, but it more naturally develops after some acquaintance with the subject matter, not before. I'm not picking on *The Compact Reader*—it's been around in various iterations since 2003, and has some nice features—but *Image & Nation* is modeling an enhanced sense of description, such as the French philosopher Maurice Merleau-Ponty used in writing about Cézanne:

> We see the depth, the smoothness, the softness, the hardness of objects; Cézanne even claimed that we see their odor. If the painter is to express the world, the arrangement of his colors must carry with it this invisible whole, or else his picture will only hint at things and will not give them in the imperious unity, the presence, the insurpassable plenitude which is for us the definition of the real. That is why each brush stroke must satisfy an infinite number of conditions. Cézanne sometimes pondered for hours at a time before putting down a certain stroke, for ... each stroke must "contain the air, the light, the object, the composition, the character, the outline, and the style." Expressing what *exists* is an endless task.

This passage is quoted in Diane Ackerman's *A Natural History of the Senses*, and a few other quotes from that rather amazing book appear in subsequent chapters. We can't all be Cézanne, of course, but we might be able to share his ambition: to understand what's actually happening in the visual world around us, and to express that understanding in our own ways. And for that, we need to develop new skills to describe what we see.

"There is no one way of describing something," writes Ludmilla Jordanova, from whom we'll hear more in a moment, although "the basic features of an artifact, such as size and medium, certainly need to be included." She goes on to mention other functions of description: to identify features that interest the writer, to engage the audience(s), to convey the materiality of the object being described, and to build and share a common understanding. But rather than trading in more abstractions, let's see her preferred method in practice: this is the first paragraph of her book *The Look of the Past*:

> To write this chapter I am sitting at a cheap, oval, gate-legged table bought at IKEA in the early 1990s; the wood is yellowish, and I have worked at it intermittently in the intervening years. I could describe where the IKEA store is, the journey there and back, the person I was with, where the table has been positioned in places I have lived, its dimensions, and what is currently on its surface. One item stands out. It is a female figure about six inches high and two inches wide, made of a grey, stone-like substance. She has long hair, flowing robes, a simple, stylized feminine face and is holding a jar. A gift from someone I worked with long ago, she is, I find, beautiful and evocative. I assume my little statue is a modern replica of an early Christian figure, although I am not expert enough to date its template without research. Presumably the figure it represents is Mary Magdalene, whose attribute is a jar, to suggest the ointment she carried to Christ's empty tomb on Easter morning. We can compare her with other three-dimensional depictions of this widely depicted woman, such as Donatello's standing wooden figure and Canova's statue of the repentant Magdalene. Mine is different: small, serene and mass produced – there are obvious marks from the mold on the sides, suggesting that the material was originally liquid in form. Mary Magdalene shares my table with a simple elegant modern lamp, purchased at a major department store, which takes a tiny halogen bulb, as well as books and papers, items such as paper clips, a stapler that must be at least forty years old, Tipp-Ex, assorted pens and pencils, cards, envelopes, files, sticky labels and much more. (15)

And they say descriptive writing is boring! This account shows, I think, how the objects we're surrounded with in everyday life all have potential stories: first, we need to notice them, then tease out the possibilities. Moreover, while it's clear that Jordanova is a highly intelligent scholar who probably knows a lot more than we know, this account doesn't feel intimidating; what's valuable about it, besides the carefully noted details, is her inclusion of intriguing personal stories—

which, counter-intuitively, tell us more about the desk—as well as her admission that she's *not* an expert and is merely supposing, suggesting that academic writing can incorporate tentativeness and discovery along the way to final articulation.

If we were to adopt a similar model for writing, we'd start with an image, for example, *Winter Landscape with Crows*, by the French painter Jean-Françoise Millet: https://reproarte.com/en/choice-of-topics/style/barbizon-school/winter-landscape-with-crows-detail

It's important to begin the process without much (or any) identifying information, the better to activate the attention: captions are their own kind of description, and some images in the chapters are only identified at their end. But we can start by just looking, on a screen in a face-to-face class or in a module of an online class, and students should be encouraged simply to write down what they see, perhaps using think-aloud strategies (https://vimeo.com/10118244). Another effective method is what Dr. Marva Cappelo calls the "Learning Glass," described in this video (https://www.youtube.com/watch?v=QpVHXbakRVY): the teacher stands behind the image and writes down impressions from the class based on the senses ... what they can see, but also what they imagine they might smell, hear, taste or touch. This would just be informal writing, perhaps in pairs or small groups, and if the instructor can act as "scribe," as on Capello's video, so much the better.

The next step would be to delve a little deeper and try to see more in the image than our first casual glances might have revealed. Too often, we let our first recognition define the image for us—"tree" or "city" or "landscape"—and, classification accomplished, move on to other pursuits. That's why the transition from looking to seeing is important: if we stay with the initial perception and recognition, a more complex image begins to take shape. (Whenever possible, these images should be seen face-to-face, and not just in the book or on the internet; if time and opportunity allow, field trips to local museums or other visually-rich sites might be in order). By now, we'd have identified the image—in this case, *Winter Landscape with Crows*, by the French painter Jean Francois Millet—with more or less detail depending on the origin of the source: this particular image was found on the David Pollock Photography blog, but not all images need to be artistic or have titles.

One example of how to negotiate this necessary deeper exploration can be found on the University of Maryland's Visual Literacy Project, for example, this photograph of two young musicians (http://vislit.arhu.umd.edu/exercises/recognizing_ebb.pdf). This closer looking might, in turn, be an occasion for slightly more formal journal entries and/or micro-themes, writing of a few paragraphs or pages that summarize the most important aspects of the image. In our image, most people will certainly notice, at this point, the wooden plough and the harrow, even if that particular vocabulary is unfamiliar; some of us might see the crows at the upper left, thin black smudges of paint that others might interpret as smoke; those students who have taken art history might be aware of the rule of thirds and the placing of the horizon.

Some acquaintance with the "grammar" of visual elements might be important here—a basic encyclopedia (http://archive.artsmia.org/artists_toolkit/encyclopedia.html), or Kent State's visual literacy community (https://www.kent.edu/vcd/about-us)—to further enable the burgeoning descriptions. But again, this isn't a textbook of visual literacy, and I'm not overly fond of the metaphor that one can "read" images in the same way that one can read text; for one thing, it leads to the idea that there's only one meaning to be found in images, and even political cartoons, which might have been constructed to communicate one basic meaning, are often ambiguous in nature. The most important thing is that students enter more deeply into the images in this book and elsewhere, and imagine more in them. "My aim," writes W.J.T. Mitchell in his essay "Showing Seeing," "has been to overcome the veil of familiarity and self-evidence that surrounds the experience of seeing, and to turn it into a problem for analysis, a mystery to be unraveled."

At this point, as description moves into analysis and interpretation, some previous criticism might be introduced (or researched by the students). John Berger's view might generate some reaction: "In 1862 Millet painted *Winter with Crows*. It is nothing but a sky, a distant copse, and a vast deserted plain of inert earth, on which have been left a wooden plough and a harrow. Crows comb the ground whilst waiting, as they will all winter. A painting of the starkest simplicity. Scarcely a landscape, but a portrait in November of a plain. The horizontality of that plain claims everything. To cultivate its soil is a continual struggle to encourage the vertical. This struggle, the painting declares, is backbreaking." Some similar images might also be introduced (or found), like Van Gogh's *Crows over Wheatfields*, or the famous photograph from Dorothea Lange, *Tractored Out, Childress County, TX, 1938*: (https://www.artsy.net/artwork/dorothea-lange-tractored-out-childress-county-tx)

Other Millet paintings might also come into play here, like *The Gleaners* and *Angelus* (a lovely short video about the former from Khan Academy is available at https://www.khanacademy.org/humanities/becoming-modern/avant-garde-france/realism/v/millet-gleaners-1857), as might very different landscapes, more romantic or contemporary in nature, as well as photographs and screen-savers. The questions this criticism and additional images might provoke will vary: how they changed student views of the original painting, if they did, by creating a deeper context; whether students agreed with the criticism, or felt the new artists had different purposes, or thought one or another image more successfully realized, and why. What now might they say about Millet as a painter, or about artistic representations of landscapes? Prompts for expository and/or research papers that focus on other problems wouldn't be far behind, including one that this entire book is based around: does "visual literacy" actually exist, and if it does, is it useful? How?

From what's been said, it should be clear why this text hasn't been written to help with standard five-paragraph essays that might "see" very little of their subject matter. It's not only that thesis statements and research questions are most profitably generated midway through a process of discovery rather than at its beginning, or that informal writing activities are as important as more formal essays and reports; simply, academic writing can assume many shapes and forms, including more personal and immediate modes, what an influential study by James Britton in 1975 called "expressive" writing. Here's John Bean's description of it in *Engaging Ideas*:

> Britton calls it writing that is close to the self. One of its main functions is to help the individual assimilate new ideas by creating personal contexts that link new, unfamiliar material to what one knows or has experienced. It is writing to discover and explore, to mull over, to ruminate on, to raise questions about, to personalize. It is often fragmentary and disorganized, like talking to oneself on paper. (56–7)

Although "intended for the self," Bean continues, "it seems to be the seedbed for ideas that later emerge in products written for others" and takes the form of "journals, in-class freewriting, thought letters to classmates, blogs, personal reflection, and so forth" (57). Such writing can also be the "seedbed" for critical thinking, which this book wants to encourage as much as it does descriptive writing. *But everything starts with looking and seeing*, and to that end, quotes from writers about that fundamental activity appear throughout the book in all four chapters, on Place, Gender, Cartoons and Icons, and Class and Ethnicity.

In the preface, art history was mentioned as the discipline most often discussed in essays about visual literacy, but it's another discipline, anthropology, that has featured the kind of enhanced description I talk about here. Roger Lancaster's *Life is Hard*, a book about Nicaragua during the Sandinista regime, has become "mainstream reading in many anthropology classes," according to a study by Thaiss and Zawacki in 2006, even though, they say, "it misbehaves." Here's a section from Lancaster's introduction:

> All too often, ethnographic writing removes the ethnographer from the scene of his or her investigations and reduces the real men and women who are its subjects to so many abstractions, themselves carriers of abstract structures or principles.... This book is written deliberately against that grain. It is disorderly. It misbehaves. Sometimes it may seem trivial. In working against the grain, I hope that some of the apparently trivial aspects of life in Nicaragua will reveal their real depths. I have tried to keep everything as personal as possible, the better to see the humor, the better to see the tragedy. (xvii)

The distance between expressive accounts like Lancaster's book and what another anthropologist, Clifford Geertz, calls "thick description" isn't far:

> If anthropological interpretation is constructing a reading of what happens, then to divorce it from what happens—from what, in this time or that place, specific people say, what they do, what is done to them, from the whole vast business of the world—is to divorce it from its applications and render it vacant. *A good interpretation of anything—a poem, a person, a history, a ritual, an institution, a society—takes us into the heart of that of which it is the interpretation.* When it does not do that, but leads us instead somewhere else—into an admiration of its own elegance, of its author's cleverness, or of the beauties of Euclidean order—it may have its intrinsic charms; but it is something else than what the task at hand calls for.

Those were my italics, but the paragraph itself calls to mind the somewhat clumsy pun of this book's title. I hope the texts, images and quotations in this book help students and teachers discover their own voices and concerns in the work of this class, whatever it may be, and thus exercise their imaginations. "Seeing comes before writing," began, famously, John Berger's *Ways of Seeing*, but what came after that was important as well: "It is seeing which establishes our place in the surrounding world; we explain that world with words, but words can never undo the fact that we are surrounded by it. The relation between what we see and what we know is never settled" (7).

More about the Process

Structure is a central concern in writing as well as in visual images, so it might be well to link the steps in the process I had mentioned earlier with suggestions for the writing assignments that might correspond with them. One feature is that possibilities for different kinds of writing—narrative, descriptive, expository, researched argument, and even letters, ads and designs—are available in each chapter, rather than those genres themselves relegated to different chapters. But to steal a creative writing term, all essays can be "creative non-fiction," and I hope the ones created from using this book will be.

NAME	ACTIVITY	KIND OF WRITING
Preview	Looking/ Perceiving	Tweets, notes, brainstorming, in class as a whole or in groups

The "Preview" introductory essays contain images & galleries interspersed by running commentary, including some introductory questions and considerations in italics. I'll use them in my classes for introducing the topic of the chapter and for generating class participation through discussion, perhaps in groups. Active engagement and participation from students has been a part of every successful class I've ever taught, and at the end of the semester (if I'm not using contract grading), I usually make participation worth about 10% of the final grade.

NAME	ACTIVITY	KIND OF WRITING
Reflection	Seeing/ Image Making	More substantial journal entries; could be personal or posted on an online discussion board or blog

Prompts for "Reflection" and the next section, "Description," are also based on the introductory gallery of images and often ask students to compare and/or contrast them; the prompts might also incorporate the assigned readings and "Vision Writing" quotes included in the chapter. Journal entries are informal by definition, so I don't usually correct the spelling or grammar. What I'm looking for are ideas and opinions: I want students to have a chance to "think out loud" and articulate their first ideas without worrying about how they're written or whether they conform to standards of correctness. Style is an important consideration in all writing, but content comes first. If I do assess them, I tend to frown on rushes to judgment without evidence that particular details have been considered; I usually make them worth another 20% of the final grades.

NAME	ACTIVITY	KIND OF WRITING
Description	Enhanced Description	Short expository essays and/or think-pieces

Here, students write about one or two images or perhaps an image and one of the readings, in a first attempt at synthesizing their ideas. These might feature "enhanced description," as described in the previous section, writing that integrates the observer with the observed, but should be relatively short, in the spirit of summary/response essays. The writing will, of necessity, adopt some of the principles of "visual grammar" that come into play while interpreting images, but also might veer away from the images to make more general points.

Since so much of this book is based on this enhanced mode of description, I'll list here, one more time, some of its possible qualities: it might include narrative, or the story of why the students see what they do; it might include emotion, on the principle that how an image feels isn't less important than how it looks; if possible, it should incorporate other senses besides sight, like taste, touch and smell; it shouldn't just "surround" or stifle an image, but open it up for further discovery; while it attempts to give an account that enables readers to know what the image would feel and look like if they were there, it should have the courage to perceive imaginatively and metaphorically as well as literally. Elliot Eisner's definition of education is relevant here: "By 'educational' I mean providing the material through which perception is increased and understanding deepened." If I were to assign one of these short essays for every chapter, they'd make up another 40% of the final grade, or 10% each time.

NAME	ACTIVITY	KIND OF WRITING
What's the Issue?	Interpreting	The generation of research questions and/or thesis statements

These issue proposals don't have to be long, but they're an important part of any formal essay or research paper, and I make them a part of the overall assessments for those papers. What's essential here is to begin to put the images and texts in some kind of context, and that will involve research. Some basic questions students might ask themselves are: Who cares about these images? What's important about them? Why is place (or gender, or icons, or class) important? What are the authors/artists trying to show and say? Which image was most evocative or provoked more thought? Why? What have similar authors and artists said that was similar, or different? What kind of images or texts might I seek out in the future, for the sake of a final essay about this topic or for my personal pleasure? What image or images would I create if I had to communicate my ideas visually? (This last might be more appropriate for a developmental English class, or any class that doesn't require research papers per se; it would be valuable if students got some experience in creating images and not just interpreting them).

NAME	ACTIVITY	KIND OF WRITING
What I Think	Translating/ Evaluating	Formal or informal academic writing of some length (perhaps 5–10 pages)

This is the "action" or trans-mediation stage, when students assemble the various observations generated in the previous activities and "translate" them, or put them together into coherent persuasive essays, theses for which would have been developed in the previous stage. Writing a good research paper—one that gracefully surveys what other people have seen and thought while persuasively asserting one's own point of view—is one of the most important outcomes of a college education; I plan to require two of them, which will each be worth another 15% of the total points possible for the class.

Afterimages conclude each chapter, with some Vision Writing quotes—which could be occasions for discussion and writing assignments themselves—spread throughout.

A Personal Note
Everyone who writes a book like this has mixed purposes. My two most important goals have been to share what I've discovered about how to "see better"—not in terms of visual acuity and motor abilities, but in

integrating our visual perceptions with other senses, and with memory and imagination, thus becoming "critical viewers"—and most of all, to generate good writing from such practice. The idea is that doing the first will naturally lead to the second.

If you haven't thought much about visual literacy, this introduction might help. But the goal isn't new: to write clearly, simply, with attention and openness to the world around us. Why would a text with visual images help that process? For one thing, it brings into play other meanings of the word "composition": the arranging of objects in space, "the state or quality of being put together," says my old *Webster's* ("put together" was once a compliment in a different linguistic era). "A poet's occupation / is to compose poetry," wrote the American poet Edward Dorn, adding that "The writing of it / is everywhere" ("A for Ism"). This is a poetics that privileges observation, seeing patterns in order to compose rather than starting with a pre-determined form, whether that be a sonnet or a five-paragraph essay: as Jack Kerouac had it, "Don't think of words when you stop but to see picture better." There's also the intransitive meaning of the word: to compose one's self, to calm or quiet, as if having things "in place," within and without, is somehow grounding and stabilizing. This book, I hope, touches on all the meanings of this important word.

The process of writing has forced me to examine my own teaching principles and pedagogy, and I hope I'll learn from using it as much as anyone else. I've just given some ideas for assignments that use the images and texts in the book, but teachers and students should feel free to make up their own; the order of the chapters isn't sacrosanct either, and often the suggested exercises and assignments call for research, which will take students away from the book, as will the many supplied links. I do think it's important that we begin to understand the immense range of sensory data that surrounds us, especially the visual variety, but other strategies—more scholarly or ekphrastic, or more focused on the basic elements of visual literacy (i.e., dots and lines as analogs of words and sentences, etc.)—might do just as well. As John Lennon sang, "Whatever gets you through the night / it's all right." Or as Molly Bloom said ... "Yes!"

We live in turbulent times, often imagined as unsettled waters; *Image & Nation* wants to be in the crow's nest of a boat that can help navigate them.

—Encinitas CA, 21 December 2015

Acknowledgements

"Poetry and Heresy," the title essay for this volume, was also published in a chapbook called *The Secular Divine* (Spuyten Duyvil, 2022) and will be republished in Matthew Cooperman's book of essays on Edward Dorn, *Empire's Occasion and the "Problem of the Poem."* The other essays and the journals in which they first appeared follow:

Academia.edu: "Charles Olson and the Bolinas Nexus," "Satire, Edward Dorn, and the Via Negative"

Caesura: "Kent Johnson and the Future of Poetic Satire," "Resurrection of the Ancillary & Ghost Talk"

Cento: "Once Upon a Time with West Ed"

Chicago Review: "From the Warring Factions"

Dispatches from the Poetry Wars: "A Defense of Satire," "Like A Dark Rabbi"

Jacket: "Ed Dorn and the Politics of Love," "Isn't It Romantic?"

Jacket2: "Politics and Time: Gunslinger"

Journal of Poetic Research: "Charles Olson and Finding One's Place"

LA Review of Books: "In the House Un-American"

Letters to Olson: "Letter to Olson"

Rain Taxi: "Damage," "Dreamland Court"

Restless Messengers: "jes' sayn'"

spoKe: "Charles Olson and Brooks Adams"

This book took my whole life to write. In that sense, it's dedicated to my wife Sara and to my teachers along the way.

About the Author

Born in Oklahoma City, JOE SAFDIE moved with his family to Los Angeles in the early 1960s, attending public high school and UCLA there. His real education, however, began when he transferred to the University of California at Santa Cruz in 1973: he took a class in Ezra Pound's *Cantos* taught by Norman O. Brown, and afterwards life was never quite the same. His first chapbook, *Wake Up the Panthers*, was published, with the assistance of George Hitchcock's Kayak Press, while still an undergraduate in 1974. On his first trip to Europe in 1975, he attended a performance of *Oedipus at Colonus* in Athens and was puzzled when the audience gave a five-minute standing ovation for a speech two-thirds of the way through the play: the next day he found they were applauding the idea that Athens had always been merciful. At the time, there were many petitions circulating in the streets for the recently deposed generals to be put to death: life and art, he realized, had an actual relationship in some parts of the world. While a graduate student at UC–Boulder, he was fortunate to study with the great American poet Edward Dorn, whose memory he honors in several essays here. Before and after that he lived in Venice Beach, participating in and leading the public poetry workshop at Beyond Baroque. He moved to San Francisco in 1980, editing the literary magazine *Zephyr*, and then to Bolinas, CA in 1983, where he met many fine poets and writers, including Sara Schrom, who would become his wife. He published two chapbooks in Bolinas: *Saturn Return* (Smithereens Press, 1983) and *Spring Training* (Zephyr Press, 1985), as well as editing the literary magazine *Peninsula*. In the early 1990s he lived in Czechoslovakia, teaching English as a foreign language at the law faculty of Palacky University in Olomouc and George Soros' Central Europe University in Prague. Returning to Seattle, he continued teaching English, publishing the chapbook *September Song* from Oasis Press in 2000. His last 14 years as a professor were spent in San Diego, where he published the chapbook *Mary Shelley's Surfboard* from Blue Press (2006), *Scholarship* from BlazeVox (2014) and *Coastal Zone* from Spuyten Duyvil (2016). Since retiring, he's published *The Oregon Trail* (2021) and *The Secular Divine* (2022), both from Spuyten Duyvil; after this volume, a book of selected poems on Greek mythology called *Greek to Me* is scheduled to come out next year with Chax Press. He lives in Portland, Oregon with his wife and his cat, where he studies the language of trees.

www.ingramcontent.com/pod-product-compliance
Lightning Source LLC
Chambersburg PA
CBHW031315160426
43196CB00007B/538